PELPOLA

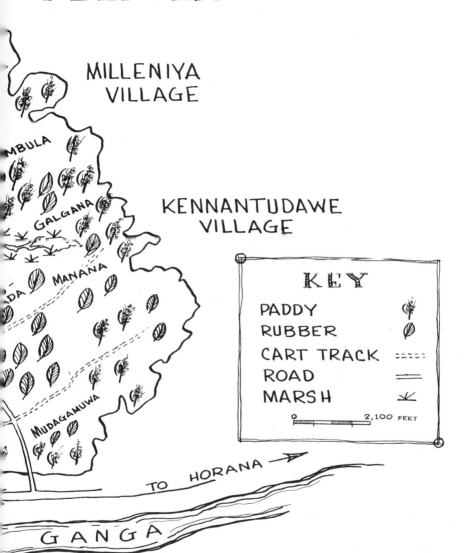

MILLENIYA
VILLAGE

MBULA

GALGANA

KENNANTUDAWE
VILLAGE

DA MANANA

MUDAGAMUWA

KEY

PADDY
RUBBER
CART TRACK ·····
ROAD ══
MARSH ⅄

0 ▱▱▱▱ 2,100 FEET

TO HORANA →

GANGA

Sinhalese Village

Man of Pelpola: Cultivator, Laborer and
Leader of Pilgrimages

Photographs by Kenneth J. Somanader

Sinhalese Village

by

Bryce Ryan

in collaboration with

L. D. Jayasena *and* D. C. R. Wickremesinghe

UNIVERSITY OF MIAMI PRESS

Coral Gables, Florida

1958

Printed in the United States of America
by McGregor & Werner, Inc.
Washington, D. C.

TO

THE PEOPLE OF PELPOLA

WITH

APPRECIATION AND AFFECTION

PREFACE AND ACKNOWLEDGMENTS

The study reported upon here represents one part of a research program initiated by the senior author while serving as the first Professor of Sociology at the University of Ceylon, 1948-1952. During those years a broad, exploratory research program was developed in which basic understanding and documentation was sought of Ceylon's rural society and culture. Villages and plantations were studied in each of Ceylon's major socio-cultural regions. Pelpola was selected to "represent" the Ceylon Low Country, the most urbanized part of the island. Obviously no claim of statistical representativeness is intended although this village is generally similar to many others in the region. While the various studies have not been fully reported, publications have appeared in different media from time to time. In addition to the village study program and associated inquiries, independent researches were led by Dr. Murray A. Straus, then also of the University of Ceylon faculty in Sociology. Pelpola was also included in Dr. Straus' project. On pages 217-219 below a full bibliography is given for publications arising from work initiated in the Sociology Department of the University of Ceylon during the 1948-1952 period.

The village study program was originally designed to gain elemental knowledge of Ceylon society and cultures, and also as a means for bringing Ceylon University students into close, objective understanding of their rural countrymen who compose more than four-fifths of the island's population. Since modern sociological and cultural anthropological studies had been virtually non-existent in Ceylon, the program was first conceived as a series of "baseline" studies. Due to a number of circumstances, more intensive and longer attention was given to Pelpola than to any other of the communities. Among these conditions was the fact that Pelpola is quite accessible from Colombo, then the University seat; further, it is a village in which urban contact is well along, and, of no small significance, it is the home village of Mr. Jayasena. The Pelpola study which began in 1949 as a directed student

project was continued and intensified after the junior members of the team were graduated from the University of Ceylon. Mr. Jayasena is currently serving as Social Services
Officer with the Ceylon Government and Mr. Wickremesinghe,
also in government service, is Divisional Road Transport
Officer.

As the descriptive facts of life became more clear, the
study was partially re-oriented toward direct analysis of the
pervasive changes going on in village life. Survey and other
structured techniques had been applied to community organization and institutional structure to verify and expand knowledge gained through unstructured research methods. In turning to problems of change, the use of structured instruments
appeared to be even more desirable, given the groundwork
laid by unstructured observation, participation, and interviewing. Our attempts to integrate structured and unstructured methods were influenced partly by the recognition of
complementation in these approaches and partly by the ultimate need for research instruments which permit measur-
able inter-village and even inter-cultural comparisons in
regard to processes of change.

Our conceptual basis for the analysis of change stems
from a theoretic tradition now most closely associated with
the respective writings of Dr. Robert Redfield and Dr. Howard
Becker. To the works of each of these men we are indebted,
as we are to the foundation work of Dr. Carle C. Zimmerman
and Dr. Pitirim Sorokin in rural-urban sociology. In an exploratory and tentative fashion we have attempted to give
quantitative expression to the processes of secularization.
Our approach to the local manifestations of the contemporary
Asian transition were personally stimulated by the brilliant
perspectives of Dr. Ralph Turner of Yale University.

Other scholars to whom we would express appreciation
include: Dr. Murray A. Straus, University of Wisconsin;
Dr. Richard Lambert, University of Pennsylvania; Dr. Burton Stein, University of Chicago; Dr. William W. Stein, University of Miami; and Dr. S. J. Tambiah, University of
Ceylon. Dr. Straus' companion study was valuable to us and
his cooperation at every stage has been deeply appreciated.
Dr. Lambert and Dr. Burton Stein have each made valued
suggestions at different points in the research. Dr. William
W. Stein has generously read the manuscript with both a

conceptual and an editorial eye. The independent and col-
laborative analyses of related series of data by Dr. Tambiah
have been of great value to the present study.

The cooperation of many Ceylon residents is gratefully
acknowledged, especially that of Dr. R. L. Tiruchelvam,
Director of Social Services, Ceylon Government, whose cooperation was of inestimable importance. We are also grateful to Mrs. E. C. Fernando, of Colombo, and to Mr. K.
Kumaraswamy of the University of Ceylon. A special debt is
owed Mr. Kenneth J. Somanader, now of the Ceylon Government Information Service, for his generosity in taking the
photographs used in this work.

To the people of Pelpola themselves we must express our
humble and most sincere thanks. Like most Sinhalese villages, Pelpola is a place of hospitality and human warmth,
a condition never qualified even by our occasional breachs
of good taste in questioning and the senior author's lapses in
the folkways. To work with people having such rich cultural
roots and such personal tolerance and good humour is itself
an important lesson for the academician who might be tempted
to confuse "learning" with "wisdom." To these friends we
ask indulgence for our frankness, yet we feel that our efforts
toward objectivity have yielded a village picture for which
even the children of an ancient and proud civilization need
feel no call for apology.

It is doubtful if a single family in the village did not con-
tribute directly to this study. Special thanks are due those
who served frequently and freely as our mentors, informants,
and cooperators: Messrs. L. D. Alfred, L. D. Thomas Appuhamy, L. L. Sediris Alwis, and L. D. Sandol Appuhamy.
The cooperation of the Priest of the Pelpola Temple, the
Head Teacher of the Pelpola School, and the Village Headman is also gratefully acknowledged.

Support from the University of Ceylon and the Rockefeller
Foundation has made this study possible. Appreciation is
expressed to these institutions, with special thanks to Sir
Ivor Jennings, then Vice-Chancellor of the University of
Ceylon, and to Dr. Robert B. Watson, Dr. Marshall Bal-
four, and Mr. Roger Evans of the Rockefeller Foundation.

We are indebted to the editors of The Milbank Memorial
Fund Quarterly and Rural Sociology for permission to draw
upon materials previously presented in those journals.

No attempt has been made for precision in transliteration. Sinhalese words are rendered here in rough phonetic equivalents. Thus, for example, the frequently used word and suffix "Gɛ" is here shown simply as "Ge" and "dēvāle" as "devale." Ordinarily words not found in the Oxford Universal Dictionary have been underscored.

In final acknowledgement, the senior author wishes to make clear that the collaboration of L. D. Jayasena and D. C. R. Wickremesinghe was of an order amounting to co-authorship. Their field research and their continued counsel provided the basic materials out of which the study is contrived.

Bryce Ryan

South Miami, December 1957

CONTENTS

x   CONTENTS

Chapter I

INTRODUCTION TO A COMMUNITY

That voyagers to the East once thought Ceylon to be the lost Garden of Eden is not surprising. From Matara, on the Southern Coast, to Negombo, north of Colombo, lush, green lowlands rise toward the equally green but clouded mountains. The coastal low country rarely extends thirty miles before meeting the foot-hills of the Kandyan Highlands. It is a region of abundant rain, well distributed throughout the year, and with a temperature varying little from a delightful, if somewhat ennervating, eighty degrees. Nature expects little of man, so long as man himself is not overabundant. Productive greenery abounds, flourishing with little or no human toil. Jak trees, coconut and other palms, mangosteens, pawpaws and scores of other bearing trees thrive upon man's minimum effort. Indeed, in this verdant Eden, man has not fêlt the need of building social values in which a life of unremitting labor is his proper fate. Even misery is cloaked by the luxuriant tropical beauty of ever flowering trees and shrubs.

The village of Pelpola is six miles inland from the coastal city of Kalutara. Like hundreds of villages in these densely populated lowlands, its houses, temples, and boutiques (small retail shops) are hidden in heavy foliage which in modern times has been supplemented by extensive rubber plantings. Stretches of paddy land stand out like lakes and inlets in the darker rubber and garden plots rising above them. Houses, about four hundred in all, are scattered in the arboreal gardens, scarcely visible in the air-view from directly above. Village lanes and pathways are cut through the rubber lands and gardens to converge on a main cart-track leading to the hard surfaced road just beyond the village boundary. Here busses ply to the coastal and to the interior towns and cities, for this is an important artery connecting the interior with the seacoast.

Like most interior Low Country villages, Pelpola is ex-

clusively Sinhalese and exclusively Buddhist. With its four
hundred families, including more than two thousand persons,
Pelpola is no doubt larger than most of its neighbors. Like
them she has not only the garden lands and paddy fields but
also returns from rubber plantings and wage returns from
fairly steady labor opportunities in the estates and other enterprises. In addition, Pelpola has a group of potters and
several brick and tile kilns, and a sprinkling of assorted
craftsmen and small traders. While Pelpola's size and prosperity are partially due to a varied economic base, they are
as well a function of the considerable territory which falls
within its political bounds. Covering an area of more than
three square miles, the village includes low lying and even
marshy alluvial lands and undulating hillsides. Fellow villagers sometimes live two or three miles from those resid-
ing near another boundary.

One-third of the village area is covered by three different
rubber estates, owned by absentee proprietors. Although
village folk work in these estates for wages they have no
business interest in them. Of the remaining land area, about
1600 acres, one-tenth or more is planted to rubber by the
villagers themselves, sometimes in tracts of several acres,
or again as a few trees interspersed with coconut or arecanut
palms. The latter is important as the source of "betel nut, "
the former second only to rice as a staple in household
economy. Highland "gardens, " in which the homes are situated, cover nearly half of the lands utilized by the villagers
themselves. While a considerable share of highland is wasted,
from any but an esthetic view, here are grown the coconuts,
fruits, areca nuts, green vegetables, and some condiments,
for home use and as small cash supplements to the family
income. Rice, the staple of diet, is produced in broad lowlands which here and there extend into pockets below the gardens. Although paddy is viewed as the basis of village economy
its acreage constitutes less than a fifth of the land at the villagers' disposal. In addition, however, paddy lands scattered
within the rubber estates are rented out to the villagers.
Small amounts of high land are held by the government for
ultimate disposition to landless villagers, and still smaller
plots are used for brick and tile works. Livestock is not
plentiful in the village and pasture is readily found in unused
patches of grassland in the gardens, on the government-

owned highlands, and in the paddy fields following the harvest. [1]

Pelpola is not isolated from the world. It is situated half
way between Kalutara, an important coastal city, and Horana,
a thriving market center for estates and villages. Regular
bus service can convey the villagers to either center in a
matter of minutes, and even to the capital, Colombo, in
about two hours. But if Pelpola is adjacent to the roadway,
it is in no sense a "highway village." Most homes are a mile
or more from the road and it is only in a political sense that
the village extends to it. A rutted cart-track passing through
solid rubber plantings provides the only direct outlet to the
highway. While the track can accomodate motor cars into
the heart of the community area, connections are in fact
usually made by foot or by bicycle. Loads are borne on foot
or strapped on the bicycle's luggage rack. Shipments of some
weight, such as rice, sugar, and flour are transported by
bullock cart from a nearby village which has direct truck
line connections with Kalutara and Horana. Many other commodities, however, are carried directly to or from the city
by bullock cart. Very recently (since 1952) a truck has been
purchased by a young Pelpolan and this is gradually replac-
ing cart traffic between Pelpola and the nearby villages.
Firewood, bricks and tile, all produced in the village area,
are shipped to the more northerly coastal cities by an old
Dutch period canal which skirts the locality. Although in
1950 there was only one motor car in the village, there were
four in 1957. These are rarely used either as family con-
veyances or agricultural equipment. Cars represent capital
investments, the returns coming through hiring them out
for wedding parties, emergency trips to the city, visits to
important relatives, or for pilgrimages to distant shrines.

No telephone reaches the village, but mail and newspapers
come daily. Four radios were owned in 1952; one of these,
in the temple premises, and another, at a centrally located
boutique, could be heard by all who cared to listen and by
surrounding neighbors regardless of their desire. Since
1952 the boutique has discontinued its radio service.

Most direct contacts with cities or market centers are
limited to trips for the purchase of commodities not handled
in the small local shops. Secondary reasons for travelling
are diverse. At Kalutara is an extensive bazaar, a major

government hospital with free facilities to all people, rec-
reational services in the form of taverns and cinemas, and
the seat of district government. In Panadura, a few miles
north, are the courts in which Pelpolans fight their frequent
cases. Beyond Panadura is Colombo, to be reached by train
or bus, and visited particularly on great national occasions
or en route on pilgrimages to the ancient shrines far off in
the Northwestern and North Central provinces.

 In the year 1950, a fourth of the male household heads of
Pelpola visited some town, urban or market center, at least
once each week, although nearly two-thirds made such a
trip less often than once per month.[2] As might be expected,
the well-to-do, a number of them small merchants, visited
towns more frequently than the poor. (Half of the well-to-do
averaged one trip or more a week, whereas only twelve per
cent of the poor went so frequently.[3]) As of 1957, about
forty-five Sinhalese language newspapers reach the village
each day. These represent two different publications. Many
go to the boutiques where customers coming to chat in their
idle hours are at liberty to read them, or listen to them
read. Since three-fourths of the household heads are literate
in Sinhalese, as are practically all of the youth and a half
of the married women, the majority can, if they wish, take
advantage of the newspapers. Many pamphlets also reach
the village chiefly through purchase in the towns.

 No one belongs to any organization having urban members,
and even participation in urban amusements is rare except
among unmarried young men. Barely half of the household
heads and less than a tenth of their wives have ever attended
a cinema. Affairs of the outside world are seldom discussed,
except in so far as they relate directly to rubber and paddy
prices or to forthcoming elections and sensational crimes.
Except for an occasional government officer and the home
visits of city dwelling children, urbanites rarely come to
Pelpola.

 On every side the lands of Pelpola meet those of other
communities. Seven different villages touch its boundaries
although ready access to several of them is deterred by
natural barriers, especially the Dutch Canal, Kapu Ela. At
other points the village line is lost in low-lying paddy fields
and at still others in the midst of rubber plantations. Relationships with nearby villages are of an utterly different

quality from those with the market towns and cities. So essentially similar are the surrounding villages in economy and local services, there is little reason for inter-village connections on any bases other than kinship and fellowship. On these foundations there are complex patterns of intimate relationships. Marriage customs do not insist upon village exogamy but there is a slight preference for a spouse from outside the village. While the lines of marriage are not rigidly patterned, rarely does the Pelpola father look far beyond adjacent villages for a suitable partner for the readying son or daughter. Three-fourths of the contemporary household heads were born within Pelpola and of the outside fourth over two-thirds came from villages within a six mile radius. Wives have more frequently married into the village, but more than two-thirds of the migrants also come from within six miles. It is not surprising that Pelpola wives usually have siblings in neighboring villages. Nearly three-fifths of them have sisters in nearby villages, under ten miles, and nearly half (forty-six per cent) have nearby brothers as well. Even among the male household heads, most of whom had parental homes in Pelpola and brothers who likewise settled there, more than a fifth have brothers in surrounding villages.

These figures give only a hint of the ubiquity of kinsmen in surrounding localities for in addition to these relatives of first degree, there are cousins, cousins by marriage, grandparents, daughters, daughters-in-law and many persons known simply as kinsfolk because of the complex relations arising through generations of preference in marrying certain classes of relatives. And while marriage is patrilineal and usually patrilocal, it is a sacrament sealing two family lines by bonds of loyalty. The "immigrant" Pelpola wife maintains throughout her life a close contact with her parental home and siblings. Furthermore this allegiance extends to her husband and to their children. Nearly three-fifths of their Pelpola husbands usually join them on their frequent home visits, and rarely are the children left behind. The village family dressed in its colorful best and bearing baskets of goodies on head or by hand is a familiar sight along the lanes and cart-tracks. Pelpola is deeply and intricately immersed in its own self-contained life but the ties to kin in surrounding villages are complex, close, and very nearly universal.

These bonds are expressed mainly in family visiting and reciprocities, but sometimes in attendance at special religious observances in the neighboring village temples or other social events outside the immediate kinship sphere. The nearby villagers of course reciprocate in visiting Pelpola much the same as the Pelpolans visit them.

With all these contacts with the immediate, and even more distant, outside world, daily life is closely contained within the community. And, although Pelpola is highly articulated by neighborhoods and segmented by paddy field lowlands and rubber groves, it is indeed a community. Though we must turn to neighborhood life for the realm of intimate and constant association, the many, and often scattered, clusters of homes look toward a single area of the village as the hub of community wide activity. The very name "Pelpola" meaning literally, if today somewhat inappropriately, "place of huts" is a designation not only for the entire village as a political entity, but also for its central, hub neighborhood. (See map on inside front cover.) Pelpola Central, as we will term the neighborhood, is undoubtedly the original core of village settlement. At the virtual termination of the barely motorable village lane, a dozen small boutiques serve as the local bazaar. These are the only ones in the entire village sufficiently large to stock expensive merchandise like cloth. One even provides a tailor with hand-powered sewing machine. Here too is one of the privately owned rice hulling machines serving the village, a hand-powered rubber press and smoke house, and the site of the weekly fair where some Pelpolans and many persons from nearby communities bring their produce for sale. The government-sponsored cooperative store is here, drawing to it most Pelpolans to benefit by its well regulated pricing. Nearby is one of the major home bakeries, important because today bread has become a competitor of the more expensive, but more prized, rice in the poor man's diet. While most of the neighborhoods have modest boutiques which hold stocks of foodstuff valuing perhaps fifty or seventy-five rupees at most, Pelpola Central offers diversified foods, condiments, and minor utensils not to be found in greater abundance or variety outside the bazaars at Horana or Kalutara.

In addition to Pelpola Central's commercial attractions, the most important institutional facilities, the principal temple and the school, are nearby. Each of these institutions reaches into virtually every household, except for the small group of potters who are of distinct caste and possess their own temple. Pelpola children today seldom miss out entirely on education, although few of them persist longer than five years. Fully three-fourths of the village look upon this central temple as their usual place of worship. These institutions, like the shops, are utilized almost exclusively by Pelpolans and draw their constituents from nearly every sector of the community.

The integrating power of Pelpola Central extends beyond its institutional services into the primary, informal and even casual life of the village. Pelpola is unified to some extent by its legal status as a village and associated political bonds. There is a single headman for the entire village and one elected representative to the regional "Village Committee." Still another all-village functionary is the "agricultural officer," a local farmer burdened with few duties but having great informal influence. Apart from these functionaries there are a number of men of influence, trusted by the villagers, and effective leaders in community affairs as well as sage counsellors in private matters. Not all, but a high proportion of these men live in or near Pelpola Central. Here are the verandahs upon which important matters are discussed, just as within this neighborhood are the boutiques at which men idle their leisure hours. While some important persons, like the "native doctor," skilled in the lore of herbalism, do not live in this immediate vicinity, it is significant that no person with an important leadership role in the entire community lives in the more outlying neighborhoods. Infrequently is this leadership expressed through community-wide formal organizations. To be sure, for the temple there is an active body of almsgivers who provide the daily food for the priests, but beyond this and the cooperatives, formal organizations have never prospered in the village although the people occasionally unite on some project holding common interest.

It is not to be thought that all of the bonds of the community are centripetal, converging upon a central core. This would be to underestimate the important kinship ties between cohesive neighborhoods, and also that intangible, subjective unity which reaches the articulate level in that frequent phrase, "my village." While Sinhalese villages usually lack

the strong communal attachment amounting in some lands
to almost nationalistic localism, the village per se is a beloved spot. The neighborhood is typically a strong area of
kinship but nearly thirty per cent of household heads and almost a fifth of their wives have brothers living in different
neighborhoods of the village. It would be a very small minority of the population without some kinship ties running
across the boundaries of neighborhoods.

That Pelpola may be termed a community, there is no
doubt, but it is a community critically differentiated by integrated, albeit precise, neighborhood units. The differentiation is more striking than the cohesiveness of the whole.
Even where several neighborhoods are closely clustered together, as in the vicinity of Pelpola Central, they are distinct
in the minds and in the neighboring patterns of the folk.

The vicinity of Pelpola Central is the most densely populated. Within this general area there are several adjacent
neighborhoods bearing distinctive names. A second vicinity
lies along the Dutch Canal, and includes Theppuwa and
Miriswatta, linked together by direct footpath. Several neighborhoods, e.g. Manana, Kuruppu Gammedda, are islands
in the rubber estates. Still others are cut off from most of
the remainder of the village by distance and by marshy lands,
making short cuts to other neighborhoods difficult, e.g.
Kuda Imbula, Galgana, and Galagama. Although a nominally
motorable lane brings some of the more isolated neighborhoods into contact with Pelpola Central, Galagama is sometimes viewed as a distinct village in itself. While this is not
true in the political sense, Galagama is less integrated than
other areas with the village as a whole. There is also a
tendency for neighborhoods toward the northeastern boundaries to integrate themselves partially with a nearby village,
many residents of which are physically closer to them than
are other Pelpolans.

Not only do the specific neighborhoods have distinctive
names in village parlance, but some of them possess distinctive characteristics, either in fact or in village opinion.
Kaluwalagoda and Delkada are the homes of members of the
"potter caste" (Badahela) whereas all other areas are the
homes of "cultivators" (Goyigama caste). Only in Delkada
are the houses of the "potters" separated from those of
neighboring Goyigama families, but in most primary relation-

ships the "potters" are a distinct "communal" group. In regard to institutional services they participate with others
of the community in all but temple activities and are in
friendly though not egalitarian relationships with their
higher caste fellow villagers. Since the Badahela depend
chiefly upon their traditional craft for livelihood they are
apart from the predominating economic concerns of the remainder of the village.

Pelpola Central is both village center and neighborhood.
In its capacity as a neighborhood it is in a modest sense an
area somewhat better off financially than most. This is due
less to its commercial activities than to the fact that as the
original village core it hence has a disproportionate number
of families with inherited lands. Its most outstanding features
are visible to the naked eye--tiled roof cottages interspersed
with small boutiques, facing on the cart-track lane which
is the village's central thoroughfare. Generally among the
neighborhoods adjacent to Pelpola Central distinctions are
minor.

It is well known that Acharigoda is "poor, " having more
simple mud-walled homes scattered among the substantial
kabook (clay brick) houses characteristic of those families
with average to good incomes. Another neighborhood, also
of low economic position is Katuketiya, settled in the last
twenty-five years as the Crown has made unutilized highland available to Pelpola's expanding population. Here the
simple mudwalled houses and some entirely of thatch, are
general, and the newness of the development, as well as
the inferior hillside land, means that shrubs and trees are
less dense.

Quite different are some of the outlying neighborhoods,
which, having least intercourse with Pelpola Central, are
weakly integrated in the community. Galgana is a place of
fearsome reputation, gained by the lawlessness of earlier
generations. The folk of Galgana long stood apart among
the typically easy going Pelpolans by their loud talk, their
pointed knives and their solidarity in thievery and brawls.
Old residents of other neighborhoods, who incidentally are
oftimes their kinsmen, bless the day that Galgana leadership died out and "the breed became so weakened that they
hold no more toddy in their bellies than do other men. "
Pelpolans of other vicinities seldom find reason to visit this

section of the village, although Galgana people patronize
the boutiques in Pelpola Central and worship at the principal temple. Singularly enough, Imbula, close by Galgana
has little to distinguish it by. Perhaps its dissimilarity to
the once rough neighboring locality lies in the fact that it,
like Katuketiya, is a fairly recent settlement and composed
of families drawn from throughout the other neighborhoods.

Marked neighborhood differentiation in character exists
only in reference to the mixed functions of Pelpola Central,
the moderately distinctive locale of the "pottery caste"
group, and the rather isolated Galganians with their hood-
lum past. Beyond these matters there has been noted a
tendency for some neighborhoods to vary from the norm in
regard to their material well being. Thus a fourth of the
most wealthy village families live in Pelpola Central although this same area includes less than ten per cent of the
village poor. But yet in that total of four per cent of Pelpola
households judged "wealthy," one or more representatives
may be found in eight of the fifteen distinct neighborhood
units. And at the other extreme no neighborhood is without
members of the poorest class, although proportions vary
between areas. Nearly every neighborhood possesses at
least a few prosperous landowners, a larger number of
peasants whose daily rice is at least secure, and a still
larger number of families who get along from day to day
with little or no land other than their gardens.

Whatever may be the extent of cultural differentiation be-.
tween neighborhoods, real significance lies in the fact that
neighborhoods hold neighbors. In Pelpola this primary locality group is rooted in lifelong proximity, and often kinship as well. It is second only to the conjugal family as an
intimate world for the individual. Only the neighborhood
boutique will usually extend credit; it is on the neighbor's
verandah that the important matters of the day are first discussed; here that children find their playmates and parents
their aides in the minor crises of daily life. The strong tendency toward patrilocal settlement means that few households are without nearby kinsmen. It is hence not surprising
that nearly half of the household heads (fifty-six per cent)
have brothers living within the immediate neighborhood.
Over half (fifty-five per cent) have adjacent siblings, brothers
or sisters. Over a fifth (twenty-one per cent) of the wives

also have nearby brothers. These figures reflect the fact
that many husbands and/or wives were born in the neighborhood within which they are now living. More than three-fifths
of the men had been born in the neighborhood wherein they
are now settled as householders.

In the formation of neighborhood affiliations it is doubtful if kinship is a conscious criterion of association. The
typical Pelpolan is apt to respond, when asked who are his
best friends, that all members of the village look much alike
to him. Yet this is scarcely true, for in some instances
there are enmities, and more important, analysis of actual
persons named as close companions in various types of activity reveals a strong neighborhood bias. Thus when the
household heads specified the men with whom they were most
intimate, in terms of chatting and idling together, nearly
nine-tenths of those named were found to be members of the
neighborhood. That two-fifths of these were also kinsmen is
perhaps coincidental. Similarly, in naming a "best friend, "
thirty-one per cent named unrelated neighbors while an additional forty-one per cent named neighbors related to them
by blood. As we might expect, wives are as closely bound
by neighborhood contacts, but within that area less frequently
move with kinsfolk, either their own or by marriage. While
the Pelpolan's spirit of independence is such that he is reluctant to confess "borrowing" from his friends, the importance of neighborhood lines are nearly as significant as
in friendship cliques but with greater dependence upon nearby kinsmen. Thus sixty-two per cent of the men borrowed
from neighboring relatives, while only seventeen per cent
did so from unrelated neighbors.

Despite the obligations of kin to kin, the ethos of the Sinhalese emphasizes and values independence and individuality.
There are situations in which kinsmen are expected to assist
one, and in daily life both unrelated neighbors and kinsmen
live in relations which are usually, although informally, cooperative and accomodative. Under such conditions it is understandable that neighborly relations do not extend into
economic cooperation except on a casual basis or upon
strictly commercial understandings. Yet it is to the neighbors one turns first for help in harvest--although their help
will be properly hired, usually in terms of cash or paddy
rather than in "work exchange. " At family ceremonies other

than rites of passage, neighbors assist on purely informal
bases. In the formalized crises and ceremonies of the family,
and in events calling for financial assistance, the primary
obligations fall first to kinsmen regardless of residence,
and secondarily to helpful neighbors. Individualistic or not,
the Pelpola household lives in a daily reliance upon those
surrounding it. Good neighbors create good neighbors, and
for a bad neighbor help at harvest may be difficult to find
even at a going wage rate. When the Pelpolan speaks on the
character of a fellow villager, the crucial tribute is, "He is
a helpful man. "

To the eye Pelpola is a symphony of tropical greens lent
further color and movement by human beings. To the ear
the same peaceful beauty is reflected in the rustle of palms
and the very quietness of man-made sounds. Pelpolans may
not live out this idyll in their daily lives, but they approach
it. Caustic comments there are; bitterness there is not.
Personal enmities rise and fall; factional violence is at most
in historic memories. Economic misfortunes and meagre
livings occur here as everywhere, but abject poverty and
hunger is rare. Smiles are frequent; voices high with anger
are few. Toward their own, Pelpolans are critically tolerant. Toward the universe at large, they are insecure but at
peace. By and large good heed is given the words of their
Lord, "Happiness to all living creatures. "

Chapter II

RICE, RUBBER, AND LABOR
THE ECONOMIC FOUNDATION

The Sinhalese ideal of peasantry is that of a husband and
wife, with their large family of children, showing close
loyalty to their kinsmen but living as a nuclear unit and making an independent livelihood from their own paddy fields and
gardens. In so far as the economic independence of the marital household is concerned, this ideal is commonly met, but
many other implications of the concept, including that of
family sufficiency in simple peasant proprietorship, are frequently unfulfilled. Qualifications arise in reference to the
ownership of land, the significance of non-agricultural income, and the considerable dependence upon the market
economy even for goods which might reasonably be home
grown. Pelpolans are peasants both in popular terminology
and in their own eyes, but scarcely in the simple significance
of tillers working their own subsistence crops, eschewing
the role of laborer as well as that of commercial producer.
When one thinks of village agriculture in Ceylon, paddy
cultivation comes first to mind. Although in point of fact the
Sinhalese are among the world's most inefficient rice producers, deep in the peasant's ethos is the understanding that
paddy is the foundation of life, and its cultivation the proper
and most honored sphere of toil. To be a cultivator very
nearly means to be a paddy cultivator. Other crops, other
food crops at least, are viewed more as gifts of nature than
as the object of the farmer's productive labors. The poor
villager's goal, in so far as it is oriented to peasant life at
all, is in terms of owning rice land. In other regions, where
the government has provided landless villagers with abundant
high garden and paddy land, the highland "gardens" resemble
jungles more than tended gardens.
The paddy ethos is strong in Pelpola and to its seasons
the annual rhythm of life is bound. Yet scarcely half of the
household heads find their chief employment in paddy cultivation.[1] However, paddy cultivation is the most general

13

economic activity in the village since, in addition to those
principally engaged in it, many (twenty-two per cent) use it
as a secondary source of income. There are very few families

Table I: Chief and Secondary Employments
of Male Household Heads*

Occupation	Chief Employment (per cent)	Secondary Employment (per cent)
Paddy Cultivation	47	23
Other Cultivation	5	12
Pottery	10	0
Rubber Tapping	10	0
Other Labor	14	28
Business	7	6
Professional and Clerical	7	1
None	-	30
Total	87 cases - 100%	87 cases -100%

*Based on a one-fourth sample of all households. See Appendix A.

in the village which conform to the simple peasant pattern of
paddy supplemented by garden produce. Most of the paddy
farmers have supplemental income through wage labor carried on by some member of the household, frequently by the
head himself.

As production groups, the households may be roughly
classified into four categories. The smallest and most prosperous group are the business, professional and clerical
families wherein the head usually does not engage in active
cultivation but in many instances owns some rubber or paddy
land. (The rubber land would be cared for by hired labor, the
paddy land rented out on shares.) For these people, about
fourteen per cent of all, the primary occupation of the household head is non-agricultural and supplemental income is in
the form of return on land rather than from cultivation per
se. Most numerous, of course, are the families mainly dependent upon paddy cultivation. Many of these combine paddy
cultivation with wage labor in the rubber estates or supple-

ment it by small returns from personally owned rubber
trees. This broad category of cultivators includes the bulk
of the moderately secure peasantry, although often all or part
of the paddy land is held on a share rental basis. Generally
of lower economic status are the households in which the
head is principally a wage laborer. These families typically
have also some income from highland gardens and, in
seasons when rentable land is available, small amounts of
paddy. A fourth of Pelpola's family heads are mainly agricultural laborers. In busy seasons, such as harvest, they
work in their neighbors' paddy fields. At other times, they
find employment in the surrounding estates or other wage labor sources. Finally, distinct from all others are the potters,
none of whom engages in agriculture. Most adults of the
"potter caste" work exclusively in their traditional craft.

In the majority of homes the work of the husband-father
is supplemented by the employment of other family members. In only thirty-eight per cent of all households having
a male head were there no regularly employed supplemental
workers.[2] It is indicative of the villager's lackadasical attitude that three-fifths of the sons age fifteen and over worked
fewer than 120 days during 1950. However, in the poorer
homes, sons, daughters, and even mothers take employment
in the rubber groves and the processing plants situated on
the rubber estates. About three-fifths of all families had at
least one member, in addition to the household head, working
120 days or more during the year. Most of these were engaged in wage labor. Over a tenth had three or more workers
in addition to the head. In the pottery craft it is usual that
all adult members participate in the family enterprise.

Paddy: Cult and Cultivation

The Production Process

Although the ownership of land, other than highland gardens, is highly variable in Pelpola, the size of paddy plots
cultivated as family operations is quite uniform. About
three-fourths of the operated units in 1951 were two acres
or less. Three-fifths were not less than one acre nor more
than two acres in extent. In spite of the primitive production
technology, a good field of even less than two acres may
provide an average household with rice for the year. Large

land owners never cultivate their holdings as a single unit.
The largest acreage cultivated as a unitary operation in 1951
amounted to about eight acres, and it is uncommon that over
three acres are handled by a single family. A field, or as
is frequently the case different plots amounting in total to
three acres, would require the help of able-bodied sons as
well as the harvest work of the entire household, and much
seasonal hired labor besides.

To the uninitiated it would be impossible to determine
where the lands of one cultivator start and those of another
begin. Paddy lands are always in contiguous fields and most
of Pelpola's some 300 acres lie in three or four great
stretches following the lowland contours through the village.
(An additional 225 acres scattered through the rubber estates
are rented to the peasants.) Although the peasant rarely has
his paddy fields adjacent to his home, the topographic dictate
of contiguity in fields has fortuitous advantages. Individualistic as is the Sinhalese peasant, every stage of cultivation
is in interdependence with the work of his neighbors. Each
operator's plot is separated from others by a low bund which
controls the flow of water from the higher to the lower land.
In maintaining these boundaries, the various operators must
be in agreement. Frequently they benefit mutually by joint
work in maintenance and in construction. If a fence is built
to protect the fields from roaming cattle, the enclosed area
will usually include the fields of a number of persons. All
those involved will work together in its construction. Where
the different operators cannot "get together, " fences are
frequently left unbuilt. Even in fertilizing, goodwill must be
present among adjacent cultivators, for an extra cut in a
bund can easily bring the fertilizer down into the lower fields.
This is perhaps one reason why fertilization is not general.

The very feasibility of cultivating a particular plot is ultimately determined by one's fellows, although this is not
realized by the cultivators themselves. The single farmer
who wished to utilize his fields in a season when his neighbors were not planting--an unlikely possibility--would be
asking for the concentration of insect pests on his own small
plot. However, this is an issue having little significance
since no paddy land is idle during the favorable season. Even
fairly uniform timing in the various stages of cultivation is
desirable from the standpoint of pest control. In the matter

of water flow, interdependence is obvious and it is in this sphere
that the traditional village functionary, the vel vidane, or
agricultural "officer, " has regulatory responsibility. For his
services he receives a small share of each crop.

In this region there are usually two rice crops each year.
These are coordinated with the monsoon seasons, the Yala
crop being that sowed during the Northeast Monsoon, and
the Maha season that of the Southwest Monsoon. The Yala
season begins in March or early April with harvest in late
August or September. Soon after this harvest, the fields are
prepared for the Maha crop, which in this region is the more
important season. Although the semi-annual harvest is typical in Pelpola, other rhythms are occasionally followed. On
extremely wet and poorly drained land a single, annual harvest may be taken from a type of seed which thrives in a
great amount of water and has also a longer growing period.
At the conclusion of a harvest fields usually lie fallow for
about three weeks while the cattle roam the now brown lowlands feeding on the stubble and occasional grasses.

The traditional, wooden, scratching plow is frequently
used in the village, but many cultivators believe that their
land is too marshy for this method of tillage. It is claimed,
no doubt rightly, that the village bulls are not sufficiently
strong to pull the plough through marshy land. Where the
soil is well drained, bulls, never water buffalo in Pelpola,
may be hitched to the simple plough for the first breaking of
the soil. Marshy land is pulverized and mudded by the hoofs
of water buffalo. Many people, too poor to own or hire buffalo for this purpose, till their land with the mamoty (heavy
hoe). Once tilled, the fields are flooded by retention of the
monsoon rains. The water, standing for ten days or more,
turns the lowlands of the village into great shallow lakes.
This period of flooding serves not only to wet the ground in
preparation for water-demanding paddy sprouts, but is important for pest eradication, and for blending the rotting
stubble and grass into the soil. During this time water buffalo wallow in the wet fields and frequently are driven through
them systematically to pulverize and "mud" the soil. When
the fields are drained the cultivator, if a careful man, will
till again but in any case the mud-clotted soil must be fully
broken up and then levelled. In the latter operation a rake-
like wooden blade is dragged over the surface leaving it a

level mud bed unevened only by the small alley-ways through
which the water is drained off the now level surface of shim-
mering mud. The field is ready to sow.

Seed paddy is almost invariably selected from the stock
of a previous harvest, usually the season previous to the last
so that the seed is suited to the monsoon. Great care is taken
that the seed be kept dry until about six days before its use.
It is then soaked for three days and opportunity given for the
seeds to sprout before they are broadcast on the fields. Although transplanting is common in some parts of Ceylon, and
Pelpolans are familiar with the practice, broadcast seeding
is the rule. In 1951 Pelpola had a "demonstration plot" of
transplanted paddy but as of 1957, the practice had not caught
on.

When the plants are about six inches high water is again
let into the fields, or more accurately in this area without
irrigation, the rains are permitted to collect in them. Although some two inches of water stand constantly on the field,
great care must be exerted in defining water levels so that
the young plants are not flooded. Within one month the crop
is on its own and is usually given no more care. About a fifth
of the cultivators do some weeding, although all know that it
is beneficial. During World War II, when the government
provided bone meal, its use was common but no one cares to
purchase it today, and, while composting is practiced by
some, it is infrequently utilized on paddy land. For centuries
Pelpola's lowlands have produced two crops a year without
soil additives other than some manuring and stubble.

In harvest, where many hands are needed, wives, sons
and daughters join in the sickling. Where the field is small
and the family large outside help may be unnecessary, but
usually workers from outside the household must be enlisted.
There is no single pattern upon which harvest groups are
formed. Generally the operator is helped by his neighbors,
often kinsmen, who are paid in paddy or in money. Sometimes
reciprocal arrangements are understood wherein no return
other than work is given, but these groups form no permanent
circles for work exchange. One person may be included this
year but not the next, and neither offense nor gratitude will
be shown at an invitation or its lack. That this system of cooperative or reciprocal assistance may once have been more
widespread and institutionalized, is hinted by the fact that

such a work group bears a distinctive name, kaiya. Today, unpaid services are common only among the poor and it is rather bemeaning not to pay in cash or in paddy for assistance received.

Prosperous farmers, especially those who do little work in the fields themselves, may hire harvest hands on a strictly cash basis. Usually these will be neighbors or less affluent kinsmen. Still others have adopted a practice, introduced in recent years, of letting out a harvest contract. In this arrangement the owner simply pays a fee to an entrepreneur, often an enterprising villager a few miles from Pelpola, who in turn hires labor, usually women, on a wage basis. Under this plan there is none of the primary group spirit which persists in the paddy field even in the modern shambles of the kaiya system. Where work groups are of fellow villagers "helping" the operator, tea and food will be served in the fields and harvest songs heard among the workers. The contract system is an explicitly impersonal introduction, derived from the common practices followed by estate proprietors in respect to their subsidiary tasks, like weeding. The harvest is a season of fellowship and it is fortunate for the preservation of Pelpola's feeling of fellowship in work that the contract plan is beyond the realm of cash possibility for most peasants.

Planting and harvesting are processes largely without ritual or formal ceremony. This has not always been true. In 1882, H.C.P. Bell, British civil servant, described in detail many ceremonies associated with every phase of paddy production in this immediate district.[3] Today it is even uncommon to begin sowing at an astrologically auspicious hour, although, an auspicious day will be preferred. Unless pests are actually found at work in the field, no magical rites will be utilized for crop protection. Nor is much ceremony attached to the setting apart of the first harvested grain in the name of the gods, although in a simplified fashion this is done today. In general the rituals and ceremonials associated with sowing, tilling and reaping are much eroded in modern Pelpola. This is considerably less true in regard to the ceremonies of harvesting, winnowing and measuring. As paddy moves toward rice most phases of the transition still have a sacred aspect. Threshing, winnowing, and measuring are matters of seriousness in a sense apart from that of mundane

economy. Turning paddy into edible rice is a technologically
primitive process but it is one hedged by formality and out-
lined in ritual. This, as well as more extensive rituals in
the past, is notable since the Sinhalese are generally un-
ritualistic.

Paddy is normally threshed on a mat covered, hard mud
"floor" made in the field itself. A post is placed in the center of this circular floor, around which teams of bullocks
are driven three or four abreast, their hoofs grinding the
grains from the stalks. As the cattle circle, driven by the
shouts, songs, and sticks of the men, the now bare stalks
are forked to the side and new sheaves added. When the
crop is fully threshed, the grains are swept up into bags
ready for winnowing. For the latter process a wooden structure some twelve feet high is built in an open place, where,
as the grains are dropped toward the ground, the breeze
carries the chaff off into the fields.

When small quantities of paddy are to be processed, the
threshing is sometimes done by hand, or rather, by foot.
A low railing is set up against which the farmer leans, supporting himself with his hands, while a wad of paddy is rolled
under his bare feet. Threshing with the feet is no enviable
task even for peasants whose tough soles can trample out a
small coal of fire without serious effect. And it is gruelling
work for the back, legs, and feet.

To describe so prosaically the work of paddy processing
violates the solemnity of the occasion. Paddy is more than
a crop; it is the foundation of life, and for perhaps two
thousand years its cultivation has been a way of life. With
the gaity and good fellowship abounding at this season,
solemnity is introduced into the utilitarian operations themselves. As sheaves are brought to the threshing floor (kamatha)
the chief farmer, usually the operator of the field, stands
with a sheaf and the implements of threshing above his head.
Facing the central pole, around which the bullocks will be
driven, he then circles the floor three times, pausing si-
lently at each cardinal point in worship of the deities of the
four directions. When he ties his sheaf to the pole, work
may commence. But work is conducted with a spirit of clean-
liness. Women may not walk on the threshing floor nor participate in any phase of this work. No doubt this is associated
with menstrual tabu, although today the restriction is

generally unrationalized. Profanity, obscenity or even crude language is not tolerated by men who enjoy rude jokes to the full. A specialized vocabulary of euphemisms and indirections is employed in reference to common objects and natural phenomena. The mat under their feet is no longer "mat, " it is "that which is laid. " The measuring unit loses its familiar name, laha, and now is goiya. Empty husks are now "that which is not filled. " A mixture of archaic nouns and descriptive phrases takes precedence over daily language.

While the paddy is being "aired" or winnowed, the sacred atmosphere is maintained; the feeling of reverence enhanced. The farmers do not even talk aloud, and when the last grains have fallen to the ground, the solemn process of measuring the rice begins.

For reasons as mercenary as they are ceremonial, the landlord or his representative will be present for the measuring. (Peasants are proverbially incapable of counting shares accurately.) But there is no hint of a watch dog role as farmers and land owner participate in the ceremonies. Usually, particularly for a large harvest, an oil lamp is lighted in the name Bahirava Devathava, the godling in charge of all treasures of the earth. Until this final moment of measuring the rice has been kept under cover since it is well known that during this critical period Bahirava has before now greatly enhanced the harvest for those who preserved the solemnity of the time. "We were measuring and measuring, " recounts an elderly cultivator, "and there was no end to it. Finally I signalled with my hand for it to stop since it is wrong to take too much.... " There are tales that in times past this godling of the grains has produced yields double that which the forces of nature had provided. And conveniently enough, when the grain has been left without watch, Bahirava is said to have occasioned the pile in one field to grow and that in the neighboring field to diminish.

To begin measuring, the chief farmer empties one bag on a mat and circles it, stopping only for obeisance at the four cardinal points. After the third circling he returns to the spot from which he rose and pays homage to the first filled measure of rice. His role completed, it is for his friends and helpers to carry forward the work from this point. The first measurefull should be set aside as an

eventual offering to the Kataragama and other deities who
protect both the farmer and his crops.[4] The rituals of production are now completed except that there is yet to come
the dedication of the deity's share. From this point onward
rice is treated with respect but not with ceremony. In earlier
times the Sinhalese maintained their reverential attitude
throughout the process of cookery.[5]

Tenures in Paddy

Ownership of sufficient paddy land for family subsistence
is an ideal of Sinhalese peasantry. It is the minority, however, which achieves the goal. Although two-fifths of all
households own some paddy land, most of them have such
small holdings that additional land must be rented if even
the family rice stock is to be assured. Nearly three-fourths
of the families growing rice rented at least part of the land
they cultivated, and of those owning land, forty-four per
cent rented some in addition. Most of the landlords live within the village although large tracts of paddy land are within
the absentee owned estates and given out to Pelpolans on a
crop-share basis.

Over the passing years some paddy land, like rubber, has
passed into the hands of outsiders. Apart from the plantations,
however, absentee ownership is inconsequential. Today land
transactions are rare, for peasants cling to the source of
rice. Even dowries, in this generation, rarely include paddy
land. As might be expected four-fifths of all present owners
acquired their land through inheritance which in many instances
involved partition. Partitioning in successive generations has
made for small holdings although it is legitimate that bequests
treat heirs unequally or on any terms which seem fitting to
the parents. The progressive diminution of holdings through
the generations has also been retarded by a long established
form of unpartitioned inheritance.

Unpartitioned property rights are common in Pelpola, in
highland gardens and especially in paddy lands. Over a
quarter (twenty-nine per cent) of all Pelpola families hold
an interest in land in which other families are also co-owners.
This system of unpartitioned ownership, know as <u>thattamaru</u>,
carries with it an institutionalized plan of land operation in
which the various owning families rotate in their use of the
field. Thus the average number of part owners per parcel of

thattamaru paddy land is 3.8, signifying that once in about ·
every four years does each owning family operate and gain
the .full proceeds from the land. For one parcel of Pelpola
paddy land, ten separate households work in the thattamaru
relationship. Never is joint ownership reflected in joint work
with shared returns. Since about half of the owner operators,
in paddy, own some land in thattamaru, and a fourth own
only in thattamaru, it is apparent that land ownership is a
highly qualified status in the village and that many cultivators shift from tenancy to ownership in regular pattern.

The disadvantages of this sytem of ownership with rotat-
ing operation are obvious. The cultivator knows perfectly
well that any improvement to the land creates returns only
partially his own. A bad season is usually equalized by a
good season, but when that comes the land is likely to be in
someone else's hands. As co-owners increase, the potential
for disagreements, jealousies and misunderstandings increases also. Indeed, it may be seriously suggested that co-
ownership in various kinds of property is a significant source
of ill-feeling and litigation among kinsmen. The presumable
rationale for such a system of property division, and the
condition under which it is commonly found, is as a means
of equitably bequeathing small land parcels of variable fertility. Partitioned inheritance would yield inequity among
children, and since paddy land is so especially cherished,
it is possible that the frictions resulting from co-ownership
are in fact less serious than would be the consequences of
partition or an otherwise balanced bequest.

The landlords of Pelpola, absentee or resident, all let
out their fields on a crop share basis. Widely varying shares
go to the cultivator, depending upon various conditions. On
land owned by absentee landlords, if the field is fertile, the
cultivator generally receives two-thirds of the harvest. On
an average field he retains three-fourths, and on infertile
lands as much as four-fifths. Under these terms the tenant
provides all costs of production. On fields owned by Pelpola
landlords, it is customary for the cultivator to share costs
of production with the owner. The latter usually provides
the seed paddy and pays half of the wages of hired hands in
harvest and threshing. Equipment, i.e. the wooden plough,
mamoty, rake and sickle, is furnished by the operator, although if buffaloes are hired for mudding the fields or bulls

for threshing, the expense is often shared. Owner and tenant divide the harvest equally. Fairly stable relationships
usually exist between owner and renter from year to year,
although this does not amount to mutual obligation. Since
there is considerable demand for land, a change in operator
is more likely to arise from the owner's dissatisfaction than
from the tenant's. If a cultivator shirks his work, the owner
feels at liberty to rent to someone else, and village opinion
would support him in the shift.

There is little resentment in Pelpola against landlords
either resident or absentee, nor is there exploitation of the
tenant along feudal patterns as is sometimes true in interior
regions. Much renting is done by men who are themselves
small land owners. Typically the landlord and tenant are
fellow villagers, often neighbors who deal together on terms
of friendly and approximately equal social positions. Universally in rural Ceylon land is the primary basis of power,
but while the landless may at times express bitterness at
their condition, rarely are there personalized ill-feelings
against the landed. Jealousy is common, but in Pelpola few
if any would wish to expropriate the rich in theory let alone
harm the well-to-do peasant neighbor. Here there is no
feudal tradition. Prestige is possible without landed power,
and the fact of being a tenant does not mean necessary inferiority in the village status system. Although the landed
are in fact the families of highest status, Pelpolans exhibit
dignity regardless of economic position.

Rubber

While forty per cent of the households of Pelpola own
some rubber trees, this crop, unlike rice, has no hold upon village sentiments and lore. Rubber is a recent arrival,
a stranger in the village, accepted and made at home within this century strictly for pecuniary reasons. In the economy of the village it has dual significance. For the prosperous,
it affords income from capital with relatively small outlays
in the form of labor. For the village poor, wage labor generally on the absentee owned estates is a steady form of
cash income. Rubber, for the well-to-do, is part of the business of being a peasant proprietor. For the poor, it is
merely the most common form of non-farm employment

readily available. Most of the rubber owning villagers do their own tapping, about the only labor exerted in their groves, although a few large holders operate strictly with hired village labor. The estates are of course impersonal, capitalistic organizations with local Ceylonese superintendents who are well known to the villagers but not as members of the village community.

Although two-fifths of the families own some rubber, only two per cent cite this as the chief source of family income. Excluding two wealthy owners, and the estates, the average rubber grove amounts to only 1.3 acres. Forty-two per cent of the holdings are of less than one acre, and nearly eighty per cent under three acres. Yet such small acreages yield considerable income by village standards, especially in postwar days of high prices. On the nearby estates an acre of rubber should produce about 1650 pounds of latex a year and even some village acres may yield 1000 pounds per year. Sheet rubber, the main product of this area, brings about one rupee and thirty-five cents per pound (about $.35). This means that the average village producer has a rather substantial cash income for a peasant proprietor using family labor and inexpensive processing.

On nearby estates elaborate care is taken of the capital investment in rubber. Budded (grafted) trees are used, fertilizers, and various disease controls are applied, and the groves are allowed a rest period annually. The villager, however, typically pushes his trees to the limits of exploitation, returning nothing to them in the way of care, and rarely replanting trees whose useful lives approach exhaustion. The carelessness with which the trees are tapped is as serious as this lack of positive safeguards to investment. Estates show tree after tree with neat series of incisions, but the small-holder's trees are invariably scarred and misshapen by careless tapping. Wandering through the village one can practically determine the boundary lines between estates and villagers' groves by looking at the bark scars. And to maximize immediate returns during the post-war rubber boom, "slaughter tapping" (second incisions high up on the tree) has been practiced without intent of tree replacement. Nor does the villager give his trees the resting period usual in estate production.

Most of the village rubber is from the original plantings

of some forty or more years ago and it is a miracle of nature that many of these trees still produce. The few larger
landowners generally exert more caution, and consequently
have better returns, but year by year the village latex production will surely diminish. Yet poor as the returns are,
compared to estate production, it is chiefly the village owned
rubber which gives Pelpola a prosperity greater than that
in most other villages.

In the family's small grove, it is frequently the wife or
a daughter who taps the trees each morning when the weather
is fine. The latex is later collected in a bucket either by
the tapper or, as is often the case, by a child in the household. Since the liquid latex must be processed before sale,
it is first coagulated with acetic acid and then carried to one
of the local processing depots maintained by enterprising
villagers. Pelpola has six of these small processing centers.
In them the latex is rolled out into sheets in the hand operated
presses and then smoked. For this service the owner of the
plant receives seven Ceylon cents for each sheet weighing
about one and a quarter pounds. When the rubber has been
smoked it is taken to town by the owner or is sold to a local
man who deals in rubber. Although the local dealer receives
a few cents per sheet for his middle-man role, city buyers
do not accept small quantities and most Pelpolans turn out
only a few sheets during the week. Rarely is the top price
received. Processing is crudely done and prices run by grade.

Less affluent villagers widely utilize the surrounding
estates as sources of wage labor. Men are employed often
as general laborers in cultivation and both men and women
find work as tree tappers. About 135 Pelpola workers are
employed. There is no strong feeling attached to employment of women and aside from home employment as potters,
rubber tapping is typically female wage work. To be sure,
womenfolk do not work outside the home unless the family
is close to the border of poverty, but when they must, rubber tapping is well suited to fit in with household chores.
On the three estates segmenting Pelpola, about 65 Pelpola
women are regularly employed, along with others from
nearby villages and some resident estate workers.

Usually the tapper completes the day's work well before
noon. Normally this includes drawing the latex from about
200 trees, carrying it to the estate factory and there

coagulating it with an acetic acid preparation. From this
point the processing is taken up by regular factory hands,
some of whom are regular, non-village, resident estate
workers. The day, starting at seven o'clock in the morning
is completed by eleven on fair days and the village women
have the full afternoon for the multifarious household tasks
at home. While tapping by estate requirements calls for
skilled work, it is not heavy, the worst burden being the
transport of the collected latex to the factory. In the morning
hours one may see groups of women with the filled buckets
on their heads moving through the groves, laughing and gos-
siping. Rubber work has its sociable aspects, and young
people sometimes look upon it with considerable favor since
it can offer brief but relatively unchaperoned moments with
members of the opposite sex.

In addition to the regularly employed household heads and
women, the estates provide casual employment opportunity
for older children who earn small sums in weeding.

Garden Lands

Practically every Pelpola home is set in its "garden, "
almost invariably owned by the householder. (Infrequently
a producing tree might be held in joint ownership [thatta-
maru] with a kinsman.) Even the non-cultivating potters
have a few coconut and fruit trees surrounding their house-
workshops. The "garden" is as much a part of the village
home as is the "backyard" an integral part of the middle
class American home. Usually a quarter of an acre or more
surrounds the house, separating it from neighboring dwellings, giving play space for children, and returns to the family larder. The majority of homes have gardens of less than
two acres surrounding them, the average being around one
acre. Usually there is no barrier between property lines,
and the village hillside becomes a congerie of rubber, coconut, jak, and other trees and shrubs with houses set among
them, at some points as close as houses along a city street.
Elsewhere, houses are scattered to easy shouting distance
between neighbors.

Since gardens are mainly arboreal it might be presumed
that they are under intensive cultivation. Perhaps in some
sense this is true, but it would be difficult to imagine pro-

ducing lands receiving a smaller labor input. Where rubber
trees are interspersed with others they should be tapped
daily--no arduous task. Coconuts must be plucked at irregu-
lar intervals, as must jak fruits, plantains, limes, papaws,
and areca nuts. Not one of these bearing trees requires
tillage, pruning, or any other care other than in the original
planting and in plucking the well-nigh perpetual harvest.
They would be benefited by care, but care is not essential
for bearing. Most of the products are for home consumption
or for sale at the weekly village fair or to local boutique
keepers.

By far the most important garden crop, excluding rubber,
Paddy cultivation is a business of living; garden cultivation is to receive the good things of a bountiful nature. Drains
are to be found in some gardens but mainly these are located
in the lands derived from Crown holdings wherein drain construction was required as a condition of title. Less than a
fifth of the villagers even make composts and they are the
ones who are doing a little true gardening in the sense of
raising yams, green vegetables and pumpkins.

By far the most important garden crop, excluding rubber,
is coconuts. Most families have at least a few trees and
some have several acres. For the latter we should consider
coconuts as a cash farm crop rather than home garden produce although few families have more than sufficient coconuts
for their home use. The coconut is important as a food,
especially when grated and mixed with chillies, dried fish
and other ingredients to form a flavorful adjunct (sambol)
to the bland rice. In addition, the milk formed by squeezing
the soft, young coconut meat is an essential base for the
preparation of many curries. Not the least important product
is toddy, a readily fermented liquor drawn from the coconut
flower. Few trees have such infinitely varied uses. Food
and drink are basic, but from the palm comes also the material for cadjan (the woven frond) for thatching and fencing.
From the nut there is the shell, a collecting bowl for latex.
From the fruit is derived oil, for cooking and also for votive
lamps and for human hair. (Actually most villagers purchase
coconut oil.) Timber, from the fallen trunk, is ideal for
bridges or for housing. Several types of brooms are made
from the ekels and fibres. Most of these secondary products
from the coconut palm are locally made and used but rarely
produced for sale. Although Pelpola is very much part of a

market economy, if necessary, a resourceful villager could
live for months at a time with no more than his paddy crop,
a few chillies and a dozen coconut trees.

Industry, Labor and the Self Employed

We have seen that a half or more of the village families
receive substantial income from activities other than the
cultivation of self operated fields, and a sizeable minority
depend largely upon non-agricultural income. While rubber
estate labor is the chief source of non-farm return, well
over one-half of the households have members who practice
some economic activity unrelated to land operation or to
estate work. The majority of these engage intermittently in
agricultural labor in the village paddy fields, and in local
casual labor. A few are permanently employed, although not
usually on a regular weekly basis, in the tile and brick works.
A few others work for the entrepreneurs at rubber presses
and rice hullers. Still others are employed on the canal
barges transporting Pelpola's ceramic products to the city.
Many engage in any of several tasks, depending upon the
season and their immediate need for money. Sons living in
the parental home follow much the same pattern as the householders, working in the family paddy fields when needed and
as hired labor in the estates or in tile works or as harvest
helpers for neighboring farmers.

The clay beds of Pelpola undoubtedly have been worked
for many centuries, first by the potters, and since Dutch
times at least, by tile and brick kiln proprietors as well.
Today it is believed that the best clay has been exhausted,
but nonetheless there are six tile and two brick "factories"
along the village banks of Kapu Ela, the Dutch Canal. Locally
owned, frequently in partnerships, work is carried on with
sufficient regularity to provide several days employment per
week for thirty or forty village men and women. Some proprietors work at the kilns themselves alongside the hired
labor.

The kilns are no more than bricked ovens covered with
cadjan thatching. Molding of the bricks and tiles is done entirely by hand, using wooden and metal forms, after the clay
has been mixed by driving water buffaloes through it time after after time. As the tile or brick comes from the molding,

it is immediately carried to the nearby yard where it must remain in the sun until it has dried. From the yard a carrier transfers the product to the kiln for baking. The process is concluded by moving the finished products onto the barges in the nearby canal. Equipment used throughout is of the simplest nature. Molds for the bricks are rectangular wooden frames, those for the tiles are formed of thin iron; rollers to flatten the clay are of wood; buffaloes mix the clay; fire and human hands and legs do all the rest.

Division of labor, however, is present throughout the process, although men may double now at the mixing and again firing the furnace. One or two men drive the buffalo through the clay, while men and women both participate in carrying; other men fire the furnace and stack the bricks for firing. The boat crews are outside the process. They are employed by the boat owners, several of whom are among the wealthier villagers. Boats, like all parts of the production process, are hand driven, by men with long wooden poles. Except for the barge-men, all concerned with the tile and brick production process look upon themselves as basically paddy cultivating peasants. None, except for a few barge-men, is of "potter caste." This work is considered a less desirable but fortunate adjunct to proper peasant life-- though many workers rarely cultivate in fact. Compared to other villages, Pelpola has little underemployment. This is chiefly due to the varied wage labor opportunities. However, if further employment were available, the semi-landless peasants would welcome it despite the fact that ample leisure is valued by rich and poor alike.

The forty families of potters have clung to their craft through many generations, and probably through many centuries, for they are all of the distinctive potting caste, Badahela. They are the only people of Pelpola, other than a few "washermen," professing no skills in agriculture and not looking upon agriculture as their proper traditional calling. Today all local Badahela households are associated with the craft, although a few of the men are also employed on the canal barges and in other unskilled and semi-skilled occupations. Eight are masons who work in and out of the village as opportunity arises. Curiously enough, the development of the local tile and brick industry has remained outside the hands of this caste group.

Potting is a household enterprise, and one in which nearly
every member of a family participates. Although practically
all of the families are intricately related to each other, the
craft is organized on the nuclear household basis, almost as
strictly as is agricultural enterprise for farmers. Inter-
family cooperation is evidenced mainly in the construction
of kilns--not in fabrication. Kinship between cooperating
families is fortuitous rather than basic to the cooperative
pattern.

The Dutch tombas (village registers) attest that potting
was carried out in Pelpola in the eighteenth century, and
there is every reason to believe that it has been uninterrupted
since. Unlike agricultural lands which seem to retain fertility despite their constant and even careless use, clay
banks are today showing signs of exhaustion and supplementary
supplies are brought in by canal barge from other points
along the Kapu Ela. Whether dug locally or transported to
the village, the clay is heaped in domelike piles in the potter
neighborhoods, near the canal, and covered with cadjans to
protect it from the sun and rain.

After careful puddling, done entirely by hand, the clay
goes to the wheel. While the wheel is turned by one person,
another, normally a woman, shapes the vessel which, unless it is to be one of the great water pots, is then carried
to the yard for sun drying. Large pots are produced by skill-
fully beating the smaller wheel-molded creations until they
are expanded symmetrically to the desired size. When dry,
the pots are collected for firing in the kilns, which are situated in the house yard or garden. Pots themselves help form
the kiln. Stacked one on the other over a brick base which
holds the fireplace, they are then plastered over with clay
to form the oven. Gradually built up heat is applied for
twenty-four hours. Firing does not take place every day in
each household since often it takes several days or even
weeks of preparation before a sufficient quantity of pots is
at hand to warrant the expenditure of fire wood. Wood is the
largest cash outlay which the potter faces and sometimes
families join together in the firing operation.

Most Pelpolans would agree that the potters are the most
energetic and hard working people in the village. In their
craft there is little seasonability. Nor is there much bounty
from nature, for the craftsmen do not count heavily on even

garden produce. Men, women and children live the life of
their craft, all participating in one phase or another of the
production process. Adult men do the digging and handling
of the raw clay, as well as the work connected with firing
and marketing. The art of molding on the wheel is, as in
many other countries, distinctively a task for adult, often
elderly, women. Women, especially girls, sit on the verandahs, surrounded by pots in various stages of processing,
"beating up" undried pots into sizes twice the dimensions
of the largest ones fresh from the wheel. Children do the
running and fetching, particularly in lining up the utensils
for sun drying in the yards between the houses.

A great variety of vessels is produced, most of them
conventional Sinhalese household utility pots for cookery,
and food and water storage. Designs are simple and without special attempts at artistry or distinction. It is unlikely
that any important innovations either in techniques or design have occurred in centuries. The products of one household are identical with those of any other and, for that matter, practically identical with the utensils produced in other
villages of the caste far removed from Pelpola. One family
deviates slightly from the pattern by making elephants of
rather crude design, a fairly common novelty item in the
town bazaars. All told there are at least a dozen styles of
pots produced, each with a distinctive name and each for a
specific purpose. Some are designed for boiling rice, others
for cooking curries, still others for carrying and storing up
to six gallons of water. In addition a popular item is the
small oil lamp, actually nothing more than a shallow basin
to be used in the home and also in worship.

The market for finished wares is chiefly in the coastal
market towns. Middlemen, however, usually come directly
to the village to buy in quantity and then to cart their loads
directly to Kalutara. Wares are also sold in the local fair and
in similar ones in nearby villages. Occasionally direct
vending is done, the potter man walking through village lanes
with strings of assorted vessels hanging from his pingo, the
light, six foot long shoulder yoke commonly used for burden
carrying.

Pelpola has no known tradition of feudal or status service
by the artisan castes to the cultivators. Nearly all economic
dealings are on strictly contractual bases, although payments

within the village economy are sometimes made in paddy.
In this latter exchange the present rate of payment gives the
potter some disadvantage compared to a cash transaction.
Prices calculated in paddy have not been kept in balance
easily during the current inflation and the village is rapidly
departing from the traditional grain equivalents. Until very
recently some of the potters would visit leading families of
Goyigama caste on Sinhalese New Year bearing a pingo load
of pots. This homage, probably a survival from long forgotten days of status service, virtually required a reciprocal
gift in paddy in traditionally determined amount. As of 1957,
the transitions in the caste system and an enveloping money
economy has thoroughly broken this practice.

Other than the potters there are a few self-employed
craftsmen. Six carpenters, of Goyigama caste, fill orders
for other members of the village, working usually in shedlike annexes to their homes. No work is produced other than
on specific order, and all of these men consider agriculture
as their economic way of life. although most of them derive
more from carpentry than from cultivation.

Since most transport into the village is non-motorized,
carting is an essential service industry. Pelpola has thirteen
carters, and of course many persons own their own carts
which are not for hire. Most of the professional carters maintain the occupation as a supplement to paddy and other cultivation, and the work might reasonably be considered more
an unskilled labor supplement to farming than as entre-
preneurship.

Rural Ceylon has but a tiny leisure class, often descend-
ents of the feudal aristocracy, living on the rents and services due them as large landholders. While Pelpola has a
few large landholders, there is no leisure class and no direct
feudal tradition. Landowners also work and, as testimony to
changing times, they are no richer than the village businessmen. Since landed position is typically inherited, the present
generation of proprietors tends to be well educated in the
Sinhalese educational system. Of the half dozen or so landowners sufficiently well off that employment might be unnecessary, several are school teachers either in Pelpola or
in nearby villages. Apart from these persons of professional
as well as landed status, the small professional and semi-
professional world of the village is composed of school teachers,

a number of whom commute from nearby home villages to teach in Pelpola, the "native doctor" or ayurvedic physician, and a few functionaries such as exorcizers who live more by wage labor than by their professional practices.

Less than a tenth of the village families have a head principally engaged in business enterprise. In addition, however, a number of persons (about six per cent) carry on small enterprises, especially boutique operation, as supplements to other employments, usually agricultural. Full time businessmen include the prosperous owners of the brick and tile enterprises, canal boats, and a few large boutiques. A few others operate rubber processing stations, and paddy hulling machines, and still fewer act as rubber brokers. Although boutique keeping is the most common entrepreneurial activity, it is not the most lucrative and is often combined with paddy cultivation or even wage labor. Since both security and prestige lie in the ownership of land, there is a persistent tendency for the wealthier traders and manufacturers also to become landed proprietors, although their lands are often outside the village.

Chapter III

THE HOUSEHOLD

The elemental unit of Sinhalese society is the nuclear
family, not, as in many parts of India, the joint-family
group. As an economic unit and as a going primary group,
the family, centered about husband and wife, is precisely defined and delimits the greater part of the closest and most intimate relationships of the individual. To be sure, this household established in marriage is intricately enmeshed in community and in kin, but the latter groupings are less precisely
defined than the household, which is typically limited to the
husband and wife and their children. Marriage is a sacrament of kin, but the marital household is the principal functioning unit within the kinship web.

The ideal Pelpola household is composed of one husband
and wife and all unmarried children, and leads an economically
self-sufficient and harmonious life under the beneficent and
mildly patriarchal rule of the father-husband. Dissolution
of the family through divorce is countenanced in law, but not
in the local mores, and while there are rare instances of
desertion, divorce is practically unknown locally. (Polygamy
is not legal nor is it practiced.) The family is united not only by internal reciprocities and affections of common life,
but by the recognition that its solidarity, moral goodness,
and security are the criteria by which lineal familial worth
is ultimately judged. Every couple realizes that by their
actions their kin gain or lose status, and the protection of
the honor of lineal and collateral kin is a conscious factor
in the disciplining of children, the encouragement of their
education, and even the wife's attention to her cookery.

Household Composition

Vicissitudes of age, death, and poverty do not always permit the family to conform to an ideal pattern of composition.
If a parent is aging, and either health or economic insecurity

35

precludes separate dwellings, then the married son, often
the eldest, takes in the aged parent or parents, or alterna-
tively moves into the parental home with his spouse. The
most basic of all loyalties is that of son to parents. Three-
fifths of Pelpola's households (based on a sample of 100
homes) are composed of single marital units while an additional fifth are of one marital family plus miscellaneous
single relatives, often the widowed father or mother of the
husband. Seldom do parents and married children permanently
share the same home, unless one of the parents is deceased.
However, dual family households frequently arise temporarily
as the young married couple moves in with the groom's parents
until sufficiently well off to construct a separate dwelling.

Nearly one-fifth of the village homes are abnormal in the
sense that one marriage partner is deceased or, as is true
in very rare cases, the husband has deserted. Nearly all of
these households headed by a widow or widower have children,
and frequently these are depended upon as the primary
earners. Where a widow with small children survives, she
is likely to turn to the rubber estates for employment. Rarely
would she seek a home with her own or with her husband's
people. Doubling up of families is ill-thought of and it is
generally recognized that petty quarreling is likely to result.
However, married children, especially sons, often build
their houses on the parental property, sometimes a few yards
from the parents' home.

The family by marriage goes through the same cycle as
that known in most lands where the nuclear unit is emphasized.
However, the significance of filial responsibilities here means
less isolation in old age than is found in many countries, and
the ever present kinsmen keep the marital unit in a milieu
utterly unlike that of Western, urban, nuclear households.
Yet couples marry, rear their children, and the children in
turn move out to establish their own homes, whereupon the
original parental home reverts to the now aging couple.
Pelpolans have a most limited conception of birth control,
abhor abortion, and look upon a large family of children,
especially sons, as the proper and valued fruition of the marriage compact. Families are large, though birth rates are
not outstanding for a peasantry. The average existing completed family has included 5. 7 children. In recent years, death
rates have been low.

Housing

There are three types of houses common to the village.
These are roughly correlated with family wealth. Pelpola's
best homes are constructed of kabook, a reddish clayish
earth which hardens to a rocklike consistency when exposed
to the air. Blocks of kabook are used like cement blocks in
house construction, and with much the same permanency
and effect. Covering the blocks is a coat of plaster, either
white or color washed. Homes of this type invariably have
red tile roofs, a few windows with heavy wooden shutters
and often bars, and cement floors. Typically, such a home
has two rooms and a kitchen and front verandah, although a
few of the well-to-do families have houses of five or six
rooms all on the ground floor. Less than half of the village
homes are of the substantial "upper class" type, the remainder being of mud construction or built entirely of cadjans, i.e., strips of coconut palm leaf woven into sheets.
Mud houses, made on the "wattle and daub" principle, with
mud plastered over a lacework of sticks, form comfortable
and long lasting dwellings. The cadjan house is the poorest
type of dwelling and is most commonly found in the new
neighborhoods built on land acquired from the Crown in recent years. Both types have the hard mud floor and thatched
roof, thatching in this area usually being of cadjan rather
than rice straw as found in some communities.

Only in the homes of the very well-to-do is there much
furniture, and this, as well as a differentiated use of rooms,
follows the European pattern. Most homes, however, make
little distinction between sleeping quarters, storage, and
"living," and to do otherwise would be difficult for large
families living in such close quarters. Each house will have
at least a table and usually one or two wooden chairs, and a
large box in which are kept a few dishes and often the good
clothing. Richer homes may have an "almirah," the large
wooden wardrobe of European origin, and the wealthy have
European style parlor furniture. Typically, in a fairly prosperous home there is a single bed on which sleeps the man
of the house. Often this is on the verandah where it provides
a lounging place during the day. Beds are almost always
simple rectangular frames, criss-crossed with laced cane
or string. Most Sinhalese unroll their reed mats at night-

fall and sleep wherever house space and convenience dictate.
Virtually every house has at least two distinctive "rooms,"
the verandah and the kitchen, even though the latter, in
poorer homes, may be nothing more than a cadjan lean-to
at the back of the house. The verandah, as well as the garden before it, is an important part of the family living
quarters. In the better homes, it will be furnished with a
table, wooden chairs, a bench, and perhaps pictures on the
wall, such as German lithographs depicting scenes from the
life of the Buddha. At all economic levels it is here that
friends congregate in the evening and the place where small
household tasks may be done by any and all members of the
family. The kitchen on the other hand is usually a dark and
none too well kept part of the house, having little significance
other than as a place for food preparation. Cooking is done
on an open fireplace or, in poor homes, on small open fires
over which bricks support the cooking pots. The Sinhalese
have no tabus associated with the hearth and only on Sinhalese
New Year does it become a place of ceremony.

Every family has three meals during the day, although in
many homes the early "morning tea" may be very little more
than that. If rice remains from the night before, this will be
eaten, and in season, the wife may prepare some yams or
manioc for the breakfast. Bread is often used as a morning
filler. Popular items, distinctively associated with "morning
tea, " are various sorts of rice flour cakes eaten with plantains or coconut sambol. The latter is widely used with rice
and is prepared from shredded coconut and chilli peppers.
At noon, along with sambol and vegetable curries, rice is
generally cooked, although rarely does the family eat as a
unit. The housewife will serve the husband on his arrival,
she herself nibbling from the pots in the kitchen. The husband may take his plate of food to the verandah. Children eat
as they arrive from school or have the inclination. Only at
dinner is the family present together but even then little
ceremony surrounds the meal; "eating together" has no ceremonial significance and nothing is thought of family members
eating separately--or together. Indeed, as in many lands,
the women usually eat after the men have been fed, and small
children receive their evening meal early. Always the evening meal is of rice, with as many curries as the family can
afford; one in a poor household, as many as five or six in a

wealthy one. In the latter, on festive occasions, ten or fifteen might be served. A meal which is not basically rice is
not considered a real meal, and the test of abject poverty
is the absence of at least one rice meal during the day. Few,
if any, Pelpolans meet this extreme criterion.

Lights are out in the village by nine or ten o'clock at the
latest. Oil for lamps is costly; the next day starts early,
and even on festival occasions the evening meal, served well
after dark, signifies the conclusion of the day rather than
the beginning of an evening. The husband-father, as the
guardian of the household, often retires to the couch on the
verandah. All others unroll mats on the inside floors, and
windows and doors are securely barred. Since the poor
families of the village are large and have few rooms, it is
obvious that many persons share the same rooms for sleeping purposes although in daytime the house space is expanded
by the garden. In the ninety houses judged to be the poorest
in the village, there was an everage of eight persons per
household with rarely more than two rooms for sleeping purposes, and often only one. [1] If the husband chooses to be with
his wife, he waits until other members of the household are
asleep, the front door having in this instance been left un-
barred.

In addition to the house proper, all well-to-do families,
have one or more outbuildings, often little more than dilapi-
dated sheds or cadjan rain breaks. These will be used as
shelter for the bulls and for protecting large equipment
from the rains. Pit latrines are to be found in many gardens,
especially those of the well-to-do. They range from simple
mud and cadjan huts to neatly whitewashed out-houses with
tile roofs. During the past few years more and more of the
poorer mud type houses have been matched with a latrine of
similar construction. Today some sixty per cent of all
families have a latrine. Those without one use the garden or
a nearby grove.

The well is also an important part of the home unit, although only the more prosperous have one or more for their
exclusive use. Always privately owned, they are generously
shared. Wells are more than a source of drinking water.
Typically, the house with a well has two of them; one near
the house and deep, for drinking purposes, and the other
more hidden and shallower, for bathing. The Sinhalese value

baths highly and all members of the household have one or
more daily. This is an important part of the day's business
and sociability. Clad in a sarong, or for women, a cloth
tied firmly above the breasts, bucket after bucket of water
is poured over the body from head to foot at the edge of the
well. A Sinhalese bath often takes an unhurried hour to ac-
complish properly and great stress would be required for
the villager to cut short his normal number of buckets full.
Wells for drinking purposes are protected, and cleaned at
intervals. Many families living near the canal use its waters
for all purposes, rarely boiling the water for drinking.

The Household as an Economic Unit

Home economy varies with the source of family income,
and the potters as a group deviate most widely from all others.
Except for the potters, the normative ideal is that of the
husband-father as the principal worker outside the home
with the wife-mother the hub of household activities. Sons
would assist their father in the fields while daughters help
with cookery and the care of younger children. Circumstances
dictate variations from the norm. These are usually associated with economic stress and involve outside wage labor
by the wife or older daughters. Frequently, also, lack of
family fields leads to wage employment among the household
males and hence their dissociation in productive activities.
Potting, ideally and actually, is pursued as a craft in which
all family members participate. Cookery and child care are
simply added burdens upon the women. Men of any caste or
of any occupation rarely assist in the home chores. Cooking,
child care, fire wood collection are all women's work. On
the other hand, at the busy seasons in the fields, womenfolk join in with the men, particularly in harvesting. Work
with the plough and mamoty is almost strictly reserved for
men, while threshing operations are exclusively male.
    Although a man's work in the fields is heavy and hard,
rarely is it a regular day-in-and-day-out routine. Men
usually have much leisure time. The average household head
estimated that he had worked 198 days in 1950, and this is
probably an exaggeration since some days were spent at
nominal labor, e.g. looking over the fields or at small tasks.
On the other hand, in this land of curries, woman's work is

literally never done. Until very recently even the rice was
hulled by hand in the wooden morter, and curry cookery itself involves hours of preparation. In addition, fire wood
must be collected, perhaps a few rubber trees tapped, the
children cared for and water fetched from the well. As the
years go by many of the minor chores fall to the growing
girls in the family. It is not uncommon to see a girl of eight
or nine out at play with baby brother on her hip. Firewood
collection is a popular task among older girls for it offers
a breath of freedom from parental scrutiny amidst other
neighborhood girls who can giggle together over small gossip and the passing comments of passing young men.

In the cultivators' homes, handicrafts are few. Women
generally have little time for them and men have little interest. Reed weaving is widely done, strictly for home use,
and some women engage in lace making although this also is
usually on a non-commercial basis. For a peasant society
the subsistence arts may seem very scanty.[2] Even in food
it is surprising how dependent are most households upon
money and the "fair, " or boutiques. Most families produce
their own rice and coconuts, but the vast majority purchase
the bulk of their vegetables and curry stuffs.

Family Roles and Relationships

The position of the husband-father is in theory and to a
considerable extent in practice, one of patriarch. His dominant position is formally recognized in all expressions of
family values, and in the behavior patterns of wives, sons
and daughters. This does not mean that the wife is a chattel,
nor is she treated as one, although folk expressions often
include the word "property" in describing the wife's position.
This has no literal support in law nor in Buddhist philosophy
which, while supportive of patriarchalism, is sensitive to
the responsibilities of the husband toward the wife. We are
instructed by a village woman of middle age that:

Once a girl marries she wholly belongs to her husband, and her duty is first toward him. If she invites
his displeasure, who will look after her and her children? A man's first loyalty is to his [blood] family
and aged parents. He should never neglect them just

because he has a wife. She must put up with it although it may be unpleasant for her.

Yet patriarchalism is not harsh, though the husband is
set apart by dignity and dominance. Pelpola husbands have
a keen sense of disregard for matters which reasonably lie
within a woman's province and the woman quoted above recognizes that:

> A woman need not be educated to know how to get
> on harmoniously with her husband. If she is sensible
> she can get around him. If she is gentle about it he
> will come around to her point of view. . .

Although decisions are the prerogative of the husband,
important matters are usually discussed with the wife and
her voice may be an influential one. Pelpola, like all communities, has its "henpecked husbands, " although this usually
takes place through subtle techniques which in no way reduce
the man's sense of dignity before other men.

In many homes it is the wife who holds the family purse.
In rare instances where a woman is the chief wage earner
she herself will control the finances. No husband would so
define patriarchal prerogatives as to insist that her money
be turned over to him. In the normal home, the wife will be
given the money for household operation and with it full latitude and freedom in expenditure. It is generally agreed in
the village that women are more thrifty and better shoppers
than men. Immediate control of the household purse tends to
devolve upon the wife through mutual consent.

Yet the household is focused toward the care and comfort
of the husband-father. For him there is no ill-conscience as
he basks in the sun on the verandah while womanfolk pound
the rice, prepare the curries, and perhaps bring him betel
to chew. In the fields he works, at home he is served. All
conventions of etiquette and propriety confirm this. There
is no toil in which the husband assists the wife, yet she may
assist him in many explicitly male tasks. If there is but one
bed it is his; his meals are served; and language behavior
reflects his special dignity in the home.

To the stranger, the relations of husband and wife might
seem cool, and formal, as well as inegalitarian. No wife

sits to eat with her man. More accurately no wife sits with
her man. There is little friendly camaraderie on the verandah, if and when her chores are done. Close affectionate
behavior in public is unthinkable, and even within the home
wives never address their husbands by name. With others a
wife avoids even such a reference as "my husband, " speaking of him rather as "the one of our household, " or by other
indirection. A husband, however, frequently uses an en-
dearing term in addressing his wife (ooyi) and reference to
her as pavula, meaning "my better half, " is common. While
joking is common in the household, it will not be between
husband and wife. Any open suggestion of intimacy is avoided,
and most especially so by the wife. It would lower the dignity
of the husband in the eyes of onlookers and children, and
might lead to speculations among the neighbors as to the
probability of this wife's general looseness in morals. Nor
is the dignity of the father much compromised by a show of
affection toward children. Only toward small infants can he
express emotion, although toward them he is lavish indeed.
Similar behavior does not occur in reference to either the
wife or the growing sons and daughters since "a father must
be respected and familiar conduct would make this impossible."

It is generally acknowledged that women are more frugal
than men. Men tend to be less dependable, prone to gambling
and drinking. Women abhor such activities. Not only do these
stereotyped conceptions exist, but there is a basis of fact
for them. Large money matters are certainly decided by the
husband, with the influence of his wife, but small matters
concerning household expenditures and activities are in her
hands, and most agree that this is the safer way. On matters
of marriage for a child, the wife is invariably consulted. In
sex relations, however, we believe that the dominance of
the husband is greater than in any other spheres of relationship. [3] As a sexual object the wife most nearly approximates
the concept of property, and some women privately express
bitterness on this score. There is a widespread feeling
among women that in this area of relations men are tyran-
nical and selfish.

Far too easy is it to interpret the conventional distance
between husband and wife as evidencing lack of emotional
regard and the absence of love and affection. To the contrary,
loving attachment is an ideal in the Sinhalese marriage and

is unquestionably present between many, probably most,
couples. Depth of feeling can never be inferred from public display. The Pelpolan believes that the outward show of
affection between man and woman is indecent and suggestive.
In a sense it is a profanation of a sacred bond. The non-
chivalric tradition, coupled with male-centeredness and
emotional restraint, can be grossly misinterpreted by the
Western observer. Even the few romantic unions in the village conform completely to village mores in their visible
relationships.

Parents hold a dignified position in reference to children,
the father one of distance and formality, the mother one of
warmth tinged with the reverence for motherhood widely
known in the East. Toward small infants the father lavishes
his affection, cuddling the small child to an extent which
might be thought womanly in some Western societies. As
the child begins to walk and talk, this warmth is replaced
by aloofness and avoidance of bodily intimacies and other
manifestations of affection. The father turns abruptly from
comforter and playmate to mentor and example, a person
to be held in awe and respect. The mother on the other hand
makes no sharp transition in her role. It is to her that the
growing children turn for affection and through adolescence
it is she who is the intermediary between children and father,
and the special pleader to the husband in their behalf.

Murray Straus, [4] in his studies of Pelpola child training
and personality, has excellently documented the permissiveness of child training. In feeding, no drama, tension or
emotionalism is felt. Children are typically fed on demand;
weaning is relatively late and highly variable, the age ranging from under six months to over five years. Bowel training is lax and mild. Straus has found that nearly a third of
Pelpola children were not fully toilet trained until the fourth
year, yet not a mother professed any difficulty in training
her children. Despite the patriarchal theory and the idealization of child obedience, and some ritualization of parental
respect, punishment is not common and childhood is relatively free of restraints. Even disobedience is often treated
laxly. Closer scrutiny is given girls than boys since their
moral development is a more grave parental responsibility.
Most discipline is imposed by the mother, but mothers confess their ineffectiveness, and severe punishments while

uncommon, will always be dealt out by the father. For boys, childhood is a highly permissive period with wide-ranging play activity through the village groves and lanes. For girls, life is more circumscribed and household duties more confining although the younger girls especially, have rather wide latitude in their play. While little girls are typically shy in the presence of strangers, boys are generally exuberant and bubbling over. Childhood in Pelpola is a happy time.

Chapter IV

THE KIN

The family system of the Sinhalese, and of Pelpola in
particular, exemplifies a complex integration of conjugal
households with loosely defined groups of kinsmen and collaterals by marriage. Although it is the large sib-like Ge
(from gedera, meaning "house") with which the individual
shares his family name, it is the household and the kindred,
especially the local kindred, which have greatest importance
in his social life. A joint family is rare, but so also is a
conjugal family without some relatives within the village
and many more in surrounding ones. Outside the home few
actions are without some significance to the local kin at
least, and for certain events the conjugal home is literally
the surrogate of blood kinsmen. For different types of events,
the boundary of kin interest varies. Fundamental facts of
economic life, the business of rearing children, marrying
of sons and daughters, and burying dead are matters first
of all of households, but such actions take place within a
community of kinship and within a moral framework wherein
the kin have rights and responsibilities. Often the latter
are but vaguely defined though not the less significant. The
individual must respond, positively or negatively, to the
calls for loyalty exerted by the voices of the "house," the
immediate blood kin of husband and wife, the amorphous
body of neighboring relatives, and even that broad quasi-
kin group, the caste.

The Ge or "House"

No one knows how many Ge are among the Sinhalese. In
Pelpola there are about a hundred different Ge names among
the household heads alone. The Ge has no organization and
no formal functions except as it provides a name which is in
some degree a badge of status and implies some sharing in
the legends and realities of ancient prerogatives and duties

46

of ancestors bearing the name. Upon this loose basis, local
loyalties can at times develop but these are usually transitory and cut across by internal cleavages and more powerful
bonds of neighborhood or true kinship affiliation. Never does
the power of the Ge as a social grouping move far beyond
the village limits, although the same "house" names may
be found in hundreds of localities. Without the added bonds
of known marriage unions or unity bred of localism, the Ge
is not a functional group. In the Sinhalese Low Country, and
hence in Pelpola it is a patrilineal name group in which members assume common heritage but less in the sense of clan
than in the sense of an exceedingly loose collection of family
lines presumed to have held a common status in ages past.

The significance of the Ge name is commented upon by
Denham in his Ceylon at the Census of 1911":[1]

To the Sinhalese his name and names of his garden
and property are matters of the greatest importance.
These names are indications of his ancestry, his family
history, and his social position.

The gé name is a surname used before the personal
name--a prae nomen--and is so called because of the
ending gé [from gedera - house]...it usually reveals
the name, rank, occupation, residence, native place,
or some particular characteristic or achievement of
the original ancestry of the family bearing this gé name.

The term "gé name" is loosely used to cover village
names...and house names, which may be subdivided into names actually referring to the place or house from
which the person came or where he resided, and names
derived from ancestors.

So fully is it realized throughout the country that the
name is an index of respectability and position that
petitions to government for permission to change names
are very frequent...

Many surnames adopted from the Portuguese and
the Dutch...came into existance during the periods of
their rule in Ceylon; for instance, such names as
Abrew, Alwis, Costa, Dias, Fernando...

A further title or addition to the names which the
Sinhalese adopted from the Portuguese are the words
"Don" and "Dona, " which are widely used, especially...
after the gé name...

The Ge is composed of patronymic families, although these definite blood lines have no distinctive names and no organization. Neither it nor the family can be conceived as a lineage in the proper sense of that word. Within any given village there is some tendency for families to extend their relationships throughout the local Ge group. The Ge is irrelevant for marriage restrictions. Recognition of lineal family usually does not extend in active memory beyond three generations. The reputation of one's father and grandfather is important in village prestige considerations, but beyond this little practical account is taken of the ancestors. It is a fair analogy to say that the Pelpola patrilineal family line corresponds to the Lodges or the McGintys of Boston, Massachusetts, while Ge refers to all Lodges and all McGintys in the nation. In actual fact it is neither the ultimate boundary of common name nor of common descent which is of most significance for the individual. Rather, in Pelpola as in Boston, it is to one's first degree kinsmen that strongest loyalties are due, and it is with the local kinship community or kindred that one interacts. The chief difference here between these two very different locales is that in Pelpola no one is without a community of kin, and the reciprocities of kinship, especially in the first degree, are wider and stronger, though little more precise.

Since the Low Country Sinhalese generally follow patrilineal naming and patrilocal residence, in regard to the village wherein the newly married couple settles, greater stress is placed upon one's father's forebears than upon one's mother's. Typically, however, there is no family name in the sense of a distinct lineal name for those of common descent. Hence Low Country Sinhalese and Pelpolans have no name which distinguishes families within the same Ge. Some Ge names, however, carry with them a place name--presumably the village of paternal ancestral origin. Also within some Ge, appended Portuguese names and titles have come to be, in effect, distinctive patrilineal family names common to a particular locality. In Pelpola, all Lokuliyanage are also "Alwis." Thus in the full name, "Lokuliyanage Simen Alwis," Ge name is followed by a given name and that by a name adopted locally by all persons of Lokuliyanage during the period of Portuguese occupation. Families of other Ge adopted Portuguese titles presumably, and no doubt in fact, deriving from honorable recognition by the invaders.

Thus several, but not all, Liyanage lines have added the
title "Don, " following the Ge name. These matters are of
interest mainly from the standpoint of acculturation. They
are of no great significance for the kinship structuring of
the community. Persons bearing the title "Don" or the name
"Alwis" do not form lineages or extended families. The origins of the distinctive names are unknown to the bearers and
kinship with others with the same symbol is fortuitous rather
than significant. In recent years there has been a tendency
for fathers to drop the Portuguese "family" designation from
their sons' names.

The Ge as a Status Bearing Body

Among castes other than the Goyigama ("cultivators"),
the Ge name includes reference to the caste of the individual
or, as is often the case, to the occupation distinctively associated with that caste. Thus "potters" all are "Badahelage"
with further distinctions, mainly shown in the place of origin, added as prefixes. In some instances, Portuguese surnames have been taken in addition. Goyigama Ge names do
not literally specify caste but one can be sure that such occupational and status roles as "scribe" (Liyanage) or "owner
of a village" (Gamladege) relate to this caste exclusively.
Among the Goyigama, composing most of the village, it
is generally conceded that two houses have somewhat higher
status than all others. Singularly enough, these houses are
the largest, composing together approximately one-fourth
of the village households, and were probably the original
core of historic Pelpola. Although it is recognized that the
Lokuliyanage ("major scribes") and the Liyanage ("scribes")
are first and second respectively in the intra-caste blood
status hierarchy, the recognition does not warrant much attention. The member of an undistinguished Ge, will speak of
this superiority with an ironic smile or chuckle. Yet the
Lokuliyanage and the Liyanage hold pride in their "houses"
and people of other Ge who are scarcely distinguishable in
status, realize that these folk both claim and have right to
claim some prestige on account of name group membership.
It would be an unwise Lokuliyanage who made much public display of his line's greatness.
In the daily life of the village it matters not a whit whether

one is of honored or of inconsequential G̲e̲, caste being
equal. But at the time of approaching marriage a person of
high "house" may insist upon an equally high status daugher-
in-law, though with all other factors equal such a status difference will be easily forgotten if the dowry offer is raised
a bit. A few long enduring grudges have grown through the
refusal on prestige grounds to make matches within a lower
status G̲e̲ group of the village. The fact that this is resented
testifies to the weakness of the hierarchy. Formal positions
of leadership are usually held by persons of the Liyanage or
Lokuliyanage groups. This comes about less from the status
distinction of the G̲e̲ involved than from the fact that some
very respected family lines are within these G̲e̲, and the
fact that the G̲e̲ is a unit of some weak solidarity when internal schisms do not arise. Normally a villager cares
rather little for the G̲e̲ of a man holding office but is quite
concerned as to the candidate's immediate kin, and his own
personal worth. However, there is usually some subtle
realization that G̲e̲ distinction or non-distinction is present
regardless of familial or personal worth, although the latter are vastly more important in prestige determination.

Ge Solidarity

Many of the intimate social contacts of villagers are
within the G̲e̲, simply through the facts of patrilineal descent
and patrilocalism. Although there is no principle differenti-
ating relatives within and without the G̲e̲, interhousehold
relationships inadvertently emphasize the closeness of the
patrilineal group.[2] Beyond actual second and third degree
relatives, members of the G̲e̲ are simply additional villagers
except as some name-proud member may try to whip up
solidarity on this basis on a local issue or election.

Exemplifying the weakness, but the subtle presence, of
the Ge feeling was a recent village election. Three candidates came forward, two of which were Lokuliyanage, the
highest and largest of the "houses, " and the third a member
of the small and undistinguished Kongahakankanamage. The
Lokuliyanage candidates were uncle and nephew respectively
but came from different cliques. Village opinion, frequently
and often humorously expressed in the tea shops, indicated
that the Lokuliyanage were doomed to failure since they

themselves were divided and their status rivals, the Liyanage, as well as the lesser "houses" would surely support
the Kongahakankanamage candidate. Fearful of losing face
in the village, elders of the Lokuliyanage called meetings
of their name group inviting the two factions to join together
and prevent defeat through disunity. The coalition movement was unsuccessful, some think through the machinations
of the outside candidate who foresaw a landslide victory if
the schism could be maintained. Yet in the voting it was one
of the Lokuliyanage candidates who won by a decisive mar-
gin. It was evident that most of the nondescript families, in
respect to Ge, had supported a man of prouder name, in
spite of the ironic view with which other villagers treat
Lokuliyanage self-importance. And the Liyanage were not
sufficiently concerned at their "competitor's" success to
turn their votes toward a man they did not want in office.
The Ge means enough in Pelpola that leading men can worry
over internal schism and the sullying of its name through
political disunity and failure. It means so little that the
dominant house has in fact a serious split and one of its numbers is elected in spite of this. In a country, and more particularly in a village, where voting often exemplifies caste
solidarity, the Ge cannot be conceived as a substantial social unit within caste.

The Community of Kin

Few Pelpolans could, if they saw any point in doing so,
list all their kin within the village, specifying their relationships. Within each caste, the village is a crazy quilt of kin
ties, for not only has Pelpola married into the same nearby villages for centuries, there is no strong censure upon
finding spouses within the village itself. Marriage with
lines previously affiliated through marriage is preferred.
As we pass beyond second and third degree relationships,
kin reckoning shades into recognition of "connections" and
distant cousins. Behavior toward them is defined much as
it is for unrelated neighbors, and without much concern
over the descent line through which kinship might be reckoned.
However, even the distant relative has somewhat greater
obligation to attend important household functions, although
his role is no different from the unrelated family friend who

also comes. In the practical business of living, beyond the
ties of siblings and of parents and children, and the extension of these ties to the marital units surrounding them,
most kinship reciprocities are hopelessly confused with
neighborliness. In daily affairs one lives among neighbors
and if the bond of proximity is supported by that of kinship,
this is a latent strength rather than a conscious binding
force. In times of crisis and in reference to the symbols
and ceremonies perpetuating the concept of kin obligation,
especially at a time of marriage, close relatives have distinctive significance. The kin are a security system, and
marriages are contracted with some view to enhancing the
nuclear family's strength in time of emergency. In crisis
there are more heroic expectations from the kin, blood and
collateral, than from the non-kin. Yet in most affairs of village life this bond is latent and the security it offers is subjective. The bulk of dependencies are upon neighbors and
these may or may not be related. Significantly enough, neighbors are frequently addressed in the terminology of kin and
would more likely be called in time of emergency than known
relatives of third or even second degree living elsewhere
in the village.

If kinsmen are important for security either behaviorally
or subjectively, Pelpolans should feel well secured. Eight-
four per cent of Pelpola household heads today have living
brothers and of these over three-fourths have brothers living within the village itself. Over half have one or more
brothers within the identical neighborhood. Very few would
lack first cousins, and many have locally resident brothers-
in-law, married children, or parents. Collaterals through
marriage abound in the village and in nearby ones.

The highly localized character of social life has already
been commented upon. This localization is not strictly, but
is very strongly, within a community of kin. Fortuitously or
not, three-fifths of the household heads have "best friends"
who are blood kinsmen. One-half named groups composed
exclusively of kinsmen when specifying those with whom they
commonly gossiped and chatted as close friends. Borrowing
of small items from the neighbors is even more restricted.
Except in the latter relationship it is improbable that the individual is consciously selecting kinsmen for his intimates.
His social world is that of his proximate associates; that

these are kinsmen is a happy concommitant of localism.

The predominance of the male line in forming the household's intimate social world is evident. As might be expected from the emphasis upon patrilocalism, children in two-thirds of the households have closer contact with the father's kin than with the mother's. From a kin standpoint, the wife is more frequently a stranger in the village, but ties which include both husband and children are persistently maintained with her parental home and even her married siblings. [3] Three-fifths of the Pelpola wives having parental homes outside the village, visited them at least once each month in 1950, and on their most recent trip, three-fourths of these women had taken their children. Over half were also accompanied by their husbands. Toward siblings, the wife maintains less frequent but no less enduring visiting patterns. Nine-tenths of those having sisters in nearby villages visited with them during the year, over half going with an average frequency of once each month or oftener. Although residence tends to be in a unilineal kin world, two lines are cemented in marriage and intimate contact is rarely lost with either side.

The chief manifest values in kinsmen arise in their provision of spouses and assistance in emergency. Possibly in some bygone day of stronger familial organization, and greater dependence upon whims of nature and less upon governmental subventions, kin ties may have had constant economic significance. Today, in a commercialized economy and a socialistic state, the value of kin extensions tends to be intangible. A son-in-law or nephew may hope for favoritism in job seeking or in borrowing money. In theory, and to some extent practice, strong men will rally in time of conflict, legal or physical, or in building a house or reaping the harvest. Actually it is common for kinsmen to support a man in legal battles, though this is often qualified by the fact that many court contests are between kinsmen. There are direct economic values in the form of dowry and inheritance but these are usually strictly the business of the nuclear family, although the kinsmen to many degrees are concerned that such matters be conducted decorously and supportively of their own prestige position. Yet the intermittent objective values of kinsmen, and the more constant subjective peace in knowing that their alliances stand behind one, are so treasured that wilful violation of the kin's prestige interests is rarely contemplated. The reputation of the blood-kin is a foremost consideration in the control of children. And ceremonials of solidarity are strong especially, but not exclusively, with the male line.

Although more is expected of kinsmen in time of stress than of friendly non-kin, and alienation over inattention more likely to result, neighborly behavior is not readily distinguished from kinship behavior in most affairs of daily life. Except for ceremonies surrounding the major passages in life, the special nature of kin bonds are most readily seen in the relationship to relatives outside the village. Since informal daily interaction cannot occur at this level, the formal visit to the outside kinsmen is distinct from relations to those who are also neighbors.

The "formal" visit usually arises informally, often by a remark by husband or wife that "so and so will be hurt if we don't go to them soon. " Within the household there is considerable fanfare though the distance may be short. Cakes of various types will be prepared; possibly a bunch of plantains plucked in the garden. Since Pelpolans are uncomfortable at the thought of an unguarded house someone, an older son or a grandparent, will remain in the home, but all who can go will do so. Sarees will be draped and redraped; sandals unworn for weeks will be dusted of their mold. Older girls and the mother will lay on face powder with heavy hands, and put more in a handkerchief for use before arrival. The pair of western type short pants which fit the junior son when last worn will be pieced out or pinned, or another pair taken from an older brother. The older brother, i. e. above the age twelve or thirteen, will wear the familiar sarong like his father.

Though the distance may be but a few miles, and the family well used to walking long distances, a bullock cart will be hired if it can be afforded. Eatable are packed in a distinctive reed basket used only for such trips or, if the entire trip is by foot, the gifts may be slung in a brightly colored pillow case. Arriving unexpected at the destination, the visitors are greeted by the entire host household who come into the garden with happy remonstrances over the great length of time since their relatives' last call. If chairs are lacking, children will scour the neighborhood to borrow

them and the universal symbol of hospitality, betel, is prof-
fered. Amenities attended to, the women will disappear to
the kitchen to prepare the great meal of rice and many curries, and to gossip of impending marriages, health of relatives and the latest village scandals. It will be late in the
night before the travellers move toward home and leave taking will be without much display other than smiles and good
wishes. On some occasions, a visit of this sort might last
for several days, but usually the bonds of affiliation are re-
cemented more quickly.

The type of visit described is typical of that made by a
married couple and their children to the wife's (or if distant,
the husband's) parental home, or to either of their siblings.
Similar visits may be paid periodically to any relatives on
either side, to whom feelings are particularly warm or with
whom contacts might prove advantageous.

Apart from these spontaneous but virtually obligatory
visits, there are various times at which kin reunion is expected. The most important of these is the great festive
season of Sinhalese New Year, when virtually all children
return to parental homes. Young married people usually
visit the parents of both husband and wife. Similarly, attendance at funerals, weddings and almsgivings in memory of a
departed relative practically require attendance unless one
chooses to be socially outside this circle of kinship. The effective community of kin is ultimately defined by the extent
of participation by the individual. Even at exorcizing ceremonies, a family will expect local kinsmen to attend and
assist in arrangements though their roles will not be distinguishable from those of unrelated neighbors. And if a man
falls ill, the neighbor's visit is appreciated but the local
kinsman's visit must be paid if amity between the households
is to be preserved. Only toward a kinsman would the forth-
right villager say, as he may well say, "You did not bother
to come to me when I was ill, probably it would mean nothing more to you if I died." The very looseness with which
kin obligations are defined is undoubtedly a factor account-
ing for the chilly relationships existing between some households and a few of their kinsmen. The recipient of action
frequently has more exaggerated notions as to the degree of
attention he deserves than does the actor. The very looseness of Sinhalese social structure is conducive to differing

definitions of the situation between actor and object.

Visits to the kin tend to be asymmetrical in the sense that elders and those of influence or high status receive more attention than do the younger and the lowly. If poor relatives of close degree are not called upon, they will be alienated, but visits to those of importance go beyond the closer degrees of relationship. An influential man will have scores of visitors in such an important season as Sinhalese New Year, each coming with the token offering of respect, betel. Regardless of status, sons and daughters return to the parental home at this season.

The wedding of a son or daughter is the time at which any household expects attention from the widest range of kinsmen both on the side of the bride and the groom. This also is one of the few occasions at which precise relatives have precise functions to perform ceremonially. In Kandyan, and probably in Low Country, Sinhalese tradition the choice of marriage partners was made by the parents with agreement of kinsmen to the third degree. In contemporary Pelpola responsibility is invested strictly in parents, although kinsmen of all degrees are concerned with the propriety of the match. The wedding celebration represents the public approval of the kin on both sides, and their fellowship at the event actively cements the bonds of the lines ceremonially united through marriage.

The active participants at a wedding indicate the bilateral definition of "close relatives." Besides parents, all uncles and aunts of the couple will be invited and expected to be active in the wedding party. Uncles and aunts are in a sense considered near kin. Of these the brothers and sisters of the groom's father are the closest, but his mother's siblings are also very much part of the intimate kin. On the bride's side similar relationships are important. The bride's brothers would assist in the wedding festivities and their wives would join blood kinswomen in preparation of the wedding food. Thus parents, siblings, uncles, aunts and their collaterals through marriage are the close kin, and will be so considered throughout life. Expectations in reference to them are greater; more frequent contacts should be maintained with them, and greater deference shown the elders among them, than toward all other relatives. Kinsmen beyond these are treated very much as friends and neighbors.

The most substantial and closely defined responsibilities
are those of sons toward parents. With marriage a wife moves
into her husband's "family" and shares obligations with him.
There is no counterpart in neighborliness for filial responsibility to the aging mother or father. Sons, often the eldest
though not necessarily, must see to the welfare of parents,
and live with them in the same house if that is necessary.
The first line of economic security for old age is the estab-
lishment of a family of children, and particularly male
children.

With the remarkable looseness of Sinhalese social organization it is difficult to assess possible changes in kinship
organization. Schisms among kin are not uncommon and it
is possible that they are increasing. With expanding population and concommitant increases in land values, disputes
over inheritance have likely increased. But occasional sib-
ling enmities are no new phenomenon. They have long been
fostered by the inexact rules of inheritance and the practices
of joint ownership of property among households not living
in joint communion. It is likely too that parents are now paying less regard to lineal status propriety in their children's
marriages and so more frequently outrage their kinsmen's
feelings of status integrity. While it may be hazarded that in
early times the local gamsabha or council could settle disputes amicably, today litigation is frequent and sometimes
with enduring ill-feeling among the parties. Though the
"blood feud, " is unknown, coolnesses between kinsmen, even
siblings, may be found. Today in Pelpola, there are perhaps
a half-dozen cases (we are actually aware of fewer) of brother
not speaking to brother and these splits, some of which have
lasted for years, are of course reflected in social participation. These are better described as coolnesses rather than
enmities. In each instance known to us, the precipitating
event has been a land dispute with subsequent litigation.

There is no evidence that at any time did a body of kin
above the household form an economic unit. However, there
has been a reduction in the use of the cooperative work group
within the memory span of older men. This, however, was
not limited to kinsmen, and there is no tendency for such
cooperative units to devolve upon kin. This type of group,
like the "exchange of work" group in other societies, has
been diminished through increasing dependence upon hired

labor and a consequently lowered status position for those
who depend upon gratis help by kinsmen and neighbors.

New values have in various ways contributed to schisms
within groups which by traditional standards should be soli-
dary in time of need. Two brothers of the village have recently returned to speaking relationships after several years
of coolness. Brother A had been active in support of a particular candidate for an office. Brother B felt another man
better qualified and refused to support Brother A and his
friend. By the vague traditional principles of expected solidarity Brother A could charge disloyalty. Brother B de-
fended his course on grounds of democratic responsibility.

It has been observed that the ties between family lines
united in marriage tend to be more symbolic and subjective
than manifest in daily conduct. Likely this situation has
been advanced in the development of a money economy and
increased dependence upon the impersonal subventions of
government medical services, credit associations, and so
forth. For example, traditionally the Pelpola wife returned
to her parental home for the birth of her children. In 1950,
Straus found nearly a tenth of all third grade school children
had been born in a government maternity hospital. [4] Nor do
all mothers failing to use the hospital return to their parental
homes.

On the whole there is not much evidence of decay in kinship and familial solidarities and reciprocities. Mainly
changes reflect minor increases in individualism and rationalism at the expense of imputed, but perhaps never really
functional kinship solidarities. Loose structure in Sinhalese
society is no new phenomenon and the unspecific nature of
reciprocities and of kin boundaries is no doubt of an ancient
patterning. Quite possibly new values, new services by government, and new sources of internal dissension have served
to reduce solidarities as well as functions. None-the-less
the contemporary householder lives in a neighborhood dominated by kinsmen and in a frame of mind in which they are
his security. And the great events of life are still matters
of close concern to the kin. In the daily business of living,
for matters in which we might reasonably expect kinsmen
to be active, neighbors who are often also kinsmen provide
each household with its intimate, primary world.

Chapter V

MARRIAGE: SACRAMENT OF FAMILIES

Preparation for Marriage

There is perhaps no point after infancy at which boys and girls are not being initiated into the roles required of husband and of wife. For the boys this means no more than the unselfconscious patterns of rearing. For girls many preparations, especially after early childhood, are conscious and carefully executed. The boy is initiated into the productive economic lore of his father; the girl, at a still earlier age, learns of baby-care and the intricate arts of curry preparation. The boy child learns early that he is a male to be served by females, while his sister is bred more to submissiveness and service. For neither is sex instruction included in the household curriculum, but with cattle in the nearby fields, and the bedding down of the children in a room likely used for eating, sleeping and procreation, rudimentary essentials come at least as rapidly as the child is interested in them.

Before puberty boys and girls within the family and within the neighborhood frolic together without much regard to sex differences, except that the girl is more closely confined by her household responsibilities. Insistence upon bodily modesty affects the girl at an earlier age than a boy. It is not uncommon to see a boy of age three or four naked in the lane while for a girl this would be rare.

Puberty brings little change in the boy's relationship to either his parents or the world at large, except that his association with female company is restricted. The subtle processes of marriage preparation are still largely unconscious and simply part of the route of growing up to be a man in the community. For girls, puberty marks the beginning of a new life period, and one in which preparation for marriage is conscious and dominant. For the son, puberty is simply a vague phase in the gradual loosening of parental control. For the daughter, it is a specific date, after which parental controls are stronger and many new limitations imposed. The passage of the girl from childhood to adolescence is one of the critical transitions of life and as such is marked by ceremonies dedicating her to ultimate wifehood, and, no less important, dramatizing this now conscious life goal.

When a mother becomes aware of her daughter's first menstrual flow, steps are taken immediately to isolate her from all male contact. If the house possesses several rooms, the girl is placed in one of them, but if there is no opportunity for such privacy, as is usually the case, a temporary curtain is placed across a corner of the main room. Throughout this first period she is to see or to be seen by no male, kinsman or otherwise. It is generally believed that such contact at this time would make her permanently "sexy" and, by implication of loose morals. That such an eventuality will not take place is further abetted by breaks in her seclusion during which elder women come to give warnings as to the proclivities of men, and the need for avoiding them in the interests of that supreme value in a bride, virginity. After the girl has been in seclusion for several days, and the menstrual flow concluded, her mother will go to the astrologer for a reading of her daughter's horoscope and the determination of an auspicious time to bathe her. The post-menstrual bath is invariably given by the dhobi's wife ("washer" caste) under the prolific jak tree, with full account taken of the auspicious direction in which the girl faces, and the auspicious moment. Usually the ceremony is conducted in the early morning hours, there being some astounding affinity between propitiousness and propriety. Water is poured over the girl, in the usual style of a village bath, from a new pot. At the conclusion of bathing this pot is to be dashed against the jak tree by the girl herself. Then taking a knife, the girl gazes upon the tree and stabs it sharply seven times, its milky fluid oozing from the cuts. At this sign the ceremony is completed and the girl returns to her household for feasting and entertainment. Great care is taken that she see first of all as she returns to the house a good omen of fertility, e.g. a pregnant woman or nursing mother. A view of a barren wife would be disastrous. The officiating dhobi woman is given all jewelry and clothing worn by the initiate, who is now decked out in new and more elaborate ornaments and lustrous clothing sewn for the occasion. Puberty is usually the time

at which the girl begins to wear the cloth and jacket or the
saree of mature women, although many girls continue to
wear the western gown as well. Even in the poorest home,
presents are given to the girl and special sweetmeats are
prepared for neighbors and relatives who pay congratulatory
calls. The beating of the great raban, a round drum three
feet or more in diameter, by the women of the family, announces to the entire village, if the entire village is not already aware, that the little girl is now a woman.

Although the Sinhalese have no practice of feminine seclusion approximating that of the Muslim purdah, a young
woman must eschew the company of males, especially mar-
riagable ones, and should demonstrate personal attributes
of shyness and subservience to the wishes of father and
elder brothers. If there is no preparation for marriage in
the sense of heterosexual contact, there is ample preparation for it through training in the role of submissive housewife. Outside the home the adolescent daughter moves in
the company of women. Before puberty she would run er-
rands to the village shop or walk in a mixed group to the
school. Now she will be accompanied by a small brother or
a married sister when she visits the shop, and walk in a
party of girls to the school. A meeting with a village boy in
the lane may offer the opportunity of a few words, but every
girl knows that her reputation may hang in the balance of
how many words pass between them. Daughters of rich
families are somewhat envious of their poorer friends who
work in the nearby rubber estates, where, although in company of older women, they have ample opportunity to be in
the company of young men. Even a public conversation, however, with several feet between the couple, if continued
long, or a matter of frequent occurance, becomes a signal
for the village gossips to infer "the worst." And once such
gossip starts, the girl as well as her parents, knows that
her chance for a good marriage is in jeopardy and concerned
kinsmen may show displeasure. Until her marriage the girl's
only safe contact with males are with those of her own household and perhaps a parallel cousin, i.e., one who is called
by the term of "brother" and with whom marriage is tabu.

Not only is great care taken in situations involving physical contact with eligible men, there are supernatural views
which support the protection of an adolescent. Young women

are peculiarly susceptible to a condition known as the "illness of loneliness" (thanikandorsa or thanikanleda from leda
or dorsa meaning illness and thanikan meaning loneliness).
This depth of loneliness occurs when adolescent girls are
left alone without company and it provides the bodily condition essential for possession by that evil demon The Black
Prince (Kalukumaraya). Possession by The Black Prince
yields a madness.

It goes without saying that the Pelpolans are not wholly
successful in effectuating their theory of adolescent sex
seclusion. To some extent children manage to circumvent
immediate controls but in addition, there are conventionalized parental blindspots. It takes no direct physical contact
for girl and boy to feel aglow at shy or flirtatious smiles
covertly given in the temple or the village lane. Nor can the
activities of a young man be wholly missed when he makes a
point of demonstrating some new finery in the lane by the
garden, or even in the neighboring garden. And in the school,
there is considerable room for contact, although no boy or
girl would dare become a matter of talk. Occasionally love
notes are waylaid by teachers and the culprits are severely,
but quietly reprimanded. Upon a second offense the parents
are likely to be informed and this will be no joking matter.

In some households, particularly among the poorer folk,
evening visits by an interested young man may be permitted,
not of course with the admission that it is an attractive girl
which brings him. The boy would ostensibly come to impart
the latest gossip or talk over the news with her father, the
real object of the visit shyly doing her household work somewhere half in evidence. If the daughter should be employed
outside the home, she might also be on regular giggling terms
with the young man as she passes down the lane. He in turn
will dress in the latest rakish styles, a silvered belt, an imported knife, and perhaps a colorful kerchief or muffler
around his head or over the shoulder. If carried on with
great circumspection this type of romance might incur no
community disfavor particularly if between cross cousins.
It is not to be thought however that many cases arise in the
village wherein it becomes public knowledge that so and so's
boy is interested in thus and so's girl. Such linkages of
names are deteriorating to the marriage opportunities available to the girl and the liklihood is that when the subject of

marriage arises this young man will be considered in terms
no different from those of a dozen others unless he is in a
preferred relationship. Interest in the opposite sex is general.
The association of such interest with any specific individual
especially with the idea of courtship is rare.

For girls the opportunity of pre-marital sex relations seldom is found, even if the girl's desire could exceed her fear
of disastrous consequences. There probably have been instances of pre-marital pregnancies in which with great secrecy folk abortives were used. One or two "shot gun" weddings are rumoured to have taken place in the village, although no one wishes to be pinned down to specifics, and any
marriage which climaxes a romantic attachment is subject
to some suspicion. It is our conclusion that pre-marital intercourse among girls is rare in the village.

In regard to boys, the adolescent period is not one of re-
pression, except in so far as restrictions are placed about
the girls. The village has its gay blades who dress "sharply"
and a few, of well-to-do families, sport racing bullock carts.
While such behavior is calculated in part to stir feminine interest, there is little sexual access to unmarried girls. On
the other hand while any pre-marital intercourse is tabu,
some proportion of the village youth have had sex experience
before marriage. It would be difficult to believe that this
were not so in view of the late age at marriage, i.e. usually
above age 25. Supporting evidence also leads one to conclude
that some grooms, but not brides, have lost their virginity
before that sacrosanct hour of marriage, possibly through
intercourse with married women, perhaps in the village or
with prostitutes outside it.

The Criteria of Spouse Selection

Personal preferences in marriage are not valued highly
by village folk but nearly every marriage match meets the
test of a large number of criteria which the Sinhalese hold
essential. The most fundamental of these is parental approval.
Even in those few instances where individual choice of partners is made, sanctions would be imposed upon the couple by
the entire community if the marriage were effected without
parental approval. This would likely be done even if the two fulfilled every additional requirement of an approved marriage.

In traditional Sinhalese law such approval had to be registered
by all adult relatives of each party to the third degree. In
Pelpola today, the more distant relatives may advise, but it
is the father, usually in consultation with the mother who
makes the binding decision. In most marriages the issue of
parental approval is irrelevant because the entire process
of getting married is directed and managed from start to
finish by the parents.

The criteria upon which parents judge the suitability of a
spouse for their son or daughter can be crudely dichotomized.
There are those which are fixed and universal, and there are
those which are variable, or subject to compromise and
balancing. The universals usually provide limits within which
compromise takes place and in a very approximate sense
can be regarded as the mores of marriage selection.

Other than the usually unthought of prohibitions upon in-
cest, in which a cross cousin is exempt but a parallel one
is not, the most basic considerations are endogomous ones.
Is the partner of Sinhalese ancestry and of identical caste?
Since the liklihood of anyone of outside ethnic origin being a
candidate for marriage in Pelpola is remote, caste identity
is usually the most fundamental conscious criterion applied
to any candidate. No parents of any caste would tolerate marriage union across this line, and no cross caste marriages
exist within the village. Actually it would probably be easier
to establish an inter-racial alliance with a Pelpola family
than an inter-caste Sinhalese one. If a proposed candidate is
of unknown family, simple verbal assurances from the marriage broker or the candidate's father will not be enough.
An emissary will surely journey to this other village to
carry on a sleuthing operation. Fear of caste mixture is perhaps the strongest of all supports for the arranged marriage
system and a source of the greatest intolerance for romantic
unions generally. [1]

The proposed bride must be younger than the potential
groom. Greater age on the husband's part is viewed very
seriously by Pelpolans and marriage of a young man to even
a slightly older girl is not to be contemplated. It is only a
little more variable that the bride be under thirty in respect
to age, and by strong preference, under twenty-five.

The suitable ages at which couples wed are surprisingly
advanced for a peasant people. The mean age at marriage

for living husbands was twenty-eight years and for their
wives twenty-two years.[2] Over a third of the men had married after reaching the age of thirty, while less than a third
had married at ages below twenty-five. The greater perish-
ability of girls on the marriage market is evidenced not only in the fact of their lower average age at marriage, but
also in the paucity of those marrying in the late twenties.
Four-fifths were married before the age of twenty-five.
Nearly one-half married in the five year period of age through
twenty-four.

A delay of several years beyond the age of twenty-five
would, for a girl, cause village talk. Ordinarily, this would
be prima facie evidence that the girl's virginity is in question
or that some other liability is present. If the young lady is
excessively ugly or handicapped in some other obvious way,
no censorship would arise and neighbors might commiserate
with the unfortunate father. There are few women in Pelpola
above the age of thirty who are unmarried, certainly not
more than three or four. One of these, a school teacher, is
the highly independent daughter of a wealthy family. Since
her parents are dead, and she has property in her own right,
she and her brothers can afford to indulge in unusual choosi-
ness in respect to the personal characteristics of her suitors.
Such a condition is rare, for without both prestige and economic power no family would dare trifle with the chances of
permanent maidenhood. Although the dowry power of a man
decreases with advancing years, his point of diminishing returns begins well after the age of thirty. Twenty-five is a
dangerous age for daughters.

From the difference in marriage ages of men and women
it is obvious that considerable disparity in the age of marriage partners arises. This is a matter which village folk
feel is right and proper. Over half of a sample group of
eighteen married women asserted that the ideal age of marriage for a girl was twenty and for a man twenty-five. The
average woman wished the husband to be four years older
than his bride; one woman thought a ten year difference was
ideal and still another, an eight year difference. In marriage
the girl moves away from her father's eye and in doing so it
is important that her husband have sufficient maturity to
control and look after her. And, since age itself brings respect, village opinion is unanimous in condemning a union

wherein the husband has not that added reverence accorded
one of greater age. Marriage transfers the girl from the
authority of the father to that of the husband; the latter must
fill both roles.

With proper assurance of age and of caste, there must
come also assurance of the virginity of the bride. No pre-
nuptial tests of chastity are provided for in Sinhalese culture,
although post-nuptial evidence is, as we shall see, systematically scanned. It is, however, in the time of the marriage
planning that the scandal mongers, and possibly an unsuccessful candidate for the bride's hand, make the most of whatever defections they have noted from the path of rectitude
during her years of adolescence. In the village proverb "a
broken box is not welcome for a lakh" i. e. a dowry of a
hundred thousand rupees would not make a non-virgin welcome in the kin. Since most brides are from villages near
Pelpola and often with Pelpola kinsfolk already in them, gossip is an effective means of preventing a local respectable
alliance for a girl who has been indiscreet. We can safely
say that no girl is married in Pelpola unless the other side
believes her to be virginal. Belief no doubt comes more
easily to some than to others but compromise with a known
sin would be unthinkable.

The respective horoscopes of the couple must match. The
fear of marrying a person of unsuitable horoscope is possibly as strong a factor as caste endogamy in supporting the
anti-romantic attitude toward marriage. Only through the
horoscope can the suitability of man and wife to each other
be tested. This matching is done at an early stage in the arrangement process. Horoscopes are cast for every child
soon after birth and are read and interpreted by astrologers
prior to any critical undertaking. Few if any Pelpolans have
married without astrological assurance that the union would
be propitious. Assortative mating in terms of personality and
physique is practiced on the assumption that such matters
are perfectly revealed in carefully compared horoscopes.
One feature of the readings is that indicating sexual compatibility. In the perfect marriage, sexual organs as well as
various aspects of personality, should be matched. Men and
women fall into one of the various classes (yoni) such as
"rat fit, " "cat fit, " and "cattle fit. " It would scarcely be
possible technically for a woman of "cow fit" to satisfy a man

of say "rat fit, " and the marriage of such persons to each other would likely end in a shambles of frustration. If the proposed pair are not fairly closely "mated, " the matter is dropped. Needless to say a firm belief in the validity of this system by young as well as by old makes even the youthfully ardent reluctant to try the Westerner's more inexact empirical method of courtship.

No doubt some tampering is done with horoscopes, but it would be exceptional if a parent permitted his child to unite with a person clearly unsuited. If there were special reasons for desiring the particular candidate, another astrologer might be asked for a reading but upon a second trial if the future were still black, negotiations would be broken off.

With satisfactory evidence as to caste, age, feminine virginity, and psychological and personal compatibility, the variable factors in mate selection remain. (These will long since have been discussed or hinted at in actual negotiations.) Agreement rests ultimately in the balancing of various assets and liabilities of the two parties, the chief of which are the economic power and status of the family lines, the achieved prestige position of the boy himself, and the dowry power of the girl's people. (Age is also a variable assuming the bride is younger than the groom, and is to be balanced along with these factors.) If a cross cousin is available, and hence under consideration, preference in all of these criteria will be shown him, but not if such preference involves a sacrifice. That spouses are in fact sought from among the kin is evidenced by the fact that one-fourth (twenty-six per cent) of existing marriages in the village are between relatives, mostly cross cousins (especially mother's brother's daughter, rather than father's sister's daughter) or persons bearing the same terminological relationship. A father of several girls may find it particularly advantageous if his brother-in-law provides a groom, so relieving him of excessive dowry demands that might be made outside the family circle. Moreover, the money or property which goes with the daughter may be expected to flow back into the family line through continuation of the preferential system. The failure or even refusal of the kin to provide a preferred mate is not considered a reasonable source of ill-feeling or of gossip and community sanctions.

The most fundamental drive on the side of the girl is the

acquisition of a husband with high personal and familial
prestige. The most fundamental drive on the side of the boy
is the dowry to be acquired, although the family status is also quite important. The dowry is in a sense an independent
variable in the situation. The girl's family knows what it
can raise and then attempts with that amount to acquire the
highest status and most economically secure husband
available. Theoretically, and no doubt actually in the past,
equal lineal (Ge and paternal) status was one of the rigid criteria. Actually today, inexact lineal prestige positions are
subject to balancing by other considerations.

Other things being equal, marriage into a family having
many stalwart males is considered good business for one
never knows when a time of crisis and need for aid may arise.
On the girl's side, among the poor peasants, a boy who will
inherit land is likely to be a good catch. For the wealthier
land owning villager an attempt will be made to find a groom
who has higher prestige of occupation than that of a cultivator. The exceptionally dowered daughter can usually attract
a school teacher or minor government officer who is probably also a small landowner.

Although personal characteristics of the bride are not
overlooked, they are overshadowed by her family status and
her dowry power. Proven ability as a cook or as an energetic
worker or even an unusually light complexion, or superior
educational accomplishment may yield a higher status husband than the available dowry could otherwise command.
Conversely the recognition of slovenliness, ugliness or excessively dark complexion may necessitate greater dowry
than would otherwise be required if she is to be married into a family of equal position.

It is apparent that the inexact criteria of marriage fluctuate around the dowry offer. The higher the dowry the
greater the demand for perfection in a groom. This is particularly true for the well-to-do or educated villagers where
there is the strongest urge for status beyond that of mere
wealth. Daughters are costly but they become the means for
status enhancement particularly if the father is able to command a minor employee of government or a school teacher.
At any social level, however, the dowry is the fundamental
bargaining instrument, the boy's people seeking the highest
possible offer, the girl's people seeking the highest status

husband whose parents will accept the bid. Among the poorer folk it is probable that dowry bids are for economic security, useful relatives, and personal character, more than
for the more arbitrary symbols of status available to the
well-to-do. This is not because the poor fail to revere the
government officer or teacher but rather because they cannot compete in this rarified atmosphere and must settle for
the best possible alternatives among cultivators of much the
same occupational prestige but of differing economic worth.

In the business of marriage arrangement, the greatest
discussion centers around the matter of dowry for the girl,
and the economic and occupational position of the boy. However, villagers like to feel that the secondary factors of
personal worth are actually the dominant criteria for matching. Thus mature village women assure us almost unanimously that the most important single criterion in selecting
a husband for their daughters is that of "good moral character." Similarly the majority feel that a husband with a loving disposition is to be valued above one with wealth, or of
even good family name.

From the standpoint of choosing a bride for an eligible
son, they also point to moral character as the first prerequi-
site. The girl's ability as a homemaker is likewise valued
above such crass consideration as dowry, and even above
her disposition, working capacity, and family "name." These
responses are, of course, no more realistic than the prayers
for peace by the general staff. A loving disposition is cherished and ability as a homemaker sought after, but infrequently at the expense of prestige, and dowry, unless the
individual is grossly inadequate.

Dowry in Pelpola consists mainly of money but in addition
it is expected that the bride bring with her in marriage,
clothing, jewelry and whatever finery her family can fur-
nish. Sometimes jewelry is specified in the dowry arrangement. Well-to-do families may also offer land and possibly
furniture. Land, however, along with livestock is seldom
used in recent years since it is growing increasingly scarce,
and paddy land has the added premium of high subsistence
returns for a minimum of labor. The girl's brothers would
not happily see land leave the line although they might mort-
gage it so that their sister could be suitably mated. Of the
dowered marriages existing in Pelpola today about a tenth

included items other than money in the dowry. Usually "high
land, " i.e. coconut, rubber, or garden trees, was included.
    The amount of dowry proffered varies widely depending
upon the economic position of the family, the degree of sacrifice they will make and the number of daughters for whom
provision must be made. Among all existing marriages in
the village over a fourth (28 per cent) had no dowry considerations whatever. These include a number of "love matches"
wherein the marriage not being a product of parental arrangement was hence not subject to dowry claim by the groom.
In addition, among the poor, dowry is occasionally forgone,
especially if the arrangement is with a related household.
For the large majority of unions, however, the dowry was
an intrinsic part of the arrangement. Expressed in terms
of values current at the time of marriage, the average
(mean) cash dowry of existing marriages was 220 rupees.
(By present exchange rates, about $50.) This sum is roughly
equivalent to the income from four to six months of wage labor in the village. For many families this amount would
represent sacrifice and probably borrowing. The range in
dowry payments is wide. About one-fifth of the dowered married women brought with them dowries of 100 rupees or
less. A tenth had dowries of over 750 rupees, the highest,
in a one-fourth sample of the village, being 2000 rupees.
These values when placed in the context of standards of living, represent important sums.
    The dowry is a daughter's share in family inheritance and
it no doubt symbolizes the transference of responsibility
from the kin of her birth to the kin through marriage. Formal claims by the girl upon her people are resolved in a
dowered marriage, although the new home is expected to remain in a cooperative relationship. Pelpolans are not entirely
clear as to how property rights in dowry are to be reckoned
(under Kandyan law they remain the wife's property). Money
payments are often made directly to the groom. Land gifts
are placed in the name of the bride and nominally at least
continue as her property. As a general economic fact, dowry
is a conventional payment to another line for desirable attributes in a groom. It is not returnable to the bride's family
under any circumstances, although in the rare instances of
separation haggling might occur over a return of dowry and
the husband might acquiesce rather than incur community
censor.

There is no doubt that an adequate dowry is significant
for the status of a wife in her new home, although women in
general speak of the dowry system disparagingly. There is
widespread feeling among Pelpola women that this is an unfortunate custom, leading men to seek them not for their
sterling virtues but for crass mercenary reasons. (Men take
a different view.) However, in practice no daughter will go
happily into marriage without suitable dowry for she knows
full well than an inadequate dowry might ever be a source of
friction. No doubt the difficulty in acquiring the dowry resources is a factor in delaying marriage, for a union without it places the bride in an unenviable position. She has entered the portals of new life without paying the customary
admission fee. In-laws, especially nearby females, and even
the husband, may find occasion to comment on the matter.
In family quarrels, the wife will be confronted by her im-
pecunious background. On the other hand the well dowered
wife has an ever present answer to an ungrateful husband:
"...I did not come to you a beggar..." The dowry is significant for the self respect and psychological security of a wife.

In view of dowry demand on the groom's side, and the
psychological and status value of it for the bride, one might
expect marriage payments to be made with meticulous care.
As a matter of fact they are not. Frequently the bride's
people promise more than they are able to produce. An advance payment is made with the remainder to be due at the
time of marriage. When the ceremony is actually in process,
the bride's people may offer excuses instead of cash. There
is no way of knowing how many husbands have been taken in
by over-optimistic promises, but they are probably a substantial minority. The position of the wife may not be a happy
one in these circumstances. However forgiving may be the
husband, the petty quarrels of domestic life lead to bitter
recollections of unfulfilled dowry expectations. The wife's
position in the new familial neighborhood may at worst become one in which jibes and recriminations by neighboring
women of her husband's kin must be accepted in shamefaced
silence. The well dowered and fully paid up bride can enter
her home with a firm step and face her new relatives with a
high head. While women all but unanimously oppose the dowry
system in principle, they will all work tooth and nail that
their daughters go in marriage with no misgivings. In theory

the system of dowry is disliked but as the institution of marriage exists it is a near requisite for an assuredly happy
union.

Arranging the Match

Eighty per cent of the marriages in Pelpola today were
made entirely through family arrangements. Most of the remainder were through personal choice of the partners with
parental or familial approval. About four per cent involved
some degree of parental reluctance. Arranged marriage is
deep in the folkways of the village, and parental approval of
a match is as deep in the mores. Although some young people
sigh for a romantic union, and a few consumate it, there is
general agreement among youth that "parents know best. "
This agreement is a happy one, for a marriage not arranged
by families carries considerable hardship and danger. Who
can know if romantic attachment will conform to astrological
requirements of sex union? If families do not make a marriage, there is no responsibility for dowry and no assurance
of cooperative assistance in crisis. The rightness of parental
decision is so deeply rooted that children who evade it will
sooner or later feel the opprobrium. A young wife could be
made keenly aware of her position as an outsider in the neighborhood although it is unlikely that any formal ostracism
would take place. Among boys, more latitude for personal
choice is possible, particularly if the father is deceased, as
is frequently the case for those marrying in the thirties. The
young man will none-the-less usually carry on his marriage
plan through the normal arrangement channels. Girls, even
with both parents deceased, exercise no personal initiative
in either the timing or the selection of a partner. The deep-
est familial obligation of brothers is to insure a proper marriage for an orphaned sister.

Like many aspects of Sinhalese life, marriage arrangement with an unsuitable partner approaches the status of a
moral, although not a religious, issue. It is one to be whole
heartedly condemned in the abstract, but in the presence of
a concrete violation, to be treated leniently. Marriages which
have even run counter to parental edict have not placed the
partners in the positions of "out-caste" but rather in the danger of chilly relationships with family, and with an insecure

feeling in the company of kin and neighbors. In the course of
time, parents usually forget their grievances and neighbors
do so more readily. The fear of consequences arising from
personal assertiveness in marriage seems greater than the
treatment of past cases would justify.

The power of the arranged marriage system lies fundamentally in an exaggerated fear of insecurity, social, psychological and economic. Few Pelpolans can visualize themselves as solitary individuals or heads of solitary households cut loose from familial moorings and dependent upon
their own initiative to meet all situations of life as they arise.
The subjective evaluation of kin censor appears greater than
the facts of kinship inter-dependence would warrant. Outright violation of parental desires in marriage is more
serious, for this will surely lead to cool relationships for
some time, and quite possibly to feeling among the neighbors which in time of tension will come forth in vindictive
comments. Negatively the potency of the arrangement system is preserved by the virtual absence of competing forms
of spouse acquisition. While mild flirtations go on among
the youth, and perhaps some occasional hot romances, this
is not courtship in the Western sense, socially or psycho-
logically. No social pattern of courtship is known to the villagers, and emotional attachments by an individual to one
of the other sex is part of a diffused sex interest easily
swayed by external events. Where "romance" has existed,
there is usually meek acquiescence to parental choice on
the part of the girl and an easy shrugging off of the old "love"
by the boy. That exceptions do arise occasionally is evident,
but among existing marital unions in Pelpola very few have
been in opposition to parental wishes. (No doubt additional
cases could be found among those who have left the village.)
The typical girl and boy follow parental dictates as a matter
of course, for marriage is a function of kin to be exercised
by parents. If, as is unlikely, one of the partners expresses
aversion to the proposed mate, the parents will reason with
the child and if that fails usually give in and search for
another candidate. Such a situation does not commonly arise
since by and large the child accepts the going criteria of a
good match. Love, it is said, follows naturally upon a well
matched union.

Rarely do parents engage in long term understandings

with other families regarding the future mating of their
respective son and daughter. Although the cross cousin may
be preferred, he is one candidate among many possibilities
when that day arrives for a father to be concerned about the
marriage of his child. It is difficult to say flatly whether
the father of a girl seeks for her a husband, or the father
of a boy seeks for him a wife. Either may make evident the
fact that their child is ready for marriage. Either may be
approached without any action on his part if it is known that
there is a son or daughter ripe for marriage. At all times
there are potential mates of each sex available in the village or in surrounding ones awaiting partners who fulfill
parental criteria. The rapidity with which an agreement is
reached depends upon the parent's evaluation of the present
candidate in terms of the possibility of a better alternative
at a later date. However, the father of a girl has less waiting power than the father of a boy, for the longer the girl is
kept waiting the greater her deterioration in marriage value.
Boys having a longer life of peak appeal can afford to shop
the market for some years, hoping that by fortunate chance
a superior union will become available. (No doubt this has
something to do with the advanced age of men at marriage.)
Even permanent bachelorhood has no terrors for the male
as for the female although in either case such an eventuality is most unlikely.

Typically a marriage is arranged through a broker, one
of the important functionaries in village life. In some instances an uncle with a wide knowledge of the area may act
in this capacity. The region has professional brokers, however, and many marriages are arranged through them.
Among the poorer folk the broker will be a fellow peasant,
often a kinsman, who keeps in touch with budding eligibles
throughout the neighboring villages. For him this is a vocation subsidiary to his work in the fields or possibly labor
on the estates. Since his patrons are poor and dowries small,
his fees become nominal gratuities. The professional broker
is of a different character; the arrangement of matches is
his life work and he holds a unique niche in village society.

The professional broker, dealing with families of above
average economic position, is a rustic travelling salesman
working the ground in perhaps twenty or more neighboring
villages. Whereas the part time arranger may not be well

known in the district, the professional is necessarily a distinctive and popular character. Jovial, garrulous, and extroverted, the broker makes his calling known by habits of dress that have become proverbial. A gaudy sarong topped off with a shirt and black coat, given added distinction by a black umbrella, is his traditional garb. Not all abide by the conventional costume, but for an ordinary villager to dress so ostentatiously could lead some neighbor to comment "Oh, a marriage broker no less." This is stock-in-trade to the practitioner, and his visits, filled with good humor and color, relieve the sameness of life and provide the gossipy substance for good tea-shop conversation.

Summoned to the home by a concerned father, the broker after due time for food, drink and chat, settles down to the details of the case. Usually he will view the candidate, for if a girl he must later wax eloquent of her charms. Invariably he will gather data on the financial position, the proposed dowry, if a girl, the occupation and wealth if a boy, education, and other matters useful for a transaction. Invariably he will call for the candidate's horoscope, for without this no arrangement could be contemplated. A good broker will already have potential partners in mind before the visit is over. His acquaintanceship is wide in surrounding villages, and usually he has in his possession at any time the horoscopes of several persons of opposite sex. One of the area's leading brokers, was in possession of sixteen horoscopes when last questioned, nine for men and seven for women.

Armed with personal and familial facts, claims, and promises, the broker either consults his own mental file of candidates of opposite sex, or seeks out a father known to have a marriageable child. The horoscope of the candidate is handed over and the broker stays late in the evening extolling the virtues of the other party, the excellence of his or her family, and the wealth which would devolve upon the union. The facts of the case provide merely the foundation for the glowing account given, and this is usually recognized by the patient but interested father who may in fact know the interested party much better than the broker and in any case has more objective sources of information in his own kin scattered through the district.

The horoscopes of both proposed persons are sent by the

parent to his astrologer for matching. If the horoscopes indicate the couple would be ill-suited the matter is usually
dropped, the broker retrieving his clients' horoscopes for
use with other prospects. If the astrologer reports favorably,
and the other candidate seems feasible otherwise, the broker
is then expected to arrange a time for the boy and his party
to call at the home of the girl.

The introductory visit at the girl's home is a formal occasion. The prospective groom flanked by father, uncles and
perhaps a brother-in-law, is introduced to the prospective
father-in-law by the broker himself. No female relatives
are included in the party, but there will have been prepared
tea and cakes and possibly a rice meal. No business of the day
would be talked until the auspicious moment for discussion.
At the proper time the girl enters the room with her mother.
As the young man is pointed out she presents a tray of betel
to him. In a well-to-do household, she might then sit and
listen to the men talk; in less sophisticated circles she would
retire to the kitchen.

At the first meeting little would be accomplished beyond
"ice breaking." Soon thereafter, if the girl's father is interested he and his brothers, and perhaps his eldest son, will
return the call. They will be treated with utmost concern
and the business of moment will be carried forward. If the
discussion develops to mutual satisfaction, a third meeting
is arranged at the girl's home at which the two parties pur-
sure their business in earnest, even to the point of bargaining over dowry. If each side is satisfied, an engagement is
agreed upon.

The day and hour of the engagement ceremony is fixed by
astrological calculations and takes place at the home of the
bride-to-be. It is a great and exciting occasion for both
families. The young man will dress in his finest cloth with a
shirt and coat with a buttonhole flower. Often the coat will
be borrowed from some prosperous relative or neighbor.
Possibly the youth will wear shoes, and if he does, it may be
for the first time in his life. They too might well be borrowed
from some older person who keeps them for just such festive
events. At an auspicious time the hopeful groom will set out
for the girl's home attended by many relatives, uncles,
brothers, brothers-in-law and cousins. Most of the party is
decked in finery and they will draw the admiring gazes of

neighbors as they move through the village. Only a cad
would laugh as one of the party stumbles in his unfamiliar
shoes, worn perhaps on the wrong feet. If the journey is to
another village, hired bullock carts will take them.

As the fiance and his party arrive at the girl's house they
are welcomed by the girl's near relatives. Western style
handshaking is rare, greetings being given in the traditional
fashion, palms pressed together chest high with fingers upward. The village Registrar makes a note of the fact of engagement, and the guests and hosts repair to tea or to rice
and curries. At this time a friend of the groom reads aloud
the naketh pathraya, the article of agreement and the specifications of the wedding to come. The naketh pathraya is a
traditionally patterned document drawn up by the village
astrologer, sprinkled with Sanskrit and Pali terms. It is to
be intoned in a conventionalized manner. Its language is
stately with aristocratic phrases and religious references,
many of which are beyond the comprehension of all present.
The less understandable this document, the more highly it
is regarded as a piece of classical work. The astrologer
makes clear, however, the auspicious day, hour, and minute
of each important stage in the wedding and announces the
willingness of both man and woman to enter into marriage.
Even the precise minute for beginning the construction of
the cadjan sheds under which wedding guests are to be served
their food is given, as is the moment at which the bride and
groom will enter into various stages of the ceremony. With
the conclusion of this reading, the document is handed over
to the bride's father. At this moment the couple rise to meet
each other and exchange rings. The groom also hangs a neck-
lace upon the bride. This moment is regarded with reverence
and with pleasure, and even the poorest families do their utmost to make it impressive and ornate. In conclusion,
flowery speeches are made by men from each side and by
custom half of the promised dowry is handed over to the
groom. He in turn passes it to his father for counting, and
the father either carries the money at departure or hands it
over to the bride-to-be. The latter is good form for it indicates to her people that the husband needs no help from
them in preparing for the wedding day, a process involving
considerable expense. The boy and his people return to their
homes and on both sides preparations for the wedding begin

at once. Engagements are as short as the astrologer deems
auspicious. Seldom do many weeks elapse.

The Wedding

The legal requirements of marriage are fulfilled with its
registration, but for most village families, the extra-legal
ceremonies are great occasions in which kinsfolk and friends
renew their loyalties and extend them. Although practically
all marriages in Pelpola are legally registered the poorest
homes sometimes dispense with the customary celebrations.
Wedding ceremonies and festivities usually last from one to
two days. The first day will be one of feasting; the second
will include the solemnizing of the union. At no stage in the
entire process does religion or a religious functionary enter
in. Marriage is a sacrament of families and it is kinsmen
who tie the knot.   .

Several days before the celebration, invitations are extended to relatives and close friends on either side. The
invitation "list" must be scanned with great care, for inad-
vertent ommission of a kinsman could mean permanent
alienation. On the other hand, to include a friend of lower
caste would be to create an appalling scene at the wedding
house. Even the inclusion of certain relatives who are
deemed to be of inferior status might lead to comment and
ill-feeling. And unless the invitation is extended in the traditional manner the close kinsman will not attend. The more
distant kin and friends might be given haphazard invitations
but those of close connection, although the precise degree
of relationship is not conventionally defined, must be waited
upon with betel, the acceptance of which indicates their
pleasure in attending. Usually festivities take place in both
the groom's and bride's houses, but the binding ceremony
and its festivities is almost always held at the bride's.

For several days prior to the wedding feasts, (at both
the bride's and the groom's houses) close friends and relatives have been laboring to make ready. Women come to
help in the preparation of eatables, men to work on the construction of shedlike cadjan out-buildings to protect the
guests from sun and rain. If the family is prosperous, a
phonograph with an amplifier sufficient to rouse the entire
village is set up in the garden. Throughout the entire festive

period its speaker, fastened to a tree, blares forth a poly-
glot collection of North Indian and Sinhalese recordings. If
finances permit, colored lights will be placed in the garden
trees. There is no mistaking a wedding house. Kinsfolk by
blood and by marriage, close neighbors, and even family
friends from afar, stream in during the day to eat and to
talk. Usually each group of guests places a money gift in an
envelope. This will be placed on the betel tray and handed
over to the father of the bride or the groom, depending upon
which feast is being attended. The father of the person to
wed, in accepting, will depreciate the importance of money
in words like, "Oh, we are not worried about any presents,
we are only happy that you come for my child's marriage. "

Although the attendance at wedding feasts is strictly
among caste equals and presumably by equals in blood within caste, conventionalized exceptions prevail. Among the
high caste families, helpers of inferior caste position,
usually "potters" in Pelpola, will carry water and do chores
other than cookery. No "potter" and no person of any non-
Goyigama caste would ever attend a Goyigama wedding except in the capacity of a menial or functionary. One caste of
low position is invariably represented at Sinhalese wedding
ceremonies; the Hena (dhobi or washerman) plays an important
role. For one of unknown caste or of known lower caste to
sit at the wedding feast would be unthinkable, although on
other occasions adjacent seating might be accepted as a matter of course. When Pelpola "potters" marry, the situation
is somewhat different and frequently they invite the men
(but not families) of the higher caste, if personal and friendly
relations exist between them. The "cultivator" does not
feel it amiss to accept such an invitation. Upon arrival he is
an honored guest, seated separately and offered bottled
drinks, but not food. He should give an ample money present
to his "potter" friend, and indeed no hard feelings will arise
if the present is sent without personal attendance. It pleases
a "potter" family, however, to have one of higher caste seen
at their household functions. Except that they are not served
by the dhobi, there are no significant differences in their
wedding customs.

The wedding day finds the households of both bride and
groom at a high pitch of activity, the one making preparations
for the ceremony and guests, the other, selecting those who

will go to the bride's house and arrange for their departure.
Those who go in the groom's party will be selected after
careful consideration, taking into account nearness of the
relationship, personal prestige and immediate family status.
Female as well as male relatives will be in attendance. Before the groom sets out, an exorcizer will come and tie an
enchanted string upon his arm, and a similar string will
have been tied for the bride. This magical rite prevents
enemies of the couple from casting a spell (kalava bandanaya)
upon them which might prevent sexual intercourse. The
rite has as well a generally protective function, especially
in regard to illness. Actually the practice is maintained by
sheer weight of custom. There is practically no conscious
fear of black magic being wrought.

At the auspicious moment the groom sets out. Frequently
delays occur among the accompanying relatives but the
propitiousness of the moment is saved if the groom steps
outside the doorway of his home.

Better than generalized description of the wedding is the
following firsthand account written by the "best man" in the
wedding of a prosperous villager:

It was the morning of 19th February, 1951. We went
to the bridegroom's house at about 9 A.M. There were
about thirty-five or forty visitors. Most of them were
relatives. We were invited to partake of some tea with
the other relatives and friends. When that was over, the
party got ready to leave for the bride's place. The
auspicious moment for the ceremony was 10:47 A.M.,
by which time we had to be at the bride's place at Paya-
gala, about twelve miles away. We started from the
bridegroom's place at about 9:40 A.M. The bridegroom
and I occupied the rear seat of one car. I had to carry
the bouquet of flowers for the bride. There were six cars
in our party. When we left, firecrackers were lighted.

We reached the bride's place at 10:25. All of us got
down from our cars but no one went in. A dhobi man
from the bride's side laid a pavada [ground covering]
from the entrance to the house out to about fifteen feet
on the ground. An elderly man from our side went in
first of all and gave the bride's mother, who was standing at the entrance, some betel leaves. Each betel leaf

signified one person in our party. Each betel leaf that
was bent into two signified one low caste man that went
in our party. This is to notify the bride's party that we
are so many in our party, so many low caste, etc.,
and to give them enough time to make the necessary
arrangements to entertain them--to prepare so many
seats, drinks and chairs and plates at the tables. But
today such notification does not have any meaning, because the bride's party are always ready to entertain
the possible maximum number of people that are likely
to turn up. So immediately after the betel was given,
I--the best man--walked along the clean white cloth,
saluted the bride's mother who was at the entrance to
the house, and walked straight in. I, being the best
man, was forewarned as to what I was expected to do.
The bride was seated in the center hall of the house on
a setee with two other girls, one on either side. As I
was walking into the house I heard someone say,
"Show him the bride." Then another remarked "She
is conspicuous enough." And indeed she was, in all
the paraphernalia of a bride. I walked up to her,
saluted, bowed, and presented the bouquet. She accepted
it without getting up. Immediately after I came in, the
bridegroom and the rest followed. They all saluted the
bride's mother at the entrance to the house, went in
and sat down. There is something special about the
coming in of the bridegroom. As the bridegroom came
on to the doorstep, a brother of the bride went and
washed the feet of the bridegroom with a basin of water,
which was placed there beforehand. On such occasions
the bridegroom is expected to present the person who
washes his feet with something, usually a ring. On this
occasion an unexpected thing happened. The bridegroom,
instead of giving the ring to the bride's brother, dropped
it into the basin of water. The basin was wanted inside
the house for something immediately after. The brother
did not notice that the ring had been dropped into the
basin. The man who came from inside the house to
fetch the basin threw out the water, and with it the ring.
The dhobi man whom our party took along, saw the
ring being thrown out. He picked it up and returned it
to the bridegroom, who was surprised at the incident.

Some people mistook the accident to be an unkind gesture
on the part of the bride's brother. But it was all a mis-
take, an oversight. This incident went round the crowd
and all of them were tittering about it. Some even talked
aloud about it. But the bride's brother explained that
it was just an oversight, and the incident was hushed in
jokes and laughter. Since the bride's brother was wearing glasses, one person humorously remarked that "he
needs another pair of spectacles to see better." In a
few moments the whole thing was forgotten and no one
spoke a word about it later. Meanwhile, light drinks
and cigarettes were served to the visitors. The women
were all inside the house, i.e. the inner rooms of the
house. The males from both sides were seated and engaged in friendly, loud talk and laughter in the outer
rooms and verandah. Still the bride and groom did not
meet or talk together. The bride continued talking with
the other women inside the house, seated on the same
setee as when I gave her the bouquet. She wore a sad
look on her face. Meanwhile the time for the poruva
ceremony was drawing near.

The poruva is a cage-like affair done in planks and
pasted with decorative white tissue paper. This one was
just large enough for two people to stand inside. It was
about nine feet tall and dome-shaped at the top. The
standing platform in it was not more than seven or eight
inches from the floor. The poruva was about four feet
by five feet with four pillars on the four sides, with the
two broad sides open and the narrower sides pasted all
round with white tissue paper cut into flowered designs.
In front of the poruva on either side were placed two
pots with a young coconut flower in each. In the middle
of the flowers were lighted two coconut oil lamps. The
poruva was placed in the central hall of the house. It
was placed to face north.

About five minutes before the auspicious moment, at
10:42 A.M., the couple came and stood behind the
poruva with the bride on the groom's left. Just before
that, seven nelis (fourteen measures of rice) were spread
on the floor of the poruva. This was covered later with
a white cloth. At 10:43 an elderly looking man began re-
citing a long narration, which ended by inviting the couple

to step into the poruva. An uncle of the bride and an
uncle of the groom led them to the poruva at 10:48 P.M.
On the right side of the poruva was a heap of betel
leaves arranged in hands of forty leaves. There were
about thirty such betel hands in the charge of the dhobi
man whom we took with us.

The first thing that the couple did in the poruva was
to drop a rupee each on the floor. This is supposed to
be the payment for the dhobi of the bride's side, who
supplied the clean cloth for the floor of the poruva,
and who had spread the rice over which it was laid.
Any amount may be paid for the dhobi depending upon
what one can afford. In this case it was actually two
rupees from each side. Next, the dhobi man whom we
took with us gave the bridegroom a hand of betel. The
groom handed this over to the bride and the latter
dropped it at their feet on the floor of the poruva.
Seven hands of betel were thus passed on from dhobi
to the groom and then to the bride and dropped at their
feet. Then began blessings for the couple in the form
of the recitation of Pali and Sinhalese stanzas. After
the spell of recitation, which took about ten minutes,
the groom's dhobi man gave the groom another two
hands of betel, these wrapped in a white cloth. This
the groom gave to the bride who gave it to her mother.
Next, all of the bride's near relatives were invited forward and given a hand of betel by the bride. All these
hands of betel went from the groom's dhobi to the
groom and from him to the bride, who gave them away.
This was a highly emotional moment because the giving
of betel and saluting the bride's relatives is tantamount
to her bidding goodbye to her own people. The groom
was, for the moment, forgotten. Some relatives were
highly moved emotionally. They came and kissed and
hugged the bride and shed tears. Others just came, took
the hand of betel from the bride and went off. After the
giving of betel was over, then came another spell of
recitation from the same person who recited earlier.
This lasted for another ten minutes or so. Next came
another stage when the bridegroom had to dress up the
bride. The dressing of the bride with clothes brought
by the groom symbolizes his taking charge of the woman.

The groom's dhobi gave the groom a clean white cloth
(hela) just sufficient to go round the waist. The bridegroom wrapped this around the bride's waist, over the
clothing she was wearing, and pinned it so that it
would stay on. Next a jacket was given by the dhobi to
the groom. This too, was pinned round the upper por-
tion of the body of the bride. The significance of this is
that in historic times the bridegroom was expected to
provide the bride's clothes before taking her away.
But today this is not necessary, because when the bride
comes on to the poruva she is in the best clothes that
she can afford. While the bride was thus "dressed, "
there was still another spell of recitation. When this
was over, after about five minutes, the bride's uncle
tied together the small fingers of the groom's left hand
and the bride's right hand with a gold chain. Then water
was poured on the two hands thus tied together. After
the water was poured, the two hands were united. During the pouring of water and tying the two fingers, some
stanzas were recited. After that, six girls recited
Jayamangala Gathas in front of the couple. The bridegroom gave each girl some money enclosed in an envelope after the recitation was over. After the girls
finished their Jayamangala Gathas, an elderly uncle of
the bridegroom invited the couple out of the poruva, re-
citing some verses. Just as the couple stepped out of
the poruva, some one split a coconut with one blow of
a katty knife at the entrance to the house. This is a part
of the ceremony. It was once believed that if the female
half of the coconut was larger than the male half, when
once it was split, the couple would have more female
children than male, and vice versa. (The two ends of
the coconut are known one as the male and the other the
female end. The female end is that with three "eyes"
on the shell.) But today no significance whatever is
attached to this incident. No one cared even to notice
which half was bigger after it was split. The person
who split the coconut himself did not look at it closely.
He collected the two pieces and walked into the kitchen
with the knife.

When the couple got out of the poruva the jacket and
the cloth which were wrapped round the bride over the

other garments were removed and given to the dhobi of
the groom's party. The couple was in the _poruva_ for
forty-five minutes. When the ceremony was over, the
bride sat down where she was first seated, while the
groom walked about the house chatting with people. After about fifteen minutes all were invited for lunch.
At this moment there was another incident. The people
of the groom's party insisted that the drivers who came
with them should be fed first. But the bride's people
said that their custom was to entertain the drivers later.
There was some talk about this. After some time it was
settled that the drivers should be fed later. So we had
lunch at about 12:15 P. M. Our party as well as the
bride's people ate together with the couple. Everyone
ate without much talk. No speeches were held at the
lunch table. One of the bride's uncles said that as there
were others waiting to eat we would be holding them
back if we were to deliver speeches and keep on sitting
at the table. As soon as we finished eating we got up
and went out. The couple stayed behind to keep company with the next batch of people, who came to eat.
At about 1:35 P. M. all had finished their lunch. The
auspicious time for the couple to leave the bride's
house was 1:58 P. M. So at 1:58 both of them got out
of the house, but everything was not ready, so chairs
were kept in the garden for the couple to sit and wait
till the others were prepared to go. When everyone
was about ready to leave, the brother of the bride gave
a talk. He said that it was customary to give something
for the bride when she left. He was talking about the
dowry. He said that part of the dowry was already
given and the rest has been banked in the Post Office
Savings Bank. Therewith the brother gave the Savings
Bank book to the bride in front of all the others. The
brother also said that if there were any shortcomings
or slight falterings on their part in entertaining the
visitors, to excuse them for any such faults. A person
from the groom's side, too, got up and said that there
were no shortcomings or any faults on the part of the
bride's people, and the visitors were very well entertained. And even if there were any mistakes on the
part of the bride's people, that they would all be ex-

cused. After the brother and the other man finished
speaking, the party started to set forth. Many more
people, especially women of the neighborhood, came
to bid goodbye to the bride by kissing and embracing
her. The bride was emotionally moved; she began crying at the realization that she was leaving her own
people.

Everyone got into their cars and began to leave. The
bride's near relatives and parents came along. In all
there were ten cars in our party, four cars from the
bride's side. Although the couple got out of the house
at 1:58, when we actually left it was 2:45. A woman
came in front of the couple's car with a filled pot of
water, which is considered a very good omen. So we
were now heading for the Photo Studio at Kalutara. We
came to the studio at 3:05 P.M. Most of the party
stayed in the cars. The bridal couple and some elders
from both sides, and I, went into the studio. First of
all a photograph was taken of the couple. Then there was
another photo with the couple and two other pairs of
males and females on either side. When that was over,
the party started to the bridegroom's house. We
reached the groom's house at 4 P.M. There was what
they call an "At Home Table" prepared on a grand scale.
The food consisted of apples, grapes, bananas and
many other fruits, as well as cakes of many varieties,
biscuits, cheese, patties, cutlets, rolls made of fish,
vegetables, and meat. There were a few scores of
varieties of eatables, a mixture of Western and Eastern
preparations. There were also many kinds of light drinks.
Bottled drinks, iced coffee, tea, hot coffee, etc. All
the people who came, except the bride's party, gave
something to the bridegroom. They invariably gave the
groom some money enclosed in an envelope. Before
the couple entered the house of the groom there was re-
citing of Jayamangala Gathas by five girls all aged about
twelve to fourteen. A pavada was laid at the entrance
to the house. Just as the couple entered the house a big
firecracker was burst. It was overhung at the entrance
to the house. Just as the couple came under it this was
burst by pulling a wire from a distance. In the cracker
were multicoloured confetti, which rained on the couple.

The five girls who recited <u>Jayamangala Gathas</u> were given some money enclosed in envelopes as presents.

After a while the bride and groom came out of the house and sat down on chairs that were in the garden. There were about twenty-five others already seated. The bride's party who came along, as well as those in the house, came out to listen to speeches. First of all one elderly brother-in-law of the bride spoke on behalf of their party. His speech was mostly advice for the new couple as to how they should make their married life happy. He began by giving an account of the character and capabilities of the bride as a wife and a life companion for the groom. His eulogy of the bride was in the superlative degree. He expressed his gladness at being able to get such a worthy retinue of relatives from the husband's side as a result of this marriage. He ended his speech by wishing the couple long years of happily married life, with plenty of virtuous sons and daughters. He also begged pardon from the bridegroom's side for any faults of the bride's side if there were any. A person from the groom's side replied, and speeches were over. It was about 5:15 P.M. now. Then the bride's party began to leave. The females of the bride's party kissed, embraced and bade goodbye to the bride. When the father of the bride bade goodbye, the latter fell on her knees in front of the father crying. Then the father raised her to her feet and pacified her. The mother of the bride only stayed behind. The rest left. (It is interesting that the mother of the groom did not go to the bride's house to bring along the bride. This is because she had to look after the affairs of the groom's place as the father of the groom was not living.) Visitors continued to come till late in the night.

The whole proceedings from start to finish did not take place even as smoothly as described. It was done with uncertainty and hesitancy at almost every step. To call the whole proceedings an unrehearsed play would not be inapt.

The Couple Comes Home

The bride and groom return to Pelpola before the eyes
of the village neighbors. It is an occasion where neighbor
women gape at the bride's finery or chatter at her lack of
fine dress. For the boy it is an occasion for smiles and
greetings to his friends but for the bride it is a gauntlet of
the pryingly interpretative eyes of her new relatives. She
knows that she is being welcomed--and also being covertly
dissected and that an unfirm face may even stimulate comments as to her fear of the first night of marriage. If some
kinsfolk have not been whole-hearted in the marriage, there
may be comments passing that her melancholy arises from
a guilty knowledge of spoiled virginity. On the other hand,
if she is gay, it may be openly hazarded that she is a forward hussy over-anxious for sex experience. Where the
trip to the bride-groom's home can be taken by car rather
than by cart, it is a welcome escape from a long passage
through the village lanes.

Normally the first night of marriage is spent in the
groom's parental home. Ancient texts describe the manner
of decorating the nuptial bed but all this is neglected today,
although the maximum privacy possible is provided. Anx-
iety reigns in the household, and indeed back in the bride's
own home, for the test of her virginity approaches. Before
retiring, a new aunt of the bride offers advice and best
wishes for a happy night, and then there is spread the white
cloth, (hela) given her during the poruva ceremony, upon
which the couple is to sleep. It is by the examination of this
cloth on the following morning, that the relatives determine
whether or not the new daughter-in-law was indeed a virgin.

Early in the morning the family's dhobi woman enters
the bridal chamber and examines the hela. If the cloth is
stained, by the flow from a ruptured hymen, haste is made
to announce the tidings to the waiting household. When the
girl is thus shown to be a virgin, the house becomes alive
with renewed celebration. Firecrackers will be set off, the
drum (raban) played, and so the entire village is aware that
a good girl was married into their midst. If the girl's
parents live nearby or in an adjacent village, a messenger
is dispatched bearing betel and red flowers indicative of
the happy climax. Customarily the bride's parents come to

call during the day. Parents, and new relatives as well, may give the girl presents.

In the memory of living Pelpolans, there are no cases in which the "evidence" of unchastity in a bride has been found, although it is conceivable that enmities between households have in the past, arisen from this basis. Village women say that nowadays, brides and grooms might conspire to keep the secret of a "broken box, " by claiming that the hela was forgotten or by some similar device. Actually feminine unchastity must be rare in Pelpola, but in any case, evidence of it would not be publicly proclaimed, as seems to have been expected by tradition. Neither family would wish to appear foolish and degraded in the eyes of the village, and despite some feeling of hurt the fact of a joyous union would be announced quite normally. The new couple is established in the village amid the husband's kin and friends. The wife must build her friendships among them.

Chapter VI

FROM BUDDHISM TO THE WONDERFUL WORLD

It is the claim of some Sinhalese philosophers that in Ceylon Buddhism has retained its purest expression. This may, indeed, be true, but pure Buddhism is a philosopher's abstraction. Sinhalese Buddhism is pure; Buddhists are not. The Sinhalese are Buddhists, but in the same breath we may as rightly say that the Sinhalese are believers in numerous gods, sub-gods, and demons, and that non-Buddhist supernaturalism in the form of planetary influences, wood sprites, sorcery, and ghosts is ubiquitous. To some extent Lord Buddha has been integrated with these complex bodies of supernaturalism. To a greater extent the supernaturalism stands as distinct systems of thought superficially rationalized to the agnostic, rational, and metaphysical concepts of pure Theravada. The lack of an object of faith in the Buddha's teaching has been supplied by the folk themselves in reference both to their Lord, who deplored faith and exalted reason, and in reference to a wonderful world of powers no more than casually associated with Lord Buddha and the concepts for which He stood.

When in this and the following chapter we move from the villager's interpretation of Theravada Buddhism and its concepts to a discussion of supernaturalism, the distinction is less one of analysis than of real discrimination in village thought and behavior. The teachings of Lord Buddha provide the philosophical and metaphysical bases for interpretations of life. The Buddha Himself is the object of the most worshipful and reverential behavior. Folk supernaturalism does not have its roots in Buddhism nor is it considered "Buddhism." It is a world of power, elements of which may well antedate the Buddha Himself but have not been incorporated in His teachings. The villager usually recognizes the distinction of that which is of the Buddha and that which is of the gods. Still, in a limited sense the Buddha has been rendered a supernatural being, and to certain Buddhist rites,

supernatural powers have been attributed. In the following
discussion we move from Buddhism as a largely philosophical and worshipful sphere of behavior into its areas of supernaturalism and thence, in Chapter VII, to the almost distinct
realm of folk supernaturalism.

Pelpolans are proud of their Buddhism. It is with tolerant
regret that they confess that some Sinhalese have professed
Christianity, for to them Buddhism is an integral part of being a Sinhalese. Pelpola itself is united in veneration of
Lord Buddha. Knowing less of Christian teachings than of
Buddhist dhamma, they deplore Christians, howsoever
mildly, chiefly in that they are people who believe in killing,
i. e. who do not accept ahimsa.

The Buddha is supreme. There is nothing existing in this
world not understood by Him. Every word He spoke was and
is absolute truth. Stories of the Buddha's life and particularly those of His existences prior to having been born as
the Buddha are popular. Every person knows at least a few
of the Jataka tales. For the least educated villagers, the
Buddha is eighteen cubits (riyana) in height and possesses
thirty-two individual features never held by any other person
on earth. Such folklore is not literally accepted by the better educated. Practically every house has a picture of the
Buddha, rarely if ever a figure, and many families keep beneath it floral offerings or an oil lamp.

Organizationally Buddhism is characterized by informality. In the cohesion of the folk about the temple there is a
minimum of lay organization. No person becomes a member
of the temple; no priest remonstrates with a lagging parish-
ioner; no wife pleads with her husband for loyalty in attendance at services. Every Pelpolan is born into Buddhism and
it is accepted as a matter of course that he is affiliated with
a local temple whether he in fact attends its services or not.
There are no "members of a parish, " in the literal sense,
nor are there temple rosters, and there is little by way of
organization for the development of religious activities in
the community. Pelpola does not well understand persisting
groups on any but a primary basis. Most temple enterprises
are pursued by cliques organized for the specific purpose at
hand.

Twenty years ago the village had only one centrally located temple; today there are three. The original is still the

principal one, one of the others being wholly subordinate to
it, and directed by a former pupil of the central temple's
chief priest. The construction of the third temple was due
to a split by the "potters" who took umbrage at the chief
priest's expressions of caste superiority and erected their
own place of worship. The original temple actually draws
the entire village for its special events and has been headed
for many years by the same priest of the Siamese Sect. The
"potters'" temple has as its incumbent a priest of Amarapura sect.[1] The vast majority of the villagers look toward
the old and central temple as their seat of worship and toward its chief priest as their priest.

The central temple has within its grounds the vihare or
Buddhist shrine, a devale, the temple of gods, mostly of
Hindu affiliation, especially Vishnu, Saman, and Kataragama. The latter is usually identified as the Sinhalese version of the Hindu deity, Skanda. Saman appears to be distinctively Sinhalese. In addition there is the preaching hall
in which Buddhist services are held and another structure
serving as living quarters for the priests. At one corner of
the grounds stands a dagoba, (stupa), recently completed
after several years of intermittant construction.[2]

The principal temple is staffed by an elderly chief priest
and several subordinate priests and helpers. All of these
are supported through village alms. Villagers other than the
spiritual leaders in the community have little to do with the
clergy in their daily lives. Many peasants feel that their
priests lack sympathy for their hardship.   But while lay-
men may deplore the person in the saffron robes, they pay
him great deference. Here is a fine abstraction in which
many Pelpolans share, a holy man can be deplored while
his robes are honored and his religious functions revered.

Organizations subsidiary to the temple have been attempted
many times in the village, four at least in quite recent years.
Each disintegrates after a short period of activity. In neither
religious nor other spheres have Pelpolans much conception
of a group program beyond some immediate objective. And if
objectives take too long, as in the case of the dagoba construction, the enterprise passes from hand to hand, no single
group possessing the germ of permanence sufficient to its
completion. It is no doubt relevant that leadership in these
affairs is by the village well-to-do and among them one finds
interfamilial jealousy and some back biting.[3]

Of all Buddhist teachings that which is central to its metaphysics is also central in importance to the villager. This
is the doctrine of kamma (karma), including not only cause
and effect principles, but particularly belief in rebirth. Religious instruction, relying heavily upon the Jataka stories,
emphasises kamma and rebirth above all else. Even Gautama
was tied to the wheel of life in spite of His power and super-
normal intelligence. He too had to suffer for His deeds and
only finally attain Buddhahood as a result of noble thought
and action. His previous births, now as an elephant, a snake,
and again as a monkey, serve to impress the peasant with
the vastness of the sansara sea and the inevitability of kammatic law. Happiness in this life, prosperity, good fortune,
ill fortune, all are understandable as a cause and effect relationship bridging the sequence of existences. Actions in a
previous life become the ready explanation for all that is in-
explicable. "I am a poor man today. I cannot help this since
I have done some sin in my last birth. But in this birth I
am doing plenty of merit and so matters will be different in
the next. " In the last analysis all misfortune can be explained
by karume, the local term for kamma, and the concept is
frequently referred to in daily life.

Nibbana (Nirvana), that ultimate theoretic goal of Buddhism, is no matter of preoccupation for the villager. Lord
Buddha made it clear that this was beyond ordinary compre-
hension--and it is equally beyond attainment for one of a
work-a-day world. Most adults recognize it as a condition
in which re-birth ceases, but the reality of nonreality is so
inconceivable that spiritual goals must in fact be visualized
in terms of existences. The immediate religious quest of the
villager is not nibbana but pin (merit) which in turn leads
to the tangible goal of superior rebirth. The achievement of
merit relies upon "Right Thinking" and "Right Action, " but
it must be noted that right action in an ethical sense is often subordinated to worshipful behavior and almsgiving.
Social ethics are explicit in Buddhist teaching as a means of
attainment, but the Pelpolan has come to attach more conscious significance to formal devices than to generalized
ethical behavior. The social teachings of Buddhism should
be followed, but in practice the religious emphasis is upon
circumscribed techniques which automatically produce
recognized degrees of addition to one's storehouse of merit.

At the same time, little attention is paid to "de-merit."
While downward mobility in the chain of births is as possible
as upward movement, there is little balancing of merit and
demerit in the villager's mind. One seldom thinks of deple-
tions in the merit stockpile although in instances of flagrant
sin, e.g. adultery or murder, it might be pointed out by a
local pietist that the culprit is surely headed for that specific punishment in hell reserved for such sinners. [4] Certain
types of prescribed actions may yield specific characteristics
in the rebirth. Thus, giving alms to priests yields prosperity in a next birth. Generally, however, merit is poured into an undifferentiated stockpile, the height of which deter-
mines how high its owner may climb between this existence
and the next.

To enumerate the forms of merit acquisition is to list
the principal forms of worship and almsgiving in the community. These range from the informal, personalized de-
votions of the individual to the organized expressions of worship in the preaching hall. The most common practice is
that of personal floral offerings and oil lamp lightings at the
vihare (temple) on full moon days. Typically, offerings at
the shrine are accompanied by the recitation of a few Pali
stanzas which by their very repetition are merit invoking.
Few villagers understand the significance of the words but
practically all can repeat lines associated with floral offering:

> These beautiful flowers shall fade and wither
> In the same manner my body too will someday be
>   destroyed.

On special occasions the relics in the temple are displayed
and their worship is considered meritorious. On these occasions the worshipper may make voluntary money donations
to the temple in whatever extent he feels he can afford and
thereby gain added merit through alms. Almsgiving to the
priests, apart from special occasions, is surprisingly systematic in Pelpola. No longer do the village bhikkhus
(priests) wander from door to door with begging bowls, after the orthodox tradition. The several bhikkhus and their
acolytes are provided food through an organized rotation of
donors (dayakaya). For this purpose the village is divided
into four areas, within each of which there is a chief

dayakaya responsible for the orderly operation of the plan.
Each contributing household has a regular day upon which
rice and curries, sufficient for the priests, are taken to
the temple. This can hardly be said to be the work of a religious association since it operates informally and includes
most of the village families. Other than this self-accepted
function of temple upkeep, the dayakayas have no special
significance. Others give food and other alms to the priests
as the spirit moves them.

Participation in the organized forms of worship is also
merit producing, but it is less frequently practiced than
alms-giving and floral offerings. Preaching services are
held on each full moon evening and it is recognized that a
good Buddhist attends them regularly. In actual fact, attendance is chiefly by women and children and the aged men,
unless there is some special event scheduled. Men may go
to the fields or simply sit on the verandah, "taking care of
things while the family worships." In old age the immanence
of death inspires greater interest in building up the stockpile for a rebirth.

The person who consistently attends the preaching service and is an active participant in all Buddhist rituals comes,
upon continued demonstration of such piety, to hold a
special honor. In addition to his name, he, or more commonly "she," is given a title indicative of the rank of
upasaka (feminine-upasikavi or upasika). The upasakas,
all of whom are past middle age are credited with understanding religion better than all others. This is mainly on
account of their ability to recite Pali stanzas, few of which
are understood by most villagers. The "best" upasaka is the
one who can recite the most stanzas, assuming that other
behavior is what might be expected of a devout individual.
An upasaka never misses a holy day and its celebrations, but
unlike others who may also attend services regularly he or
she spends the entire full moon day, as well as the evening
of worship, in accord with almost priestly precepts.

Although the upasakas have little secular significance,
they are honored elders and invariably consulted prior to
the organization of religious festivals by less pious but energetic neighbors. Almsgiving to upaskas is perhaps their
only secular advantage, other than the status of piety. Gifts
to them are considered meritorious by the remainder of the
laity.

The two most significant activities on poya day (day of
worship) are the observance (recital) of sil, and the preach-
service (bana). Sil is often observed in groups, not necessarily always on holy days at the temple. For the generality
of religious folk, sil involves the recitation of five precepts
(pansil) pledging abstention from killing, stealing, adultery,
lying, and drinking. Many villagers observe pansil before
retiring each night. More difficult is the way of the upasakas, for they observe (and on poya days conform to) three
additional precepts (ata sil): abstention from sitting on high
seats, abstention from eating solid foods after midday, and
abstention from activity that would unduly gratify the senses,
e.g. listening to music and the use of face creams and
scents. For the observance of sil, the worshipper dresses
solely in white, often with a string of beads--like a rosary
--for purposes of meditation. Young people, especially
young men, sometimes profess embarrassment over participation in the ritual and a considerable number of them
avoid participating.

Upasakas generally gather at the temple on the morning
of a holy day where, after the observance of ata sil, they
form into small groups to discuss the life of the Buddha,
and especially His pre-Buddha lives as recounted in the Jatakas.
An old upasaka will be heard relating such a story to the
group or possibly reading a sermon to them. In subsequent
meditations, a sacred stanza may be repeated for hours
without thought or curiosity as to the meaning.

The general group service for the laity is held late in the
evening of the holy day and is centered upon the preaching
(bana) by the bhikkhu. Sermons, unless followed by some
special feature, draw mainly the women and elders. Typically they include one or more of the Jataka stories and
perhaps the explanation of some Pali stanzas regarding the
virtue of almsgiving to priests, or comments on Buddhist
ethics. It is the Jatakas which the people love, and if the
bhikkhu should offer comments on secular affairs or imply
criticisms of their daily lives, the folk would feel that the
bounds of priestly propriety had been overstepped, and
might openly criticize the sermon as they walk home in the
night.

From time to time, special religious observances are
held. The pinkama, as such an event is called, may be a

special preaching service or special almsgiving or possibly
a large pirith ceremony (i. e. calling forth the protective
power of the Buddha). These events are usually stimulated
and organized by cliques among the laity with the advice of
the priests and often the upasakas. Their social and religious
functions are varied and complex. They imply entertainment
for the village, the acquisition of merit by all who participate, especially the organizers, and also enhanced status
in the community for the latter. Usually the pinkama is a
device of money raising for the temple, whether or not the
content of service is protective, instructive or inspirational.
Village cliques organizing them are frequently competitive
in their attempts to put on bigger and better pinkamas than
those developed by others. Rather like revival meetings in
some Western societies, one ultimate standard of success
in the affair is the size of the crowds and the amount of
money made for the temple.

The most elaborate and rarest type of pinkama includes
entertainment, and special bana preaching for which some
outside bhikkhu is brought in. A great fanfare of advertising
for the event may be given in surrounding villages. Pera-
heras (parades) of gayly costumed well wishers, acrobats,
and bullock cart floats might trail for a mile through the
country lanes ending up at the main village temple where
gifts are left for the priests. This is almost strictly an advance publicity appeal, although alms are duely provided.

On the occasion of such a large pinkama, the most recent
of which was in 1952, a family will have an early evening
meal and usually all except the head of the house will be off
for the services. Even the young men go--for the young
women also go and there is better than an even chance of
some small flirtations and other types of amusement as well.
Little parties of neighbors join in walking from the distant
parts of the village usually staying in a body through the
services, although the young men lag behind to chat in the
compound and possibly to hear the sermon from such an un-
restricted vantage point. A number of the old upasakas will
sit upon the high preaching platform itself, although no
women will be among them. Practically all, before entering
the preaching hall, will have visited the vihare to offer
flowers to the Buddha and give merit to the devas. [5]

When the time comes for the bana preaching, usually

about nine P. M. or later, the organizers of the pinkama
go to the priests' residence nearby, and bring the officiating bhikkhu to the hall under a white canopy. His feet are
washed and the service begins. Pansil is first observed
and the preaching starts. Infrequently an interruption might
occur as an upasaka comes down from the platform to remonstrate with some noisy youths in the compound outside.
A young woman inside may giggle, half an eye on a boy
standing beside an outside post. And gradually, as an upa-
sikavi may drift off into sleep, an increasing disinterest is
displayed throughout the audience except by the faithful on
the platform. At the conclusion of preaching, all greet the
priest with "Sadhu, Sadhu" and he in turn wishes his listen-
ers the bliss of nibbana and gives merit to the devas through
the recitation of a Pali stanza.

If the priest is thoughtful for his popularity, his sermon
is not unduly long for he knows well that the special nature
of the particular occasion is as much in the entertainment
which follows as in his presence. Pelpolans do not hesitate
to criticize a priest who takes advantage of his position to
keep them waiting over long. With the conclusion of bana,
the atmosphere of reverence ends, and fellowship and
laughter is general as people assemble in the compound for
the entertainment phase of the special service. This may
be in the form of a dramatized Jataka story, possibly enlivened by a few advance nips of arrack by the principals.
(Usually the players are from outside Pelpola.) At times
the performance is interspersed with jokes and horseplay
which, if crude, are highly amusing. After the tedium of
the long preaching, the audience is immensely responsive,
laughing loudly and occasionally hurling jocular insults at
the players, until some more sober spectator bids for
silence so that the show may proceed. As the affair wears
on, the audience may press nearer and nearer to the "stage"
until finally one of the organizers moves them back. At no
point is the performance entirely without audience reaction
but of course at no point does the jollity grow so great as
to disrupt the show. With the conclusion, the villagers walk
back to their homes laughing over the show and quite possibly criticizing the players and speaking ill of the organizers,
but none-the-less with a sense of uplift as well as the feeling of having been entertained. Adverse talk is to be ex-

pected in village life when anyone steps into the limelight
and no one takes the shortcomings or the criticisms very
seriously.

During 1951, Pelpola had one of its most memorable
pinkamas in the form of a pirith ceremony. Pirith, the chanting of holy texts in Pali by the priests, is often a ceremony
for protection against specific evils; this one was held as a
money raising device for the completion of the dagoba, be-
gun some years earlier. Such an event is designed to draw
villagers from a wide area, many of whom have loose affiliations to Pelpola through marriage. The organization of
this pirith was in the hands, and instigated by, a small and
virtually self appointed committee. At the early committee
meetings the view was expressed by the chairman, and one
or two others, that the celebration would be unlikely to be
as profitable as was hoped. This pessimistic attitude by a
minority was soon whipped into active opposition when the
chief priest without consulting the committee sold booth concessions beside the temple ground, and made certain conditions not wholly pleasing to the people. The committee was
now thoroughly divided, one side remaining pro-priest and
pro-pinkama, the other standing in opposition to the priest
and wishing to call the whole thing off, partially on the
grounds of its probable financial failure. Gossip passed
quickly through the teashops and boutiques that the chairman
and secretary were responsible for the collapse of the plan
through their unwillingness to go along. The chairman, a
devout and wealthy dayakaya, who now wanted nothing more
than to be well out of the whole affair, saw his position in
the community jeopardized. He offered to donate one thousand rupees if the remaining dayakayas would take over the
administration. This new fact, quickly turned to rumor, reinstated the chairman in the village affection, but again his
position was clouded when a representative of the priest himself came to claim the gift. Refusing to turn the money over
to the priest's clique, the now ex-chairman invited in a group
of responsible citizens who were pro-pinkama and made his
presentation to them only to have it rejected out of displeasure
at his anti-pinkama convictions. After several days of cross
currents of rumor, ad hoc meetings, and probably some influential comments by the priest himself, the money was accepted by a responsible person and the organization of the
event left in the hands of the priest.

For a month the temple was the center of greater activity
than Pelpola had known for many years. Inside the temple,
priests chanted <u>pirith</u> steadily. Outside the temple grounds
perhaps a dozen stalls grew overnight--let out on conces-
sion by the priest. Here were sold nick-nacks with appeal
to all, combs, cosmetics, and trinkets. Tea and cold drink
stands flourished, while petty gambling concessions did business well into the night. On some evenings, Jataka stories
were dramatized. The <u>vihare</u> itself was constantly decked
with flowers, and oil lamps. Drums, so essential to the
Buddhist service, were heard morning, noon, and night. A
great parade of almsbearers from a nearby village came to
the temple, their parade being a mixture of twentieth century
buffoonery, religious representations, and traditional Sinhalese symbolism. Needless to say, during this month the
temple lacked nothing in the attendance of youth, and both
merit and spiritual protection was gained by many who had
not been near the shrine in months. And, people had a very
good time for a very fine cause.

Although the village was in wide agreement that the
<u>pinkama</u> had been a monumental success religiously and
socially (the ex-committee chairman and a few others quietly
dissenting), subsequent boutique gossip indicated considerable skepticism of the affair as a financial enterprise. Temporarily the original organizers of the <u>pinkama</u> were no
longer organized, work on the dagoba stopped, and the former leading <u>dayakas</u> contributed minimal alms. Time, however, brought forgetting, and by 1956, after several years
of inactivity a reconstituted committee brought completion
of the dagoba. It is probable that relatively little of the necessary money was derived from the great <u>pinkama</u> of 1951
--which is still, none-the-less, a memorable event.

The <u>pirith</u> is a ceremony which bears close scrutiny for
it is at once a Buddhist rite and yet one seemingly directed
toward ends other than worship. <u>Pirith</u> chantings become
utilizations of the sacred texts themselves for purposes of
protection against mundane dangers. In the normal course
of life, <u>pirith</u> is not associated with fund raising, but it is a
direct appeal to the supernatural power of the Buddha (in
this instance not "super-normal" as His powers are properly
described by philosophic Buddhist writers) for intervention
in the processes and affairs of men. To invoke the name of

Buddha through His priest is the most efficacious form of
supernatural intervention, but it is also the most costly and
the most soporific. In some circumstances, it is the rich
man's efficacious substitute for the more common, cheaper
and more entertaining appeals to properly supernatural
powers. Typically it is used in situations of serious illness,
protection of pregnant women, blessing a marriage, and in
the preparation of new houses for habitation. The ceremony
is terminated with an almsgiving and always the officiating
priests--usually there are several--are fully fed. If possible,
the associated almsgiving will include all manner of articles
suitable for a priest, umbrellas, robes, fans, and towels.
Food must be provided on a lavish scale for the priests, and
for the neighbors and relatives who join in the ceremony.
The sacredness of such a night is too great that its power
should not be extended beyond the household, and relatives
are sure to help with the food requirements. Frequently
lasting an entire night, and for the purification of a new
house three consecutive nights, the priests perform a ceremony having little association with Buddhist agnosticism.
In pregnancy rites, a string passes from an arecanut flower
to the woman via the priests, and it is common that participants clip from this string sections to tie around their necks
or wrists as subsequent protections from misfortune. No
demon, no evil spirit may stand against the Buddha.

If the pirith ceremony takes us one step into the border-
land between philosophic Buddhism and practical supernaturalism, the pilgrimage to sacred shrines is at least mid-
way between these theoretically distinct spheres. Pilgrimages are among the greatest events in the life of the villager, thrilling beyond description, awe inspiring, and a
source of conversation for the remainder of one's life. Occasionally trips are taken to Anuradhapura, or Polonarruwa
far off in the north-central jungles, locales of ancient royal
and holy sites. Most frequently trips are to Sri Pada (Adam's
Peak), sacred as the abode of God Saman and revered for
the footprint of Lord Buddha on its summit.[6] This is a journey long looked forward to by every Pelpolan, and once taken
is never to be forgotten. Not only is it a high point in religious ecstasy, but for many it provides the only trip in a
lifetime to strange places, made the more strange and wonderful by the living mythology guiding each step in the climb.

The very danger of the trip renders it the more satisfying,
for in this the unusual in daring and expense has been surpassed that one may honor the glory of Lord Buddha and His
powerful minion, God Saman.

Pelpola has several well known pilgrimage conductors
(gurunnanse), versed in the lore and legends of the holy
places. Usually a number of people desiring to take a trip
collect, among themselves, the money necessary for the
hire of a bus or station wagon, and turn the arrangements
over to the selected gurunnanse. The gurunnanse, looking
upon himself somewhat as a religious mentor receives no
pay, but the grateful villagers usually give him presents,
and what is more important, their sincere thanks. The ex-
pedition itself, lasting usually three or four days, and sometimes longer, is a miracle in social organization for people
who at home represent something close to the ultimate in
loose group structuring and unwillingness to be harnessed
in any form of bureaucratic or rigorous organization. Once
outside the village, the pilgrims behave as a single organism,
following their leader's instructions implicitly, criticizing
nothing, and expressing no hint of individualism in action,
and apparently little in thought.

On the night previous to departure, pilgrims visit the
vihare and the devale, offer flowers to Buddha, light oil
lamps and ask the gods for protection. The trip to Sri Pada
is awe inspiring, and until recently fearsome, not only supernaturally but physically, since the last long climb up the
peak itself is through wild jungle. Today, however, one route
is well lighted by electricity from its start in the town of
Hatton to its finish on the summit. Modernization does not
appear to have diminished the thrill of this adventure nor its
sacred atmosphere.

Once the journey starts, the bus rings with the praises
of "Saman deva" and the call, "Sadhu, " the holy exclamation
of Buddhism. Indeed, the usual decrepit nature of the vehicle
renders doubly reasonable all claims upon the deities for
protection. Throughout the trip, but especially on the foot
journey, language and behavior is guarded. No decision of
the leader will be criticized, no evil or profanity spoken and
brotherly love will be exuded toward all in the party. No one
should say that the climb is tedious or difficult, large boul-
ders which must be overcome are described as small stones,

and great trees are referred to as small plants. The insig-
nificance of nature magnifies the glory of Saman, and it is
well to magnify him here, for all that befalls upon this trip
is his doing. If one says that the journey is difficult, then
he will be incapacitated. If one thinks evil, he will be racked
by fits of chills or fevers. Intermittently, the name of
Saman is cried aloud and the Buddhistic call of karunavai,
"Kindness to All, " echoes.

Nor must any weakness or sickness befall a traveller.
(Many a broken heart has stayed back in the village because
of a miscalculated menstrual flow.) If a poor pilgrim falls
ill on the trip, his lot is not happy; for this is unquestionably by the act of Saman. The leader of the party prays
constantly to that god, and to Lord Buddha, for forgiveness
and for mercy upon the ill-fated one. A special charm will
be hung about his neck and, while his companions will express no dissatisfaction with him, his unpopularity becomes
unspokenly obvious. Ordinarily the trip is carried through
to conclusion in an atmosphere of ecstasy and brotherly
love not experienced in other situations of life.

In only one of the great crises of life, that of death, does
Buddhism have direct significance. Birth and marriage, and
puberty among girls, are surrounded with supernaturalism
but not with Buddhism. In none of these is the bhikkhu a
functionary. Death, while fraught with essentially non-
Buddhistic supernaturalism is attended by the bhikkhu functioning in his role as bhikkhu. No family would bury its
dead without the presence of the priest, strangely enough,
partly because his presence is essential to rid the house of
the departed's spirit. And here is perhaps the only time at
which the priest acts as personal comforter to the distraught,
chiding and solacing them in the name and spirit of the
Buddha.

Funeral behavior is particularly interesting because it
offers a contrast, and a paradox fully recognized by the villagers themselves, between Buddhist teaching and community expectations. Before the arrival of the priest, the
corpse is usually laid out upon chairs in the garden. Close
relatives gather to mourn, and it is common that the female
members of the kin sob and cry aloud. In some instances
the display of grief among women is highly exaggerated and
relatives or neighbors will seek to comfort and quiet the

bereaved. With the coming of the priest the display continues
and it is for him to present the lesson of the Buddha. "This
is not for Buddhists, " speaks the bhikkhu, and he may tell
them that parable of the Buddha when He was asked to revive
a dying child. "Yes, I can renew her life, but you must use
a medicine as I direct. Go now and bring mustard from a
house in which there has been no death. " Quieting the funeral
party with the Buddha's wisdom, pansil is observed and the
bhikkhu preaches upon the inevitability of death and in praise
of the meritorious life of the deceased.

In Pelpola, the dead are usually buried in a cemetery located in the Katuketiya neighborhood. Cremation is more
costly and is practiced only by wealthy families. Perhaps
one funeral in twenty-five is consumated in cremation. For
burial, the relatives and friends of the deceased carry the
coffin to the burial ground in mourning procession. Rarely
does the priest accompany them, although occasionally a
close friend will offer a funeral oration at the grave. The
coffin is lowered to its grave by the close relatives of the
deceased. In instances of cremation, which also take place
in the burial ground, a wood pyre is constructed and the fire
lit by the nephews or sons-in-law of the deceased. Where
such kinsmen are not available any close relatives will take
on the responsibility. Among very wealthy families the
ashes may be collected for permanent deposit in a small
tomb to be erected anywhere on the lands of the deceased.

On the seventh day after death an almsgiving will be held
to provide merit for the deceased, and to rid the house of
his spiritual presence. A number of priests are invited and
brought to the home with ceremony. Relatives and neighbors
come in number, with eatables of all kinds for the priests.
Alms consist chiefly of the best food which the family can
provide, and after a joint recitation of the five precepts, the
priests sit down to feast. When they have had their fill, the
preaching starts. (After long hours watching the priests eat
and then listening to them preach, one may hear such a
whispered comment as "the priests have no sense of time
and less sense of another man's hunger. ") When the conclusion comes, the chief occupant of the house gives presents
to the priests and the not wholly patient company move toward their respective homes and the long awaited rice and
curry. A hungry village man has been heard to mutter as he

went, "those priests eat at an almsgiving what a normal
man eats in three meals. " Devout and loyal as he is, the
Pelpolan cherishes his right of criticism and humor.

It has been apparent that Buddhism has in situations like
the pilgrimage and _pirith_ been merged with belief in supernatural powers and gods. In the former the power of the
Buddha is given supernatural quality, and in the latter the
merger is a wedding of convenience between Lord Buddha
and the gods. In death, the Buddhistic principles are evident, but they are expressed in a situation shrouded with
ghostly overtones. The border land between philosophic
Buddhism and various types of supernaturalism is not precise, nor is the boundary one of a single dimension. In still
another type situation, the Buddhist _bhikkhu_ himself acts
as a functionary of the gods.

The _bhikkhu_ is not generally viewed as one with supernatural powers, but under serious, uncontrolled circumstances, as in critical illness, the villager might call upon
him for an appeal to the deities. This is one of the many alternative courses possible under such conditions, others
being _pirith_, the use of strictly exorcizing techniques, or
other agencies of appeal to the supernatural. As an alternative to these latter, more common, devices, the villager
may approach the priest with a view to having him intercede
with the deities in the interests of a sick relative. This is
usually done through the composition of poems (_Seth Kavi_)
in praise of the gods. (Occasionally, it is said that similar
techniques are used to bring evil upon an enemy [_Vas Kavi_]
although this would typically be accomplished by a sorcerer.)
Since Vishnu is the leader of the gods, most poems are sung
in his praise. Here the _bhikkhu_ has transformed his role into that of direct intercessor with non-Buddhist supernatural
powers. Nor is it uncommon for the priest to invoke his
skills in reference to the gods when rain interrupts a
pinkama.

Cart track approach to Pelpola. Its scattered
neighborhoods are hidden in the groves and
gardens.

A poorer village home of
wattle and daub construction.

Front room of a superior type home in **Pelpola**
Central converted into a tea boutique.

Older girls learn a folk dance beside the well
in the school yard.

All Pelpola children attend the well - staffed, graded school.

As often as not, land is broken with the mamoty
rather than the plow.

Water buffaloes puddle the clay in the first stage
of Pelpola's brick - making industry.

From the nearby kiln, bricks are loaded on
canal boats for shipment to coastal cities.

Women rubber - tappers, on absentee - owned
estates, carry latex to an estate factory for
processing.

A pot after being formed on the wheel is being
expanded by skillful beating.

The daily chore of pounding rice is now being supplanted by small hulling machines in the village.

A villager carries food to the Buddhist temple.
In Pelpola the begging bowl is rarely used.

Chapter VII

THE WONDERFUL WORLD: GODS AND DEMONS

The Sinhalese have marvelous arrays of supernatural entities and apparitions as well as diffuse belief in supernatural power dissociated from specific personages or spirits.
Pelpola partakes of Sinhalese supernaturalism generally,
but, as is true throughout Ceylon, local definitions provide
variations upon a broad general pattern. In these practices
we find Hindu gods redefined, Tamil magical invocations,
indigenous gods and demons more or less common to all
Sinhalese, and ghost-like beings reminiscent both of folk
Hinduism and the Vedda bandara cult.[1] The different elements of supernaturalism are loosely fitted together. Any
firm systematization of belief would be a product of anthropological reconstruction rather than the villager's mind.
From his standpoint, it is more accurate to think of various
kinds of supernatural reality, more or less overlapping,
more or less integrated.

Very roughly we distinguish six types of supernatural
powers active in the life of the villager. Although these
powers are not hierarchically graded, the Buddha stands
above all others, and toward Him there is a unique reverence and worshipfulness. Surrounding the Buddha as His
minions and helpers is the largely Hindu pantheon, especially
Vishnu, and Kataragama, (the Sinhalese version of Skanda)
and Saman, a distinctively Sinhalese deity, and a host of
associated devas. All of these are considered part of Sinhalese culture with no conscious recognition of their affiliations with Hinduism. In a third category, distinct from
the Hindu type pantheon, are the planet gods influencing
every phase of the individual's life. Utterly apart from
planet gods, but affiliated with the pantheon of devas are
the yakas or demons and with them a multitude of wood
sprites, and ghosts. Loosely associated with the demon
world is a realm of diffuse supernatural power less explicitly attributable to particular entities, e.g. auspicious

meetings, evil mouth, the plethora of charms, and rituals
holding automatic power in their own right. Not fully distinguishable from the demon world is the power of sorcery.
Although black magic operates through a specific demon, it
is so systematized that we should view it as a distinct type.

Lord Buddha is, as we have observed, a worshipful reality and teacher, but He is at once in village theory a supreme power over all forms of life, including human and
superhuman. Although the Pelpolan believes in His infinite
power, the influence of pure Theravada has limited the extent to which His name is invoked in secular affairs. Supernatural powers have come into Buddhism mainly via the back
door of folklore rather than through an omnipotent position
claimed by Gautama. It is perhaps one of the great psychological weaknesses of Theravada Buddhism that it contains
no final god or gods, nor wonderful powers exterior to the
individual. This gap has been amply filled by accepting the
non-Buddhist world of gods and demons, and by the limited
transposition of the Buddha Himself into a divinity. More
surprising than the qualified deification of the Buddha by the
villager, is the very infrequence with which He is asked to
intervene in mundane matters. Appeals in His name are
usually limited to matters of health and serious sickness although purely Buddhist rites are also performed as protection against the spirits of the dead and the exorcizing
of evil influences abiding in newly built houses. Most new
homes are consecrated through pirith performed by the village priests. Pirith services for illness are not common;
here the worlds of planet gods and demons are usually ap-
proached directly. Pirith, in these matters, has the role of
a generalized anti-biotic in contrast to the specifics provided
in astrological or demonological treatments. Beyond these
limited uses, the Buddha is an object of reverence and worship; vows are not made in His name, and invocations for
success in secular achievements are unthinkable. Nor does
one "pray" to the Buddha for salvation in the form of nirvana,
or guidance in life. Such matters are well understood to be
derived from meritorious conduct in the first instance and
from meditation in the second. Yet, invocations to all types
of spiritual powers include mention of His name and while
efforts may be directed to a demon, and by a formula suited
directly to this being, the use of Buddha's name is added

insurance. "The name of Lord Buddha has before now deci-
mated armies of demons. "

The most pervasive and encompassing supernatural system is that of the planetary gods, for it is by one's stars
that all good and all evil befall one. Through their proper
understanding all events of life may be understood, fore-
casted and wisely acted upon. The moment of birth is the
determining event in life but although life's courses are fixed
by astrological law, the gods of planets may still heed invocations and rituals in their honor. To the Sinhalese the astrological system is natural science not supernaturalism. [2]

The planet gods are nine in number, each of them having
distinctive types of directive influence upon the individual.
These influences range from the dangerous and harmful to
the beneficient and success insuring. While influences of
several may be present upon the individual at any given time,
and during the course of his life, their relative powers
over him shift. In addition to these fundamental directive
forces, daily stars are also significant, particularly for the
determination of precise "good" and "bad" days. Given a
horoscope correctly drawn and given a skilled reader, the
outline of one's life, one's vocational aptitudes, weaknesses,
and strengths may be laid before one. Even the ups and downs
of a future career may be foretold with warnings of "bad"
or "dangerous" periods and with admonitions to push ahead
during auspicious times.

Every child has his horoscope cast at birth. Usually in
Pelpola this is done by the chief priest in the central temple
for he is acknowledged to have great accuracy and skill.
(This is considered coincidental to his role as bhikkhu.) The
horoscope once drawn is carefully guarded and brought out
only for scanning by an expert prior to or during critical
occasions. As might be surmised, were an enemy to gain
access to one's horoscope, his power over the victim would
be great, for the days and moments of the latter's weaknesses, and the very nature of his susceptibilities would then
be known. In event of illness, important business decisions,
puberty ceremonies, marriage arrangements and all crises
of life, the horoscope will be taken to an expert astrologer
for his study. Thus in marriages, partners must be astrologically suited, the marriage must be performed on an
astrologically auspicious day, at an astrologically auspicious

hour and minute and while facing in an astrologically auspicious direction. Or again, an individual may delay betting
on the Colombo horse races until his planetary influences
are in accord with a sweep-stake win.

The Hindu-like pantheon is of second rate importance but
unlike the planet gods is associated with the Buddha and with
worship. Vishnu is especially integrated with Buddhism.
Pelpolans recognize this diety as the caretaker of Buddhism
in Ceylon. Other associations are often vague in theory, but
close in the villager's behavior.

There are said to be 33 million devas. These include gods
derived from Hinduism, indiginous Sinhalese gods, and vague
entities, neither good nor bad in relation to man, but for
whom some regard should be shown. As has been observed,
ceremonies for protection in time of physical danger are
carried out in the devala, chiefly in reference to Vishnu,
Saman, Kataragama and Pattini, the latter an important
deity of South Indian Hindus. In time of serious illness,
among other protective devices, vows to perform some
great venerative act are offered to Vishnu in return for the
safety of one's self or the recovery of a sick relative. One
form of alms is given for Pattini, often in thankfulness for
recovery of a sick child. This entails feeding "milk rice" to
seven mothers, as an honoring to the goddess. Occasionally
coconut trees are consecrated to Pattini, or other deities,
and the fruit is not picked until the vow is fulfilled. Kataragama is the object of harvest-time thanksgiving, and alms
are given in his name following the paddy harvest. In one
type of almsgiving, e.g. kanyavarunge dana or "young girl
alms," gifts are designed to stop ill-luck for a daughter.

For the deity Saman, there is no apparent Hindu counterpart. Saman is the guardian of the Adams Peak (Samantakuta)
wilderness, sacred to Buddhists for the Teacher's footprint
on the summit. Legend says that it was Saman who invited
Buddha to place his footprint on the peak. [3] Regional deities
are also found in other parts of Ceylon but Saman is probably
the most famous, and certainly the most revered among
Buddhists.

Rarely in relations to the deities does the bhikkhu have a
role. Most vows or offerings are carried out without a professional priest or functionary. Perhaps the most common
form of relationship to the gods is a ceremony of beneficence

on the part of the villager himself in offering flowers in
their name that they may acquire merit in the proper
Buddhist sense. The gods can be great allies in times of
distress and they must not be neglected in good times, and
in harvest.

Yakas or demons are quite a different ilk. With few exceptions they are the enemies of man. As such they are not
venerated or worshipped, but rather, cursed and exorcized
and prevented from acting. [4] There is no doubt an infinite
number of demons but most Pelpolans are specifically aware
of only half a dozen or so. Their historic affiliation with
Hindu apparitions is apparent from descriptions of some of
them as cited by informed villagers:[5]

1. Mahasona:
    With the face of a bear, he is eighty-four cubits in
height and has thirty thousand henchmen including his
own apparitions which are eighteen in number [the so-
called sanni demons]. He may kill a man by striking
him on the face and when he strikes blood will flow
from the victim's nose and mouth and sometimes fin-
ger marks will show. Mahasona is everywhere and
eternal and he has been seen by men but not by anyone in Pelpola. His vehicle is a wild boar. His chest
and stomach are on the opposite side of the body from
his face.
2. Riri Yaka:
    Riri Yaka is only nine inches tall. It is said that
he tore open his mother's breasts at the moment of
his birth and drank her blood. He is the bloodiest of
all demons.
3. Thota Yaka:
    This demon is always near a place where there is
water and strikes his victims near wells or streams.
Further characteristics are unknown to Pelpolans.
4. Kalu Yaka:
    This demon is particularly fond of afflicting women.
He will make her displeased with her food, frighten
her in dreams and weaken her. She will become lazy
and unclean.
5. Gopalu Yaka:
    This is not a troublesome demon in Pelpola since
he lives with large herds of water buffalo and Pelpola

has no large herds. He carries a stick and a small
coconut shell in his hand. He might strike a man who
comes near a large herd at night.
6. Hooniyam Yaka:
    This demon, also called Hooniyam Deveta, is both
demon and a subordinate member of the Hindu type
pantheon. He is in charge of kodivina or hooniyam
(black magic or sorcery) and is above other demons
in status.

    Although additional demons are referred to in ceremonies
by exorcists, Pelpolans are generally ill-informed about
the precise content of the demon world. Everyone recognizes that specific demons (the sanni demons) are associated traditionally with particular diseases, but people are
hazy on even disease demonology. Few yakas, other than
those named above, are known by name, except to exorcists
themselves--and they are none-too-well informed. Most
persons will recognize the names of additional demons but
precise knowledge is a matter for scholars.
    In traditional lore the yakas are particularly associated
with disease. Eighteen sanni demons are recognized by
practitioners of demon exorcizing. Each has a distinctive
appearance and is associated with a specific disorder, and
each is represented by an appropriate mask. Diagnostic
demonology is not understood by the unskilled and even the
exorcists themselves are usually hazy about the nature of
all of the major demons.
    Nearly all Pelpolans believe in the power of demons as
activators of human disorders but practically all believe
as well that their powers are limited. No one would think
that demons cause most of the common disorders and complaints. Tooth-aches, colds, malaria, and the vast majority
of other familiar ailments are never interpreted in demonological terms. On the other hand practically everyone believes that demons are responsible for mental disorders,
"madness, " bad dreams, fright, dislike for food, fainting,
and some would include stomach disorders and unfamiliar
chronic illnesses of diverse types. In a survey of 100 village
heads of households only six persons expressed disbelief in
the power of demons to cause disease, but no one believed
that demons were responsible for common, "normal"

diseases. Demonological powers are great in respect to disorders which in more sophisticated circles would be described
as functional, psychogenic, or psychosomatic. In respect
to diseases which are readily curable by Western medicine,
demons have been outmoded, and much the same can be said
for many common disorders which "native doctors" (Ayurvedic practitioners) are presumed to treat successfully.
Demonological explanations are a last resort when Ayurvedic
and Western medicine have seemingly failed in respect to
disorders which are organic and not clearly psychogenic.

The spirit world beyond the major demons includes such
diverse forms as subordinate "assistant demons, " demon
apparitions, and the ghosts of departed persons. These differing beings have no carefully formulated relationship.
They all, however, are negative in relationship to man,
ranging from the mischievous to the deadly. All are viewed
as being in the same category of reality as the major demons.
None has any relationship to the more godlike planetary
figures, although inauspicious astrological situations permit
an opening which can be taken advantage of by any being on
this iniquitous and personalized side of the supernatural.

Evil apparitions of the demons and their ghostly hench-
man are particularly prevalent at mid-day, midnight, dawn
and sunset, and in specified places in the village. At these
hours it is unwise to be in the village burying grounds or to
linger at cross-roads, wells, ponds, or streams. Persons
who have eaten fried food are especially susceptible. Fish
and meat particularly are lures for demons. While some
supernatural entities have never been observed, and even
their effects known only by repute, many persons have seen
the unnamed apparitions of demons. These are manifest in
such forms as a buffalo or a black dog, and by repute, a
wild boar.

No one should suppose, as well one might from this evidence of a fearsome demon world, that Pelpolans live in
terror of the supernatural. Just as one may fear serious
disease yet lead a normal life of exposure without much
thought of falling sick, so do Pelpolans live in the midst of
a potentially threatening supernatural world. (Demon is possibly a too terrifying English rendition of "yaka. ") Thus,
although the theory of demons makes certain village locales
theoretically dangerous at given times of day, generally

people do not let this interfere with the normal course of the day's movements. Men will be seen bathing in the canal at high noon, and boys will tend cattle by the cemetery at theoretically crucial hours with no apparent reluctance.

True ghosts, prathas (or peretayas), are less demon-like than they are similar to mischievous but rather fearsome elfs. [6] It has been observed that upon death the spirit lingers in the home until an almsgiving has taken place. The pratha is a spirit which lingers longer, usually in the home of the deceased. It is hence both personalized and specific. Some spirits do not yield to the power of the almsgiving ceremony and live on in their home unobserved but active. Such persistent individuals are likely to be those who were greedy, overly fond of their wives and children, or simply those who loved life too much. There is also some connotation of physical uncleanliness in the word pratha. The pratha does not do serious harm. It is he who throws sand in the rice, makes mysterious noises in the roof, or at worst may cause the children to fall ill or lose their appetites. Prathas are rather common but usually quite susceptible to exorcizing.

Beyond the realm of spirit beings affecting the lives of men there is a vast range of magical belief and practice unspecific in terms of responsible beings. Mantrams or mantras (charms) are known by the laity. [7] These are effective in varieties of situations. Thus, it is believed that verbal charms might protect one from snakes and other dangers, or guard a young man or young woman from romantic advances. Mantrams are also an essential part of every supernatural ceremony of protection or exorcizing, and are recited to reduce pain--often by enchanting a piece of string which is then tied around the affected part of the body. Tabus, as upon a woman walking on the threshing floor in time of harvest, have no rationalizations beyond the fact that they are "bad to do." Ill and good omens, abundant in number, have no conscious affiliation with explicit supernatural beings. Much agricultural magic and ceremony is unrelated to specific powers. Fertility in paddy is, however, the provision of the godling Bahirava. Evil mouth, while no doubt vaguely a product of demon infestation, operates mainly without a theory of action.

Although very few persons in Pelpola are credited with

possessing evil mouth or evil eye, one elderly man is well
known for it. Upon his approach to a neighbor house, he is
not shunned but he is pitied and his influence feared. (Charms
will be uttered to protect the fruit on the bearing tree from
withering before his glance [evil eye] and to guard the health
of the children from his compliments.) If the threat is deemed
serious, as is rarely if ever the case, an exorcizor will be
called. Unquestionably the concept of evil mouth is related
to the villager's reluctance to engage in lavish praise for his
own or for another's possessions or loved ones. Ordinary
compliments do not create untoward effects, but lavish
praise, emotionally rendered, is suspect. This might, in
any one, yield the effects of evil mouth and provide him with
a lasting reputation for dangerous words and glances. It is
not well to gloat or brag over one's wife, one's possessions,
or one's crop. By the same token it is the part of prudence
to understate their value.

Another "force" not personified in a specific demon is
killata asuvenava. The significance of this power is generally that of making one "subject to contamination." Thus
a villager with an open wound would not attend a funeral on
grounds that this influence would lead his injury to worsen.
Again, one who wears a protective talisman would avoid
eating pork in that, due to killata asuvenava, the power of
the charm would be voided. This force also enters into one
bitten by a strangely acting dog, i.e. presumably rabid.

Black magic (hooniyam or kodivina) is made possible
through the demon Hooniyam, but its development as a magical system is directed less toward the demon than toward
formulae which automatically set or cut a spell. Through
kodivina an entire family may fall ill, persons may die,
crops be destroyed, and evil spirits set at work in the household. Once it is determined that the ill-fortune of a family
or individual is the result of kodivina, it is only through the
techniques of kodivina that normality can again be restored.
Although the power of black magic is fully recognized by
Pelpolans, this is not a prevalent explanation for misfortune
and evil days. Probably this is because of the high development and organization of alternative explanations, i.e. in
reference to planet gods and demons or even kamma. Also
it is relevant that the casting of spells is extremely dangerous to the perpetrator and to his professional agent. If the

spell is improperly set, its curses come back upon those
responsible.

The symptoms of supernaturally induced troubles must
be diagnosed before they are treated. Pirith is a generalized
purification or blessing, but one not usually utilized when
specifics can be found. The Sinhalese are not lacking in devices for determining the specific causes of untoward happenings, nor in devices for exorcizing them. The major
diagnostic skills are those of the astrologer and the "fortune teller." The principal forms of exorcizing are thovil
(demon dancing) and bali (planetary god invocation). The
treatment depends upon the diagnosis.

With recognition of probable supernatural forces at work,
the villager approaches either a fortune teller or an astrologer. These symptoms may be any of those condtions described as resulting from demon or godlike influences but
the most common situations involving such action are conditions associated with pregnancy, unexplained mischief in
the home, illnesses, especially those of functional character
or undiagnosed by Western or Ayurvedic practitioners,
fearful dreams, or a series of happenings which together
force the conclusion of some dogged period of successive
ill-happenings of many types. [8] Generally speaking, appeals
to planetary gods are made for protection against potential
evils, while demons are exorcized as actual present evils.
However it is not uncommon that existant evils are attacked
through the planetary gods, theoretically for their sympathy.
On another occasion, with identical symptoms, treatment
may be given by exorcizing demons, without reference to
planet influences.

Illness is the most ubiquitous condition involving supernaturally directed action and around it is built the greatest
structure of ceremony. Upon observing the symptoms and
suspecting other than natural causes, the villager may go
either to the astrologer or fortune teller, a choice which in
Pelpola is more fortuitously than rationally decided. Pelpola
has no astrologers other than the bhikkhu, and while he
draws horoscopes, he does not engage in analysis. On the
other hand, the presence of four well known exorcizers in
the village creates a general bias in favor of demon infestation rather than planetary interpretations. Also where the
astrological conditions are bad, demons or their minions

are the immediate trouble makers, taking advantage of this
planetary-based period of weakness. Hence except in protective ceremonies as during pregnancy, "demon dances"
are more common than are dances of invocation to planet
gods. And in some cases it is clear that the difficulties are
demonological in origin, i.e. bad dreams, madness, noises
in the house, evil mouth.

Pelpola has no fortune teller, but a nearby village has
one of great local fame who is relied upon for accurate diagnosis. He, of course, emphasizes spirit powers rather
than astrological distrubances. Typically the fortune teller
relies upon "lamp reading" (anjanam eliya) for the identification of the evil influence. In reading the lamp, the diag-
nostician applies some black plaster to the back of a saucer.
The saucer is then placed before the lighted oil lamp. After
considerable ceremony an outsider gazes through the lamp
at the black plaster and there develops a vision indicative
of the cause of the disorder. If, for example, Hanuman (the
"Monkey God" of the Hindus) appears with a red flag, this
is evidence of kodivina or black magic, and by skillful
questioning its nature and perpetrator will be found out.
Either by this or by other devices the fortune teller demonstrates the nature of the evil, always in terms of the demon
world.

Had the sufferer approached an astrologer with identical
symptoms and complaints, the diagnosis would have been
different, for the astrologer has knowledge only of the
heavens and none whatever of the demons. The horoscope
would have been studied, the significant stars determined,
and a prescription involving planetary appeals given. [9]

Tracing the origin of trouble to one or the other of its
two possible roots is an important step. Diagnosticians are
not therapeutists. Depending upon the diagnosis and related
prescription the villager must approach those who specialize
on the one hand in planetary appeals or, on the other, in
demon exorcizing.

If planet influences are operative, the villager approaches
a man of Berava caste, in a nearby village, and arranges
for a bali ceremony. The bali is never done with masks but
it is always done by members of the appropriate caste, i.e.
"tom-tom beaters, " or Berava. Images of the planet gods
are moulded in clay and a conventionalized altar constructed

inside the home. Neighbors and relatives come for the entertainment, for it is that indeed. All night the dancers
work, singing, praising, exhorting, charming. If an important guest arrives, special handsprings and dance steps
are done in his honor--and for an anticipated honorarium.

Thovil ceremonies are varied. For simple matters an
exorcizer may simply chant a mantram and set up symbols
on an affected house or tie a string on the victim's wrist.
If a dangerous disease demon or a persistent pratha is at
work then a full scale "demon dance" will be indicated. The
large thovil involves elaborate properties and the exorcist
and his assitants will construct them on the day preceeding
the ceremony. A small table is built of plantain trees and
coconut leaves; flowers, dried fish, seeds, young coconuts,
and various other prescribed articles are placed on the
table. Soon after an early evening meal the exorcizing begins. This is a set pattern with artistic variations by the
performers and involves drumming, dancing, chanting and
ad lib dialogue, often comical. In the early morning hours,
in the case of a bedeviled house, the spirit will be driven
out with a lighted torch. In treatment of "madness" especially
among women, the patient will be "beaten" in the early
morning hours with a coconut flower, and then questioned
regarding her possession. The particular demon's name
will eventually be mentioned by her, or alluded to, and a
proper sacrifice determined, often a cockerel. The offering will be given symbolically, the demon threatened from
the premises, yellow strings tied to the victim's neck, and
recovery anticipated.

Either a bali or a thovil is an entertaining event in the village and many persons turn out for it. Performers always
seek to make the affair jovial, cracking jokes and making
plays on words. Performances are as much folk dramas as
they are awful ceremonies. [10] In many places the thovil is
enlivened by the fearsome masks worn by performers in
representation of the entire array of disease demons. Pelpola performers do not use masks, but there is no doubt
that a considerable part of the popularity of both bali and
thovil ceremonies arises from their entertainment value,
and quite possibly as outlets for conspicious consumption.
That the villagers have some faith in their efficacy there is
no doubt, but it is probable that they would be much less

common were they not occasions apart from the humdrum
of village life and opportunities for playing host in a grand
community show.

Black magic is of different character. It is secret and
dangerous. No one would admit having occasioned a spell
to be cast, for obvious reasons. These are matters of ter-
rible secrecy. Although two of Pelpola's four exorcizers
have the ability to cut hooniyam, and have done so for Pelpolans, casting of spells is done through outside sorcerers,
if it is actually done. We know of no verified instances in
the village, although recent cases outside the village have
been verified. All Pelpolans fear hooniyam and believe that,
if efficiently carried out, death can be brought to an entire
family through illness or accident. Yet, ill-fortune does
not appear to be commonly attributed to sorcery and to say
that village people fear it is not to say that they live in
dread of it.

In performing hooniyam the exorcist (working now as a
sorcerer) will chant mantrams for perhaps two days over
the materials to be used in the spell. In this area a commonly known technique is to bury some properly prepared
ashes of a burned human body in the garden of the victim.
From that time forward results may be expected--and if no
results appear the perpetrators live in terror that the spell
was improperly cast and will rebound upon themselves. From
the victim's standpoint, or rather from the standpoint of a
person who believes himself to be a victim of hooniyam,
upon the advice of the fortune teller, a great thovil is planned
in which yellow strings are tied around the necks of all in-
mates of the house and a pumpkin cut amid mantram chanting. The pumpkin is decorated with a drawing of the demon
Hooniyam and its cutting in two symbolizes the destruction
of the original spell. It is the sign of an effective cutting if
drops of blood are visible inside the cut pumpkin, and indeed
one of the most successful exorcizers of the region carried
secretly a phial of blood--in case none appeared through
magical processes. [11] Hooniyam spells and cuttings are
probably the most expensive ceremonies known to the villager for this is playing with the fires of hell, and such business comes high--and infrequently. Testimony to the awe-
someness of the black spell is that the exorcizer insures
himself from the effects of failure by observing pan sil and
worshipping both the Buddha, in the vihare, and the Hindu
gods.

Chapter VIII

SOCIAL STRATIFICATION

Pelpolans do not usually think of themselves as being critically divided into status levels in any respect other than caste. Caste membership, unlike other status determinents of significance, is absolutely precise and, except as the caste body itself rises or falls, unmodifiable. It does not, however, impose fixed limits upon status in regard to other criteria, and is certainly not to be conceived as the sole status structure in the community. Subject to qualification, we may conceive of a caste as one situs within which universally recognized status criteria operate. In the following pages, from a discussion of caste structure and relationships, an attempt is made to analyze the further determinants of status. Upon this foundation the village is then viewed from the standpoint of class structuring.

Caste

The accepted hierarchy places the Goyigama ("cultivators") in the higher position, and the Badahela ("potters"), the only other group of numerical importance in Pelpola, in the lower. A few families of Hena ("washerman") caste are simply regarded as of "low caste" without much thought given their relative status. In general throughout Sinhalese society the Goyigama are considered the highest caste, but neither Badahela nor Hena are the lowest. Apart from status implications it should be remembered that the local caste body forms the communal group within which any villager lives. Less of the significance of caste lies in its hierarchical implications than in its provision of the "communal, " intimate world surrounding the individual and his kin. The caste group has a meaning similar to that of an endogamous ethnic "community" within a larger heterogeneous area community. Here, however, relative prestige position is assigned through tradition; vocational roles are implicit, and social distance is institutionalized.

119

Within caste, the lines of G̲e̲ are of a character reminiscent of caste itself but of much less importance. Among both Goyigama and Badahela some name lines have more "honor" than others. This is a matter distinct from both nuclear and lineal family prestige, and it survives mainly in a subjective sense. As has been indicated earlier, the G̲e̲, while ascribed and precise, has little behavioral significance. For most practical purposes, caste is the only status category in this village which is precise, inalterable, and in some behavioral matters, such as marriage, can not be qualified by a person's other attributes and achievements.

About forty of Pelpola's four hundred families are of Badahela caste, two are of Hena caste, one Vahumpera, and the remainder Goyigama. [1] By tradition the Goyigama is the cultivating caste, although there has probably been no time in Sinhalese history when this occupation was exclusively theirs. In Pelpola, however, all cultivators are of this caste. The Badahela are by tradition potters and the Hena, washermen. In Pelpola the Hena pursue the vocation of washing, and also maintain the ceremonial services expected of members of this caste toward the Goyigama. Badahela families are practically all engaged in potting, although some of the men also practice non-traditional vocations, especially masonry. That a number of the Goyigama families do no actual cultivating is probably due to modern circumstances. The preservation of caste-linked vocations has no support in law and not even very strong support in community attitudes. Agriculture is an honorable vocation, but it is frequently clung to in lieu of more advantageous opportunities. Similarly, the "potters," who, like the Goyigama, would eschew an occupation traditionally affiliated with a lower caste, have no scruples about leaving their traditional work when superior opportunity arises. Nor would the Goyigama object. None-the-less, throughout the village ancient occupational roles tend to persist.

Partial separation of housing within the village nearly achieves a distinct potter community in a locality sense. The Badahela are concentrated in two neighborhoods. Residential proximity in addition to segregation in some social affairs, kinship and other bonds make them a closely knit group. Unlike many Indian regions there is no formal organization or panchayat for any caste in this region. There are

numerous peripheral overlappings of the Badahela and Goyigama "communities." Inter-household visiting does not occur widely on anything like an equal basis, but none-the-less
the "potter" family does not hesitate to borrow a chair from
a high caste neighbor for an unexpected guest of importance.
A few Goyigama men have loafing and drinking companions
among the "potters." However, intermixing of this type is
frowned upon by most of the Goyigama. Actually the majority
of inter-caste contacts occur in commercial situations, in
which all participate without discrimination, in the school,
and in the normal passages of "good day" in the lanes. Even
the special interest associations of the village afford little
mixing, despite the fact that such joint participation would
be unobjectionable even to the most conservative Goyigama.
In matters connected with agriculture, the Badahela have no
concern. While they belong to the cooperative societies,
they do not take much part in society business. There is a
general tendency to leave such things to the Goyigama and,
as democratic as Pelpola is, a formal position of leadership by a Badahela would be thought unseemly. In religion
the two castes worship separately and the reason for this is
an historic matter giving much insight into inter-caste relations. The story is worth repeating.[2]

Until about twenty-five years ago, Pelpola had a single
temple in which both castes worshipped. It was, and is now,
dominated by the local Goyigama, with Goyigama priests,
and located in an entirely Goyigama section of the village.
On a poya (holy) day back in 1930, a Badahela man sat among
his friends on the high stage-like dais in the center of the
preaching hall. When the priest entered he noted the situation and gave a severe and public reprimand to the "potter"
who had "forgotten his position in life." This insult was
keenly felt by the Badahela "community" and it was forth-
with decided by them that they should build their own temple
and henceforth worship separately. Although a number of
Goyigama leaders felt badly over the incident, none dared
ask the priest to apologize, and accordingly the Badahela
began work on their own place of worship. Four years later
this was completed, with the financial assistance of local
friends of Goyigama caste, and a priest of a non-Goyigama
sect was installed.

It might be thought that an incident so strongly charged

would have brought a lasting enmity between the castes. In
fact it had no such effect. The potters simply changed their
place of worship, quietly, and without rancour. Frequently
they come to special services at the "Goyigama temple, "
and openly profess that if that priest would ask alms of them
they would give. The event has obviously furthered communal
separateness in village life, but in regard to social distance
the effect has been the reverse. The Goyigama were ashamed.
The complaisant higher caste had brought dramatically to
their own attention, th'e hiatus between concepts of caste
hierarchy and the Buddhist Way.

One should not conclude that life in the village is equalitarian. The Badahela is still an inferior caste, although the
symbols of their low birth and discriminations in behavior
are inexact and mild. The past two decades have witnessed
gradual but significant changes, both in the amount of personalized intercourse and in the diminished symbols of distance. A mild honorific (Appuhamy) is maintained as an address form for Goyigama, but is today most likely to be
used toward high caste men who also have high prestige in
matters other than caste. However, one who is knowledgeable of village ways would discern that in greetings and in
conversation the Badhela retain a deferential manner toward
any person of high caste.

In affairs centering about the home, especially in regard
to eating, there are firmer evidences both of communal
separateness and of inferior-superior positions. The Goyigama visiting at the home of a Badahela is treated as an
honored guest. The Badahela visiting the Goyigama home is
welcomed, but he does not sit as an equal, nor does he remain long beyond the business of his call to engage in pleas-
antries. It is unlikely that he would enter the house beyond
the verandah. Only among a few night-hawking and none too
well thought of Goyigama men would there be any joint eating. Thus the Badahela's Goyigama friend may be an honored
guest at a wedding but food prepared in that home is not taken
by him, though he will drink bottled drinks and accept a
chew of betel. (No Badahela would be a guest at a Goyigama
wedding.) Actually the mixing of castes in any home situation
is rare except as some business may be transacted on the
Goyigama's verandah.

Unlike the Badahela, the Hena caste holds a position of

privileged familiarity with the Goyigama. As family washerman the Hena has physical access to the high caste house, and in important rites, such as puberty and marriage, both the husband and wife of the washer family serving the Goyigama household are intimate ceremonial servitors. Such close relationships do nothing to absolve caste inequality but they are associated with affection and almost "family feeling, " often on both sides. Typically the Goyigama eschews formal and degrading caste titles in addressing a local momber of the Hena caste. Adults of this caste are normally addressed in a familiar form, the adult male called Henamama (Hena-uncle) and his wife Redinenda (Cloth-aunt). (This reference to the Hena woman relates to her traditional function at puberty and marriage ceremonies.)

There is no breath of discrimination in the village service institutions. Nor is there segregation in the school. It would not occur to a Pelpolan that caste is any basis for precedence in a shopper's cue or for segregated seating in the busses, or even the temple. Actually, as is the case in housing, unselfconscious clustering often occurs. Free participation without prejudice is the accepted rule in matters outside family and eating. And in any extra-household participation it would take a person sophisticated in village ways to detect the cues of superiority and inferiority in the personal interaction of Badahela and Goyigama.

General equality in public affairs does not extend to the sphere of leadership and formal office. While there are certain "potters" respected by the Goyigama for their piety and neighborly goodness, there is none to be classed as wealthy, as "powerful, " or "influential" outside his own group. Had any "potter" the attributes essential for community-wide leadership and the will to exert himself toward office or even wide informal leadership, we might conceivably see some caste tension in Pelpola. Leaders both in and out of office are, and always have been, Goyigama. There is no challenge to their monopoly of honors today nor is there likely to be for some years. When the matter is posed as an hypothetical issue, the high caste Pelpolan is more apt than not to turn his head in the manner of a Sinhalese shrug and observe that times are changing and no doubt this too will come. Though a minority might look favorably upon such an eventuality, the possibility is viewed with little

emotion, and many would today reject the principle if not
the fact of a strictly Goyigama local officialdom.

There is little difference between Badahela and Goyigama
in their acceptance, or rejection, of caste ideology. This is
true because Sinhalese caste has become more a communal
differentiation than a hierarchical one. Both groups, generally speaking, support the preservation of castes. The
Badahela however are united in their belief in non-discri-
minatory equality in opportunity and community life, while
among Goyigama there are some still wedded to the principles of caste superiority and inferiority. (See Chapter XI.)
Most Goyigama, however, agree that caste is not a proper
basis for any hierarchy of well-being, nor of economic and
social opportunity. The ideology of non-discrimination is
perhaps developed beyond its practice, but caste hierarchy
is dying. Cultural differences between castes have been
practically nonexistant within any known historic period. But
the castes, as discrete, endogamous units and hence with
some separation in communal life, show no signs of deterioration.

Status Factors and Gradients

The recognition of castes provides the merest beginning
to an understanding of status allocations. Nor may status
matters which are not of caste be labelled simply "social
class." In Pelpola, as in all communities, status, in the
sense of a position describable as more or less prestigeful,
more or less powerful, or honorable, is derived from a
complex set of criteria. These criteria may be any attributes or functions which the community holds in valuative
hierarchies or continuua. Some, like caste, are discrete
and circumscribe precise social levels. Others are graduated, and positions assigned with more or less uncertainty.
The various types of criteria, or determinants, overlay and
qualify one another with such utter complexity as to make
reference to an overall status position for any given individual tenuous in the extreme. We may at least be sure that
members of castes all hold prestige or honor positions in
the community which are based on criteria other than those
of caste itself.

Like every community, Pelpola has people who differ in

the respect, the honor and the esteem in which they are held. Wealth, especially landed wealth, is important for prestige, but even within a caste, status is not allocated upon so simple a basis. There is no doubt that Pelpolans treat their wealthy with added deference, and positions of wealth are no doubt related to the facts of power deriving from land as well as the various emulative accoutrements of wealth. Yet when village men discuss "stratification, " they do not speak in terms of wealth so much as other attributes which they deem status-worthy.

Pelpola's "theory of status" indicates at least five significant factors other than caste. Of these, wealth is recognized but given less emphasis than most others. Recognized, but given a minimum of importance, is the Ge line of the individual. More important than Ge is the reputation of the patrilineal family. Such "reputation" is derived from other attributes, but the very fact of "being of good family" is a significant fact. Among achieved attributes, the fact of piety, religious devoutness, or its lack, sets persons apart for special regard. But the most frequently heard valuative term relates to "helpfulness. " The man who can be counted upon for neighborly assistance, and has "knowhow" in confronting these matters, is the ideal citizen.

Beyond these conditions which villagers spontaneously recognize as bases for personal status valuations there are others of less direct daily significance, but nonetheless important. The high valuation of clerical employments runs through all village ambitions and dreams of glory for self or sons. Since white collar positions are few in village life, most persons who have achieved this enviable place have departed the village. School teachers, however, hold a high place in the status system, less from the villager's veneration of learning, which is considerable, than from the veneration of "white collar" occupations, especially as associated with government. In the general run of village work there is not much distinction given various employments. Rubber tapping is a task of low regard, but many persons engaged in it are also associated with the highly honorable vocation of cultivation. Potting is of course so thoroughly linked with caste that its status is inseparable from that of the group practicing it. The attainment of high education is highly regarded partly through the valuation of learning per se, partly as a means to clerical employment.

It is to be recognized that the going theory of status may not be reflected perfectly in the actualities of life. Further differing ingredients in status may yield distinctly different overt expressions in status oriented behavior. The possession of wealth or high occupational position brings more visible behavioral deference than does the valued quality of good neighborliness. The former yield deferential behavior even when tinged with jealousy or personal disapproval. The latter brings no signs of deference in its own right, but does bring forth qualitative judgements expressed verbally and in cooperative actions. Piety carries with it distinctive verbal symbols of deference and almost certain informal leadership in matters connected with the temple.

These seeming confusions are more apparent than real, for if they are confusing they are so to the analyst rather than the peasant. "Status" is a concept composed of many more or less related dimensions. Within this cluster of connotations the distinction of two types of ingredients will serve to clarify some of the complications of Pelpola's status system. We must distinguish between the concepts "prestige" and "esteem." Prestige relates to an "ascendency based upon recognition of power," and more literally to "dazzling influence," derived from "success." Esteem is also a condition of repute, but repute of a different sort. Esteem is favorable opinion. It is less a matter of high reputation than of good reputation. Things or persons held in esteem are precious. When we deal with the concept of general social status these two elements are difficult to extricate. Yet their distinction brings the roots of orderly understanding in this milieu. Deference paid to wealth is a product of prestige. High valuation of the good neighbor is a reflection of esteem. Piety may well partake of both. Leadership in the secular affairs of village life is clearly joined with esteem though not without prestige as well. Prestige alone, as will be seen, does not yield leadership in Pelpola though it may yield office.

Regardless of the determinants, or even the logical defensibility of the concept, Pelpolans like Westerners have a concept of "general social status." This conception is expressed in the word piligeneema connoting "one's hierarchical position in society." There is no implicit connotation of economic worth in the term nor of any single factor which might determine position. Although persons are not conceived as falling into classes in regard to piligeneema, whatever its ingredients, persons can be graded in reference to it with the implication that the grading relates to differences in "honor" and "importance." In so far as the two can be separated the connotation is more "prestige" than "esteem."

The application of this concept is circumscribed by caste. No Goyigama man reasonably speaks of piligeneema in reference to a Badahela. When pressed for a statement regarding the position of one of the lower caste, a typical response is, "He has no piligeneema." Yet such a response does not signify that the higher caste views all members of the lower as sharing a common condition of "no" prestige. It means rather that the prestige systems of the two are non-competitive, relating as they do to what are conceived as being separate communities. Piligeneema refers to a type of order within a people; "potters" are a "different people." The Goyigama, if pressed for a general status evaluation of a Badahela, may well respond that "among his people he is a good man and stands well." Because he is of a different caste does not mean that as a person he has no social status, nor even that it is unqualifiedly lower than that of some high caste persons. In pure esteem terms caste would be of little or no consequence in the rating one individual might give another. Esteem is little affected by formal status categories. In piligeneema, with its strong prestige element, each caste forms a distinct milieu. Men of different caste take personal worth into account when they deal as individuals, and to some extent symbols typical of caste superiority and of inferiority are relaxed or exaggerated in keeping with the personal esteem and prestige of the actors. Goyigama equate all Badahela in regard to prestige but not esteem. Badahela in turn recognize differences among Goyigama in esteem and probably also in prestige. The latter probability does not suggest that the Badahela reject the plural social structure. Rather as a weak and rather homogeneous status group they recognize the facts of power as much as the facts of esteem among their high caste neighbors. If a Badahela holds high piligeneema among his fellows, this is less relevant to the Goyigama than the fact of high piligeneema of a Goyigama for a Badahela. Piligeneema is associated with power and the Goyigama's power is not restricted to his caste.

Within the Goyigama caste an exploratory and partial inquiry was made into the components or determinants of general social status. Twelve well informed men of the caste were selected to rate all Goyigama household heads in our survey sample, in respect to (a) piety and (b) general social status (piligeneema). The raters were chosen to include representatives from each economic level and each of the two important Ge, with several from minor Ge as well. Ratings on the two continua were done at different times and always in privacy with the one person rating. Terms representing degrees along the continua of piety and of piligeneema were developed out of general conversation with villagers prior to the systematic evaluations. It was arbitrarily decided to classify all persons into four categories in respect to each continuum in order that comparison with economic classes might be simplified. For purposes of analysis the true position of any individual was defined as that ranking assigned him by the largest number of judges. In ninety-two per cent of the cases an identical piligeneema score was agreed upon independently by over half of the raters. Similarly agreement on piety was reached by over half in eighty-five per cent of the cases. In addition to the two variables set to our judges, we included in this analysis the economic class of the person rated[3] and the status of his Ge. The latter classification was based upon the general village recognition that the Lokuliyanage hold the priority position, followed by Liyanage and then by all others. (Measures of lineal and nuclear family status and neighborliness were not attempted.)

The distribution of ratings (Table 2) indicates the critical eye with which Pelpolan views Pelpolan. Each continuum is skewed toward the bottom of the scale, although there appears to have been some reluctance to class a great many people within the ranks of the outright impious, of which the lowest grouping explicitly consisted. On the other hand forty-two per cent were judged to be "people who amount to nothing, " the lowest category of piligeneema.

Internal analysis of the four series indicates that both financial position and piety are significantly related to piligeneema. Persons of low economic position and persons of low piety tend to hold inferior general social status positions, while those high in these attributes tend to be high in general status. These differences are statistically significant at the

.01 level. Ge position is unrelated to general social status,
although it bears significant positive relationship to economic position. (Significant at the .01 level.)

Table 2

Distribution of Goyigama Household Heads as Rated
on Status Attributes (in per cents)

Rating	Piligeneema	Piety	Economic	Ge
High	4	1	3	10
Moderately High	11	26	18	13
Moderately low	43	53	34	77
Low	42	20	45	--
Total Cases	(92) 100%	(92) 100%	(92) 100%	(92) 100%

We may not on the basis of statistical data, infer that
economic factors are of determinative importance for general social status. It is reasonable, however, that of the
factors, the financial is the most important, although it
probably operates through indirect means. Status through
piety is possibly partly a function of wealth. Men of wealth
are in a favored position to be judged pious since their almsgivings are more dramatic, greater, and more frequent.
(Unless one is an upasaka, attendence at religious services
is so erratic among adult males as to constitute no general
measure.) It is possible that the discrimination of those assigned the lowest piety rating was more frequently on ethical grounds, judging by our raters' comments. Although we
have here no measure of familial status, we know from general observation that this too correlates with wealth in so
far as the long landed families are acknowledged to be households of great honor. A general correlation probably exists
between worth in land and lineal and nuclear family status,
although it is unlikely that family honor is generally credited
to those made wealthy through trade. Neighborly helpfulness,
although a highly esteemed character attribute throughout
the village, probably has little to do with community wide
evaluations of piligeneema.

Social Class

Pelpolans do not think of themselves as divided into levels
of "social class. " Nor are there commonly used words indicating classes in terms of prestige generally. In reference
to the specific criteria of prestige, only one, wealth, appears to be conceived in class levels. The existence of an
economic class terminology is evident, but these levels are
not conceived as social classes possessing distinct interests,
cohesion, or self contained circles of social interaction.
Such groupings are construed in terms of material goods,
security, and varying living levels. These categories have
no conscious prestige implications, and the words expressing them refer as readily to the poor Badahela as to the
poor Goyigama, or to the most honored landed proprietor
and the despised but equally wealthy trader.

In popular conception the village possesses four economic
grades or classes. At the peak of the hierarchy are the
pohasath, "well-off people, " or, as sometimes described,
the sallikarayo, "people having money. " The second layer
is composed of the "middle people" madyama, while the
next lower are the "day to day" folk or "ordinary, " samanya.
At the bottom are the duppath, literally, "those fallen in
sorrow, " or as otherwise termed "one rice meal a day
people. " It is fully recognized that variations exist in each
level but these are the classifictory devices of the village
for spontaneous reference to one's economic position.

To gain further knowledge of the economic hierarchy,
four of the most widely informed men of the village were
selected and asked individually to classify all Pelpolan
householders as to their economic class positions. The
raters each came from a different level, but apart from
this were chosen for their community wide information.
The "true" position of each household head in the village
was taken as the class rating assigned him in at least three
out of the four evaluations. (In three instances an additional
rater was used to break a tie.) Consensus was high, as
might be expected in a community where secrets are kept
with difficulty.

The results of this inquiry show the economic class pyra-
mid to be very squat. Forty-four per cent of all householders
were classed in the lowest economic level, while thirty-six

per cent fell into the next to the lowest class, the people
with a "day to day" living. Thus, only a fifth were deemed
to fall into categories which might be termed prosperous,
sixteen per cent "middle people, " and four per cent "people
who have money. "

The objective correlates of economic rank are many, and
no doubt in some senses directly prestige inducing, e.g.
through emulative valuation, and power. The "well-off" folk
are well off in even urban terms, although not of great
wealth. [4] They are composed of the larger land owners, especially in rubber, and the major entrepreneurs in ceramics,
canal transport and other enterprises. The homes of this
small body are all of plaster, usually over a kabook base,
with tile roofs and possessing five or six rooms, each with
cement flooring. Many items of Victorian design are found
within the houses. Chairs, some of which are upholstered,
and tables are common. In some homes there are writing
cabinets and a phonograph. Beds of local construction are
usual. None has an atmosphere of luxury but most are prosperous homes furnished with some regard to turn-of-the-
century British styles. In well-off houses, rice is eaten
two or even three times a day and with many curries. The
man of the house wears a coat when he walks through the
village, and often has sandals below his sarong. Younger
men of wealth own bicycles, and most own shoes saved for
special occasions. Perhaps most outstanding of all aspects
of wealth, these families will send their children to urban
boarding schools that they may ultimately make their mark
in the English-speaking world. And in the present generation
of prosperous men, it is notable that only seven per cent of
those in the two upper classes are illiterate in Sinhalese as
compared with more than one-third of the lowest level.

Ostentatious display is not pronounced, but the great private almsgivings and similar events are necessarily prerogatives of the more prosperous. Weddings among these
families are also affairs of considerable display in decora-
tions and especially in food.

With the "one meal a day" folk, living is quite different
in its physical surroundings. Houses are rarely of plaster
and tile. Instead, they are commonly constructed entirely
of thatch, although many are of the somewhat superior wattle
and daub (mud) with thatch roofs. Such houses are built by

family labor, whereas the upper classes' kabook and plaster houses require specialized workers. Daily wage or home labor is here the major means of support, and although frequently two or more persons are employed, a wage rate of one rupee and a half to two rupees per day does not buy much material comfort. (Nearly all potters fall into this category.) Most homes are of two rooms with virtually no furniture except a table, a rough chest, and occasionally one or two straight wooden chairs. Instead of the well adorned and frequent rice meals, only evening rice is served, often with little more than a coconut and red chilli sambol (relish) for zest. Signs of status emulation are seen in the widely owned nickle plated flashlight and less frequently a jack-knife. The householder will likely possess a white shirt for dress occasions but his village attire is limited to the sarong.

Except for the wealthy, there are few certain signs of economic class position. Housing is probably the most accurate, ranging as it does from the neat plastered homes of the upper level families, distinguished among themselves rather inexactly by size and maintenance, to the typical "wattle and daub" of the "ordinary people" and the thatch construction of the very poor. This is far from an exact index of position, however, except in the extremes of wealth and of poverty. In no single objective measure can one stratum be sharply distinguished from the next.

It has been observed that Pelpolans do not think of their economic classes as constituting real social groups. Nor is there pronounced development of economic differentiation by neighborhood. (See Chapter I.) To test Pelpola's theory, typically expressed by one man that "every villager looks much the same to me, " the economic ratings of persons specified by household heads, as being "best friends" and those named as being in their intimate friendship circle, were compared to the rating of the person specifying them. [5] (In this analysis the full survey sample of 100 cases was used.) Forty-six per cent of the householders in the two highest economic classes named a best friend who was beneath them in financial rank. Thirty-one per cent named a person also of high position. However, it is notable that not one named a person of lowest economic class although this is the largest single category in the community. At the other

extreme of the hierarchy, nearly one-half of the poorest
heads named a best friend one step above them in economic
status. Thirty per cent claimed best friends within the two
highest strata. Those of moderately low position, the "day
to day" people, appeared to be entirely random in their
selection.

Similar results appear from the analysis of the economic
positions of persons with whom householders most frequently
spend their leisure hours. Although fourteen individuals,
some probably from outside the village, were named for
whom we had no financial rating, and six householders
claimed to have no intimate circle, 267 known intimates
were specified by ninety-one household heads. Sixty-three
per cent of the persons named by upper class respondents
were also members of the upper classes, i.e. the two highest levels. Only eight per cent of the intimates named were
of the lowest class. Respondents of the lowest class, however, tended to name persons above them in rank. Only
twenty-three per cent of their intimates were equally low
in financial position, while over one-third came from the
two highest categories.

While these rough methods are unworthy of refined statistical analysis, it is apparent that the well-to-do tend to
nominate as their friends persons who also are of some
economic worth, and rarely persons who are in the poorest
class. The poor, on the other hand, widely profess friendship with those above them in economic rank. Unfortunately
we have no statistical basis for determining the actual composition of friendship cliques. It is apparent that spontaneous
claims to intimacy with the well-to-do made by the poor are
not fully reciprocated. Probably in point of fact the poor do
associate themselves with the wealthy, exaggerating somewhat the intimacy of their ties. In part the more circumscribed friendships of the well-to-do may be ecologically
influenced but this is surely no full explanation. In general
the tendencies toward exclusiveness at the upper level and
the upward climbing at the lower, display a remarkable
consistency with what seems to transpire in Western communities.

The composition of Pelpola's aristocracy of wealth
symptomizes the village's mid-passage from a stable peasant community to a composite of folkness and commercial

expansiveness. Peasant societies are not typically ones of rapid social mobility but Pelpola has in this generation demonstrated unmistakable signs of a growing entrepreneurial elite. The families of new wealth all owe their position to business and industrial enterprises. Families of old wealth have the roots of their fortunes in the land.

Selecting arbitrarily the ten richest families in the village, only three owe their positions chiefly to landed proprietorship, which in each case extends back through several generations and possibly centuries. The remainder are, with a single exception, families in which the contemporary household head has achieved his position through some form of business enterprise. The exception arises in the case of a family in which business enterprise in the last generation laid the foundation for landed proprietorship in this one. The richest man of the village achieved his wealth through various trading activities mainly outside the village and subsequent land investments here and elsewhere. Others have achieved wealth through brick and tile manufacturing, local boutique proprietorships, and one through various local enterprises such as mechanical paddy hulling, a bakery, and a boutique. Only one of the business elite was born outside the village. He came to Pelpola as the groom in marriage with the daughter of a wealthy landed proprietor. Nearly all of these men have origins which would be classed as "ordinary" or "day to day." While several now own agricultural lands through investment of business profits, in no instance did operations in agriculture lay the basis for their prosperity.

The wealthy landed proprietors each inherited wealth, and, particularly the agricultural sources of wealth, in paddy land and rubber. Two of these men are in family lines known to have been wealthy long before rubber came into the region, i.e. about 1900. Only one of the contemporary family heads has branched out into business activities. This man, a school teacher by profession, and highly educated in Sinhalese, owns one of the well used rubber processing stations at which villagers pay a small fee for coagulating, rolling and smoking their rubber. He also owns a hiring car.

The attitudes of the rank and file villagers toward the men of wealth contrast sharply when we speak of the landed and of the enterprisers. Business men, particularly the traders,

are generally viewed as squeezing their riches from their
neighbors' purses. No similar attitude is exhibited toward
the landed who put out their paddy lands to share renters
and who hire villagers to tend their rubber. This is in the
proper order of things. Buying cheap and selling dear has
no basis in indigenous ethical values. Each of our ten men
receives deferential treatment by less affluent neighbors,
but the business men are in the main disliked and distrusted,
while the landed proprietors are held in honor and esteem.
Of the business rich, two are virtual isolates in the village,
and the only one regarding whom favorable comments are
spontaneously offered is he of inherited wealth made honorable in this generation through landed proprietorship. Most
are commonly referred to in terms ranging from "useless
fellow" to "cheat." Only two of the enterprisers engage actively in community affairs, one holding an important official appointment. A considerable proportion of the village
would hoot in derision if it were suggested that this man
was indeed a leader of the community. The other is in
formally active, and is generally respected.

On the other hand, the landed proprietors in our small
group are typically spoken of in highly favorable terms, an
observation we have tested through a number of separate
observers and in widely varying contexts. All three are out-
standingly active in village affairs, and two of them are
sought out for counsel by many villagers. Only one of these
men currently holds any office in the village, but it is certain
that each could do so if he wished. Although one is engaged
in minor business activity this has no detracting effect in
the face of his generosity to the temple and his personal and
financial assistance in village problems both public and private. These men differ from most of the enterprisers in
viewing themselves as responsible leaders of the people,
and they find satisfaction in this role. The rich generally
have prestige but it is the landed rich who have also esteem.

Chapter IX

THE CHANNELS FOR SECULARIZATION
(CONTACTS WITH THE OUTER WORLD)

There is little hope today of reconstructing much of Pelpola's life and world prior to this century. Since at least Dutch times, however, the village has been in direct touch with urban centers and their markets. Cart-track travel from the village to the coastal center of Kalutara, and possibly an inland one as well, is no doubt of ancient origin. Only in recent times, however, has anything other than footpaths led into the village proper except for the unique and significant water channel which has existed since the Dutch period. The Kapu Ela, which to a slight extent has isolated Pelpola from her neighboring villages, has for the past two hundred years been a channel of trade and communication. The tile industry, dating to Dutch times, has been dependent upon canal boats carrying the finished wares to the more northerly coastal centers. It is said, too, that Pelpolans have been famed as boatmen since long ago, but what effect these travellers may have had upon local ways and thought cannot be guessed.

Long before the Dutch, whose interest in Pelpola is attested in archival records, the Portuguese had been in direct contact with this village. Their influence is indicated in many contemporary family names. [1] Apart, however, from the canal instigated by the Dutch, and its stimulus to ceramic production, there is no sign that Pelpola underwent any influences not general to the Ceylon Low Country. Several centuries of European rule have contributed to the moderate cultural distinction of the Low Country and the Kandyan Sinhalese. The Dutch originated the process which brought all Low Country Sinhalese under a legal system of European origin, but the precise charting of the effects of early European contact would require historical research well beyond the scope of this inquiry.

Rubber, introduced to this area at the beginning of the

present century, holds a direct significance for contemporary life and changes. With adjacent estate development,
Pelpola's footpath to the world became a cart-track, and
the existing cart-track beyond the village was transformed
to a roadway. Quite early Pelpolans took employment upon
the estates, and women, as well as men, were thrown into
wage work outside the village milieu. Rubber plots on villagers' holdings set up important new interests in a market
place, and a market place responsive to world affairs. The
chain of events associated with rubber brought local boutiques, new money to spend in the town bazaars, roadways,
and dependencies upon economic and political forces outside both village and country. For the first time, Pelpola
in a real sense became part of the world at large.

The Second World War gave the next jolt to Pelpola's
quietude. This conflict stirred the village in many diverse
ways. Ceylon was subject to imminent invasion by the
Japanese. Colombo harbor was bombed by them. But even
closer to home, the war brought a sudden end to the cheap
Japanese merchandise popular with villagers. Soon also the
excellent knives associated with a vaguely recognized place
called Germany, disappeared from the markets. The official
position of Ceylon, aligned with the Allies, was well known,
but there was some equivocating over the attitude to take
toward peoples who had supplied them with good things, particularly when one of these nations was said to be Buddhist,
and the other honored a symbol similar to one venerated in
Buddhism. Pelpolans were loyal to their government, but
they were concerned. More significantly the new economic
facts of life were brought home to the village. Rubber prices
soared, as did consumer prices. Paddy production and control schemes plagued the peasant producer. Rationing systems were introduced. Textile scarcity led at one point to a
short lived weaving venture in the village itself. All of these
conditions contributed to a new personal concern with the
state of the island and the conflicting world outside it. News
of the day was now valued in terms of protecting personal
interests in rapidly changing markets, and even in one's
own paddy plot.

More intimately the outer world was felt through military
establishments in the nearby towns. Pelpolans found jobs in
the military workshops in Kalutara. Euclids, tractors and

bulldozers came into their fund of knowledge. A nearby air-
field made real man's conquest of time and space. Some
contacts, on the whole friendly ones, were established with
Australians, Americans, and Indians serving in war-associ-
ated enterprises.

On the whole the war did well by Pelpola, and indeed the
post-war tensions, with inflated export prices, have not
treated the community badly. Enhanced prosperity set the
stage for new standards of living, and expanding contacts
gave to these a more Western hue.

It would be unfair in this impressionistic account of Pelpola's introduction to the world, if the influence of government were not stressed beyond mention of wartime controls.
Although national independence followed war, suffrage has
been exercised in reference to colonial government for many
years. Few Pelpolans have been without intimate knowledge
of courts and their workings, since civil suits have been
common among the villagers. This generation has also had
familiarity with the government health program, especially
in reference to an important hospital center at Kalutara.
Functionaries in a variety of government bureaus visit the
village from time to time regarding health programs, agricultural production, education, and larceny. Postal and telephone services are familiar to all as are many other governmental services. Pelpola knows that it is an officer of central
government who appoints its village headman. The people of
Pelpola themselves elect one of their numbers to represent
them in the "Village Committee," a regional body with minor
governmental responsibility. Most of all, national consciousness has been stirred by the events of independence and general recognition that Ceylon is an independent state with her
own elected rulers. And, if people know little of political issues, they know a great deal of their politicians.

Almost a hundred years ago a government school was established in Pelpola. Today there is only one very elderly
man who recalls this institution, in which he had eight days
of schooling. Disinterest both by teachers and villagers
brought an early end to this venture and it was not until 1899
that another school was opened, this time under the auspices
of the Buddhist Theosophical Society, and the local priest.
It is this institution which serves the village today. No longer
under the control of the priest, it has been certified by the

national government. In recent years nearly every child
has attended the school for at least a few years, although
relatively few complete its approximately nine-year course.
Here, among other subjects, Pelpola's youth learn the
rudiments of world geography, history, and in the last few
years, English and civics. (Only two residents of the village
can converse in English and one of these is the newly installed English teacher.) Recently a radio has been purchased,
and pupils listen to educational broadcasts produced through
the Dominion educational administration. School excursions
are made periodically to points of national interest such as
Colombo and the ancient cities, and there is some participation in nation-wide school contests.

As Pelpola becomes increasingly enmeshed in affairs of
the outside world, it is to be expected that there should be
direct contact with cities and city centered media of communication. No adults are wholly apart from urban contact
and many males are in frequent and varied touch with the
city. In our household survey not one male householder had
failed to visit an urban center during the preceeding year and
exactly half made city trips more often than twice each month.
While the frequent travellers are weighted by shop-keepers,
it is obvious that Pelpola men are in close touch with the
nearby towns, especially Kalutara. As a matter of common,
but not regular practice, wives and children join in the city
trips.

Usually the villager's affairs in the city are limited to
those of a consumer-purchaser, but Kalutara has other attractions as well, the cinema, the taverns, and the chit-
chat with bazaar acquaintances and similarly trading friends
from other villages. In a minority of cases, kinsmen living
in the towns provide some point of real integration with the
more personalized side of city activities. It is significant that
about one sixth of all households have one or more sons living in a city. A few have married daughters who are urban
residents. Close relations between urban children and village parents are almost invariably maintained. Even great
distances do not prevent the return of married children with
their families for Sinhalese New Year.

Apart from kinship connections with urbanites, the villager's participation in city affairs is largely impersonal
and transitory. No one belongs to any organization centering

upon a city, nor to one including any urban membership.
Cinema attendance and, when wives are not along, tavern
participation are the main forms of urban group activity.
Cinema attendance is particularly interesting since vicari-
ously it involves still further participation in life beyond
the village horizon. A little over half of the household heads
have ever attended a cinema. During 1950 only twenty-nine
per cent of the household head sample had seen a movie,
and most of these had seen only one during the year. Significant for change, however, is the fact that of the male
youth, age fifteen to twenty-four, separately surveyed,
three-fifths had seen at least one cinema within the year,
and most of these had seen several. Women of any age rarely
attend, although it is relevant that as many as five per cent
of the wives did so within the year.

Few urbanites other than migrant children and businessmen come to Pelpola but the city is represented through
many , and increasing, secondary media. About twenty
copies of Sinhalese language newspapers were delivered
daily in 1950. By 1956, this figure had more than doubled.
News of "significance" is likely to pertain to the rubber
market, sensational criminal cases and political events of
outstanding importance. (Little world news is included in
Ceylon newspapers.) In the household sample, nearly thirty
per cent of the heads professed to read the newspaper regularly, as did fifteen per cent of the wives. Children over
fifteen, practically all of whom are literate, appear to read
even more generally than their parents, although no attempts were made to ascertain just what regular reading
constituted.

Few of the men and still fewer of their sons fail to listen
to radio programs from time to time. Formerly programs
were usually heard in the boutique. Today only two private
radios are owned in addition to those in the school and in
the temple. Radio listening has probably declined since 1952.
Four-fifths of the family heads had heard at least one complete fifteen minute program in 1950 and about half as many
of the wives had been equally interested. Practically all who
listened, young or old, heard mainly religious and musical
programs. Nearly four-fifths of the most ardent radio fans,
the young men, expressed explicit preference for music
above all else.

Booklets and pamphlets come to Pelpola in considerable
number and relate to a variety of subjects but mainly religious and historical. More than three-fourths of the household heads did some reading of booklets during the year, and
in this wives too were active (sixty-eight per cent). Sons
and daughters over age fifteen read with about the same generality as their fathers and mothers. Topical interests were
different between parents and children, however. Over four-
fifths of the heads usually read on religious topics, while
practically all of the youthful preferred other topics, often
those of Sinhalese history.

No doubt the crucial test of village contact with the world
lies in the degree of perception and awareness of facts and
events lying beyond the horizon of village experience. A
survey inquiry in 1950 attempted to gain some measure of
the breadth of knowledge among family heads regarding other
nations, Ceylon national affairs, and elemental scientific-
mechanical matters. In a re-study conducted in 1951, using
the general survey sample, only questions of international
knowledge were posed. Similar data were sought from unmarried male youth, and a small number of wives. [2]

It can be assumed safely, on the basis of general observation, that practically every adult male, and most of their
wives, know such fundamentals as the name of the country's
Prime Minister, the fact of Ceylonese independence and the
names of major political parties. Similarly all know something of the major ethnic groups which compose the nation.
Most of the men know the names of their parliamentary representatives. Survey results in 1950 confirmed these observations as well as the fact that all adult male householders know
that the Sinhalese are the largest linguistic group in the island.

While refined knowledge of national affairs was less general, seventy-one per cent of the men realized that their
Prime Minister had more actual power than did the Governor
General, but only a third knew that the latter held his office
by appointment from the British Crown. In regard to economic
matters, nearly all, ninety-five per cent, recognized that
Ceylon was an importer of rice. However, the local significance of rubber led nearly as many to believe that this crop,
rather than tea, was Ceylon's most valuable export commodi-
ty.

Since the surveys of 1950 and 1951, it is probable that
knowledge of national affairs has increased rapidly. It is
certain that political awareness has grown more keen. In
April of 1956 a general election was held in Ceylon in which
it may be safely estimated that more than four-fifths of Pelpola's adult males voted, and at least two-thirds of the
women. Great interest in this election was evident and village support shifted from the government party (United National Party) to a new coalition movement headed by Mr.
S. W. R. D. Bandaranaike who, as the result of this election
became Prime Minister. While many forces were at work
to swing the Pelpola vote, an influential fact was that the
new "United Peoples Front" (Mahajena Eksath Peramuna)
was strongly and nationalistically Buddhist-Sinhalese. There
is reason to believe that popular identification with the new
government and its programs is directly responsible for the
greatly increased newspaper circulation in the village.

These results bespeak a knowledgeable peasantry, and
they are probably rather typical of Low Country, but not interior, awareness. The myriad direct and indirect communication channels have made their mark. In a society where
husband and wife rarely discuss extra-household affairs,
and where women are more isolated from the channels of
communication, it is understandable that wives are less
well informed.

For a country in which rural technology is at a rather
primitive level, it is not surprising that few men have had
much experience with, or understanding of, technical matters which might be thought elemental in most Western rural
communities. Less than a tenth of the household heads had
ever operated any device run by electricity or gasoline,
though of course all had witnessed such operations. Simple
wood working tools like screwdrivers and saws had been
used by nearly all, but only fourteen per cent had ever used
a wrench. In regard to scientific achievements in spheres
of some concern to them, there is probably a great range
from ignorance to knowledge, depending upon chance circumstan
Very few could conceive of mechanized paddy cultivation as
a possibility (thirteen per cent) and equally few believed
that machines could milk a cow. On the other hand, public
health activities have been such that all professed belief that
latrines would be a safeguard to village health--even though

many of the men do not use them with regularity. It seems
safe to conclude that the diffusion of scientific knowledge is
rather slight as compared with national political information.

The sphere of international relations and world politics
is a crucial test for direct, perceptive contact with the larger
world, for it is rarely an area of discussion within the village and it is one which hints at some broad awareness of
Pelpola's enmeshment in distant and foreign events. Our
survey questions were carefully chosen for some relevance
to Asian affairs, but, as was the case for the earlier survey, guess responses were discouraged. Usually the villager prefers to admit lack of information than to hazard a
pure guess.

For those who have noted the results of similar informa-
tional surveys in the United States with its massive development of communication media, the knowledge of Pelpola men
may be surprising. The majority were aware that Asian
countries other than their own had achieved independence in
recent years. Nearly two-thirds could specify another nation having become independent, and a fourth could name
two such countries. Over half, fifty-two per cent, knew that
Japan and Germany had been allied in the last war, and
nearly as many knew that Chinese and American troops were
on oppos... sides in the then current Korean war. All professed to have heard of the Korean conflict and no doubt this
was true. When one considers Ceylon's remoteness from
affairs of the West, it is notable that one-half of the men
recognized the existance of tensions between the United
States and the Soviet Union. The query gave small opportunity for an accurate guess since it was presented in the form
of a multiple choice question specifying three possible combinations of countries. With the emphasis upon religious matters in Asian politics, it is perhaps surprising that only
thirty-eight per cent knew that Hinduism was the dominant
religion of India. Still fewer, twenty-one per cent, knew the
religion of Pakistan. On the other hand four-fifths recognized
Burma as a Buddhist country, a matter frequently mentioned
in the press and in religious discussions.

The unmarried male youth, although more participatory
than their elders in the media of information, were generally
no better informed. Surveyed separately on identical questions they provided fewer correct responses on seven out of

ten questions pertaining to world affairs. Two-thirds of them, however, were aware of United States-Soviet Union tensions. In spheres of scientific and technical information, however, they generally surpassed the older, married men.

As might be expected from the comparative isolation of women, of the thirty-three wives systematically questioned, only six knew Hinduism to be the dominant religion of India and fewer still knew the religions of Pakistan and Burma. Accurate answers to questions on international affairs were given by none and only eleven professed to have heard of the war in Korea.

We must conclude that the men of Pelpola have moved well beyond the confines of their village in more than simply physical movement. Awareness of nation is general and there is fairly wide elemental knowledge of international matters having Asian relevance. Although inadequately tested, we may infer that scientific or technical knowledge is not so widely transmitted through available media.

Chapter X

SECULARIZATION IN COMMUNITY ORGANIZATION

The life that counts most is the life of family, neighborhood, and kin groups within the village. Most of living
is in the intimate and informal gatherings on verandahs, in
the boutiques, in the lanes, and in the fields. Few relationships are dictated by some single and conscious purpose,
and when they are they usually transpire within a framework
of intimacy. Nearly all Pelpolans find their closest friends
within the neighborhood mixture of kin and non-kin. Beyond
the neighborhood is the village at large, and aside from
specialized commercial and legal transactions, life is mainly
circumscribed by its boundaries.

There is no reason to believe that the primary life of the
village has changed significantly in recent years. The loosely
organized groups and reciprocities are probably not much
more loosely defined than in earlier days. Only in the apparent decline of the cooperative work group, kaiya, is there
clear evidence of deterioration, but while work groups are
now usually on a pecuniary footing, they are none-the-less
constituted of intimates and kinsmen. Helping a neighbor in
his emergencies is yet a function of good will and in most
instances it is not repaid in any precise or monetary reckoning. Nor do Pelpolans usually want money or paddy so badly
that they will accept harvest employment from even a fellow
villager whom they personally despise or disrespect.

The primary life of the village is so intense that we must
visualize newer forms of group life less as displacements of
the old than as, at this stage, largely non-competitive ad-
ditions. Over the long run, however, there is no doubt of a
decline in established primary group functions. The very introduction of wage labor on a wide scale has implied the
diminution of the nuclear family as a production group. It
seems incontrovertible as well that the growing market
economy has emphasized impersonal sources for commodities which were once produced within the family. Reliance

145

upon kinsfolk has been evidently reduced through government maternity hospitals, just as dependence upon a medical practitioner has shifted from the village "native doctor"
toward the government dispensary. Even the limited credit
facilities sponsored by the government mean less necessary
reliance upon kinsmen and neighbors. These are the logical,
though seldom visibly disorganizing, effects of money economy and socialistic government.

Cinemas, newspapers, and radio have already been mentioned as communication media with the outside world. They
are more than this. They also create new forms of participatory groupings unfamiliar to the traditional peasant world.
Theoretically at least, they may serve to differentiate people
in reference to new interests and enthusiasms, and bring
into the peasant's experience that kind of interaction so
marked in city life, the minimal group characterized not by
mutual inter-stimulation but chiefly by a one way flow of
stimuli. Cinemas particularly exemplify this new interaction
pattern for their attendance requires participation in that
new form of congregated group peculiar to the urban world,
the impersonal audience.

That Pelpola is not yet habituated to its most readily
available form of mass participation is indicated by cinema
attendance figures. By 1951 a little over a half of the adult
males and one-twentieth of their wives had ever seen a movie.
But three-fourths of the male youths had visited cinemas and
with greater frequency than their elders. One-fifth of the
youths saw four or more films during the single year 1950.
If we were to accept one movie a month as a measure of
habitual attendance, then perhaps fifteen per cent of the village males could be said to be regular movie goers. Most of
these are under age twenty-five. Since the younger married
men attend more often than the older, it seems probable that
we see here a growing pattern which to some extent will be
maintained after marriage. Movies are catching on. In sharp
contrast to the movie audience in the West, however, women
and girls are little influenced. Of households having daughters
over age fifteen but unmarried, only ten per cent had any
daughter who had ever attended a cinema. Most village youth
report that their parents object to their attending but this is
no burning issue.

There is no indication that the growth of movie participa-

tion among males has had an influence upon primary group
structure. Nor is this a sign that youth are any less immersed in their neighborhood and kinship groups than their
parents. When the male youth name their "best friends" they,
like their fathers, select boys of their same neighborhood.
Only five out of seventy-nine boys named a best friend who
was neither a neighbor nor a kinsmen, and even the odd five
all stayed within the village in the friendship choice. Forty
per cent had "best friends" who were kinsmen and neighbors
as well. It is interesting to note that of the five boys naming
friends outside these close circles, two had never attended
a cinema and none had ever seen more than three films.
Similar evidences among adults make it difficult to believe
that the lure of the secular world has brought new bases of
personalized association or that it has in any way weakened
the hold of families and neighborhoods. This is supported by
the daily observation of the juveniles and adolescents at
play throughout the village. Among women there is no doubt
of the continuing significance of the neighboring associates.

The introduction of radio and news implies the establish-
ment of publics and masses. Masses there are not in Pelpola,
and if there are publics in reference to these media, they
are "publics" composed of cronies, neighbors, and kinsmen.
From the types of programs heard, it is impossible that
radio creates schisms of interests and controversy. Nor are
there publics attached to figures or programs of the broad-
casting world. Program favoritism may in time develop such
groupings but they are not evident today. No fan club could
interest a Pelpolan. In this sphere the source of entertainment is new; the interests in it are, like its content, traditional. Change here is potential not actual.

Even with newspapers something of the same situation
exists. Usually these are read in the boutiques as part of
the normal socializing of village life. Here, however, there
is stimulation which breeds cleavages in opinion, but on issues unrelated to local affairs villagers usually do not take
intense interest. The important schismatic interests are
over matters of the temple, the road, land disputes, or an
outbreak of cattle theft in the area. Pelpola is awakening to
outside voices and the influences of outside events. As these
touch village life they hold significant interest, but what
Pelpola conceives as touching this life is principally that

which relates unmistakably to rubber prices and to national
politics. On the first topic there is never cleavage in interest. In regard to national politics the village has at one
period given landslide support to a single party, and at
another equally full support to its rival. Undoubtedly, however, the newspaper is the village's most important source
of contact with world events and its effect upon localism is
not to be underestimated. It is not, however, a significant
factor in the immediate organization of village life.

A third new and secular interactional pattern is that of
special interest groups. Here too is an associational structure which, if developed in an urban pattern, would cut
across the informal groupings based in kin and locality.
Pelpola has had interest group experience. Over a fifth of
all household heads attended organization meetings in 1950.
Effectively the organizations are limited to the Goyigama.
The "potters" utilize, and technically belong to, cooperatives
but take no active part in organizational affairs.

There have never been interest groups within which Pelpolans have participated jointly with urbanites. In fact, only
one group includes persons from other villages and this, an
agricultural society, has five members from Pelpola, none
of whom is very active. Neither this nor groups internal to
the village ever involve truly impersonal relationships. Yet
the interest association is significant, for not only is it a
new organizational form, it is the type of group structure
through which various outside agencies, especially government, spread new programs and activities. Even if interest
groups are superimposed upon primary backgrounds they
are more than manifestations of urbanization in social structure; they, like newspaper publics, are organizational ve-
hicles for further change.

There are seven groups in the village which in one sense
or another should be termed special interest associations
although several of these relate more to the past than to the
present. The only spontaneous organization having a long
and current history of successful activity is centered upon
the temple. But this association is too informal and too much
the concern of everyone to qualify as a group bound by a
special interest. It is the association of dayakayas, people
who provide for the village priests. In Pelpola, priests have
not followed the ancient routine of begging for their daily

needs in recent times. Instead, the dayakayas, each on an
understood day, carry food to the temple in quantity sufficient for that day. Probably ninety per cent of the householders
("potters" form a separate association) should be considered
participants, although membership is more by long understanding than by a formal device or physical assemblage.
Dayakayas do not meet together as such. Rather, they are
the village community itself viewed from the aspect of religious solidarity.

In a more real sense the upasakas and upasikas form an
association of the most religious members of the community.
Although without formal leadership, other than the priest's
stimulation, and without differentiation in roles, the devout
hold a common concern with religious matters and meet in
concert to further their ends. Their ends have generally been
those of individual spiritual attainment but their like concern
with Buddhism has been a basis for the building of a true
action group in the community. More than twenty years ago
the upasikas, women of piety, formed a society dedicated
to temple improvement. This association, the Upasika
Samitiya, composed exclusively of women, was formally
organized. In more recent years a number of men also concerned with religious life followed suit in the creation of an
organization to raise funds for the construction of the dagoba
in the temple yard. Although women participated, this association was dominated by men. The singular facts about
these religious organizations are that they are the only organizations spontaneously created by Pelpolans and that as
organizations they are both defunct today. Dayakayas go
onward, as do upasikas, but organizations have a difficult
road in this village. Just how their demise occurred will be
discussed later. There are other potential corpses yet to be
introduced.

The five remaining organizations to be considered were
each stimulated by an outside interest, in most instances
national governmental programs. For some ten years a
parent-teacher association has enjoyed nominal existence,
and in a remote sense functions today. No meetings have
been held for several years. All other organized groups
have been strictly in response to governmental stimulation.
During the second world war a shortage of cloth led the
government to support weaving schools in villages. No doubt

this was done with the hope of furthering a dream of some
national leaders, the creation of a cottage industry program.
Pelpola joined in this, and produced a few weavers and a
small amount of cloth. The school and the association behind
it died a completely natural death with the reopening of normal trade channels with the outer world. Also war-inspired,
the consumers' cooperative movement came to Pelpola. Since
the cooperative was an official mechanism for marketing
subsidized and rationed commodities, its membership came
to include virtually every family in the village. The cooperative store is active along with numerous private, retail
boutiques. It has come to be run chiefly by an inner clique
with relatively few of its many members taking any active
part in its administration or policy making.

Agricultural organizations have had a mixed history. The
national Rural Development Program opened a local society
in 1948. After one spurt of action, it was inoperative and apparently defunct in 1950. Quite different, however, was the
history of the credit cooperative, also introduced as a branch
of a nationally sponsored movement. Two credit associations
were organized, serving different parts of the village, and
these are today active and constructive organizations in the
community.

In view of the high metabolic rate for special associations
in Pelpola, it should be observed that at no time during the
past two decades has the village been without some organization of special interest. But in this history, the only real
survivors have been the two credit cooperatives, and the
consumer cooperative. (We have not considered several ex-
tra-curricular programs associated with the school and
catering strictly to the school children.) It may be inferred
that Pelpolans are not what might be called "easy joiners."
Positively, it may be suggested that something in Pelpola's
social soil makes the growth of special interest groups difficult and tenuous. Even when fostered by strong governmental
stimuli as with the Rural Development Society, survival, let
alone strength, has not been assured.

The history of each defunct organization has a remarkable
sameness. And, although the consumers' cooperative is active, it too shows some of the familiar symptoms. One of
the common characteristics of Pelpola's organizations has
been the lack of any program. Objectives there have been, and

it has been toward specific objectives rather than toward
continuing programs that most organizations were oriented.
This has been particularly true of local spontaneous groups
and less true of those integrated in national organizations.
Yet the Rural Development Society failed to survive its original and achieved objective. The weaving school had a
nominal program, although any rational evaluation of it in
higher echelons should have foreseen its doom once international trade was reestablished. Ceylon has none of the
religious and nationalistic fervor regarding home spinning
and weaving as does India. Here circumstances virtually
precluded a continuing program. If any spontaneous association has gone beyond either achievement or failure in
initial undertakings, it has been the women's Upasika
Samitiya. For many years these women, united in their devotion to all matters of religious concern, maintained a
loose but persistently functioning organization. Probably
the Samitiya will rise again for one key to its longevity has
been its capacity to go into long periods of suspended ani-
mation between objectives.

Similar to the Rural Development Society, the Parent
Teachers Association was born in an enthusiastic drive to
collect funds for a new building. This objective was successfully carried out. Although the association was to continue
in an advisory and liaison relationship between parents and
teachers, the achievement of the building fund concluded
its effective life. Nominally it still survives. The office
holders of several years ago continue to provide a useful
semblance of a "committee" to approve innovations desired
by the head teacher. The "committee" never acts as a body,
has no association to which it is responsive, and does not
initiate ideas or action.

The fundamental cause of the rise and fall of organized
groups in Pelpola, is that Pelpolans have little sense of
the meaning of organization. They have no realization, inclination, or ability to develop a systematic pattern of operations. This includes no recognition of the need for continuing objectives and it also includes failure to establish
channels for the accommodation of conflicts and the constructive expression of grievances. Never has an organization succeeded in building esprit de corps to the point that
leaders are perceived as persons carrying forward the

purposes of the followers. Specifically, Pelpolans do not understand, or at least accept, role differentiation in their programs when this involves some of their number being placed in special positions of trust and authority. The real leadership of Pelpola is informal and non-directive, and it is leadership based upon qualities of wealth, land, and personal character. It is leadership, but it is leadership through influence rather than through office and directives by office. The effective informal leaders in Pelpola are active in community affairs but their status is not derived from their offices. Office holders become "pretenders to power not rightly theirs. " They invite the suspicion of others both as to motive and as to the handling of funds.

These seem very big words to put upon a simple peasant folk. Their application becomes meaningful when we look more closely at an actual organizational history, that of the most enduring indigenous society, the Upasika Samitiya.

The Upasika Samitiya was inspired by the chief priest in 1930, less by the desire to have a continuing organization than to get the construction of a column upon which the temple bell might be placed. Appealing to the women of piety, the priest saw not only the objective accomplished but a nucleus of devout persons willing and able to continue their work for the temple. The lay leader of this group, and its formal president, was the mother of the then village headman who, in addition to holding this governmental office, was a man of "good family, " wealthy, and highly respected personally. The president was a woman of consequence in Pelpola. Upon her death, before the achievement of the bell column, it seemed only right that her daughter assume leadership of the group. This she did although it occurred to no one that she be made president in name. (The president was now dead.) During her "term" the original objective was achieved and for a time the group relaxed. A new purpose was found, with the help of the priest, again in a money raising campaign. This time the group succeeded in gaining a new table for the temple offerings. Shortly after this accomplishment the leader moved from the village and the headmistress of the village school took over the reins, and gradually the title, of office. The participants did not elect, nor even select, the new leader. As a most active worker she simply moved into the position, there being no understood mechanism for leader selection or rotation. The upasikas continued to work and to glory in it. They completed many projects, including the construction of a latrine for the priests and a staircase for the relics chamber. Practically all of their projects were directed toward raising money rather than toward direct participation in the construction of their objectives. Yet here was an enduring organization, with pride in accomplishment, and unlike others in the village, a vigorous esprit de corps shared by the strongly motivated members and the leader. The group was small, never numbering more than forty members, and composed of women most of whom had been engaging in special worship together for many years. But simple as it was, and perhaps its very simplicity was a favoring factor, it survived and thrived.

In the second decade of the Samitiya a new priest came to the temple, a man with ambitious ideas. He proposed a new residence hall for the priests, an enterprise of major dimensions. The upasikas plunged into this work. The priest, dissatisfied with the revenue being produced by the loyal women, but sensing in them a vital link with the community, stimulated the creation of a second organization within their ranks, devoted exclusively to the residence hall fund campaign. No doubt this move was given some sympathy by certain upasikas who recognized it as means for gaining formally recognized positions of leadership. As was inevitable the upasikas were split into rival camps, each working the same field, each set of officers contesting for the support of the same members. Even devotion to a cause could not withstand the usual nemesis to Pelpola organizations, the backbiting of leaders by followers and the circulation of rumor by rival leaders. The Samitiya, united by twenty years of successful service was torn apart. Today the upasikas are again simply pious women giving their individual alms to the temple. The meagerest organizational strategy would have preserved this constructive and harmonious league. In a more sophisticated society it might be presumed that the Samitiya was wilfully murdered for personal ends. Here the charge would be non-culpable homicide.

Among organizations built mainly by men there is, apart from cooperatives, none with a sustained history. Of these the Chatiya Vardana Samitiya is perhaps typical. This

organization was created to raise funds for the dagoba, but
dissolved in dissension immediately short of its objective.
(See Chapter VI.)

With the Rural Development Society the precipitating ar-
gument leading to inaction was the issue of whether or not
the leaders go to the "potters" to remonstrate with them
over their gambling or if the "potters" should be summoned
to the leaders. There was no disagreement over what might
have seemed the more fundamental issue, i.e., the propriety
of such remonstrances by officers in a Rural Development
Society.

The surviving cooperatives demonstrate how fully organizational activity depends upon an enduring, recognizably
useful program, and consecrated, thick skinned, and paternalistic leadership. The core of each of these organizations
is in reality the group which functions and which administers.
Thus in the credit societies the leadership clique holds
meetings to discuss their business, but the only other at-
tenders are the persons whose loan applications are matters
of immediate business. Annual meetings of members are
held, however, and a few non-functionaries attend. Their
voices here support the officer clique. Criticisms will be
voiced later in the boutiques. The organization's program
will continue so long as the leaders themselves remain in
harmony or until boutique gossip brings their handling of
funds into the status of public scandal--whether true or un-
true.

Much the same situation exists with the consumers' cooperative, although annual meetings at which the officers
are reinstated are more widely attended. Here, however,
there are rumblings of disharmony among the leaders themselves. Having no mechanisms for the resolution of disagreement and in a society where individual wills are rarely
subordinated to organizational solidarity, the cooperative
stands in immanent danger.

It is with greatest accuracy that we describe Pelpola's
special interest groups, as small, rather informal associations or cliques serving a public--generally the entire village or at least the Goyigama sector. That a list of seventeen men exhausts the leadership personnel of all male associations living or defunct, indicates the closely held
monopoly upon organizational leadership. With a single

exception each of these men is well-to-do. With but two exceptions, they do not engage personally in cultivation. Most have superior education and practically all have land holdings in the village. They are all of Goyigama caste.

Even brief scrutiny of organizational leadership and structure suggests that we are dealing less with special interest groups within the community than with community leadership nuclei which serve from time to time in stimulating and directing community action, and provide some continuity in leadership and service. Special interest groups from the standpoint of leadership are somewhere in passage from the historic community council or gamsabha to the urban phenomenon of differentiated leadership. Pelpola is fumbling with the secular form of life but attempts to superimpose these patterns upon a community structure rooted in informality and strongly built upon neighboring relations have not been very successful.

It is from such a background as this that the fact that even a fifth (twenty-two per cent) of all household heads "regularly attend" some special interest group meetings, should be assessed. Most of these attended the single, annual meeting of the consumers' cooperative.

Chapter XI

SECULARIZATION IN CULTURE AND VALUES

The Sinhalese, like many peoples undergoing the influences of Western society, have behind them an ancient civilization and literature. Although it is not within the scope of this work to reconstruct the ancient Sinhalese values and culture, the task of evaluating changes can proceed upon more than mere guesswork as to what the past held. To a limited extent, knowledge coming from the past has been tested through field studies in localities of extreme isolation.[1] In general, the usages and values which we posit as "traditional" would be so described by the elders of Pelpola whether or not they currently subscribe to them.

Traditionally the nuclear family has been the elemental functioning unit in the community. At the same time this family has recognized concepts of lineal honor. Decisions which might reflect upon that honor, and security, were protected against individualized whims and interests. Thus parents and the further kin made for the individual his choice in a marriage partner. Respect for parental elders was embodied in folkways of deference, and something of the same was true for the relationship of younger married couples toward their elder bilateral kinsmen.

Status structure and achievement was conditioned by a heritage which included both feudalism and caste. High position by birth was valued. Equalitarian interaction was possible only with caste equals, and within caste, status by Ge and family line was significant. The very language was highly inflected by status gradients.

Religious life, possibly influenced by the ascetic element in Buddhist ideology, related more to man's relationship to the universe than to man's relationship with man. Yet, Buddhist teachings were manifest in the veneration of holy men and almsgiving, and also in belief in the virtue of kindness and harmlessness to all living creatures. Buddhist metaphysics, while no doubt influencing conduct through subtle mechanisms, have not given the villager much con-

156

cern over realities of <u>nibbana</u>, timelessness, or selfless-
ness, nor even the self-conscious achievement of serenity
regardless of physical suffering. No doubt the ethics of
Buddhism are related to the hospitality, tolerance, and
gentle permissiveness valued by the folk, but the processes
whereby religious values are reflected in personality traits
are not self evident.

Beyond Buddhism the villager accepted a natural world
which, when beyond his own control, was guided by the
powers of a demon world, a largely Hindu pantheon, and
the planet gods. And when subjected to his own control, his
techniques were grounded in traditional truths, with a cor-
responding lack of initiative toward development of new
methods of manipulating nature. Manipulation, when not
magically grounded, was still embedded in the social heritage. Pelpola man seems always to have felt at essential
peace with his universe.

The old village economy was one dominated by motives
of subsistence and security, rather than by profit, com-
merce and speculative gain. In agriculture, paddy was the
focus of interest by the bulk of villagers, with slash and
burn (<u>chena</u>) in nearby jungle. There was no focus on a market. Wage labor was considered degrading, and agriculture
the most honorable of works other than high service to the
king. For potters, the handicraft was their economic focus,
perhaps in early times in return for the use of cultivable
land under feudal tenure. For a century or more their production has been toward a market. In keeping with caste concepts, vocation was associated with caste, and occupational
mobility was slight.

This brief epitome of a few important modes and values
of the old village life, indicates the striking contrasts that
are present as urbane and Western structures and values
impinge upon the community. The new value system encourages individualism in decisions once the prerogative of
parents and kin. It encourages egalitarian interaction and
equality of opportunity in spheres once fixed by birth statuses.
The premise of power held in an elite by birth is challenged
by concepts of citizenry and electorates as well as by businessmen. The rationalism and empiricism of scientific and
urban man contradict both supernatural controls and the
truth by tradition rather than by induction. Peace toward the

universe meets doctrines of progress, doctrines which are pursued in the name of national survival. And the very concept of national survival now has meaning to a folk whose horizons were once bounded by the Kaluganga and the Kapu Ela.

The economic values of the new world are those of the market place, and they are supported by new symbols of status procurable through market dealings. Opportunities of wage labor, and trading and white collar pursuits, test in different ways the status value of an honored agriculture. Monetary incentives have little room for ceremony and ritual in production.

The antithesis between traditional Pelpola and the commercial, democratic, and progress-oriented twentieth century is not total but it is striking. The values and structures of this new secular world have in part become the official policy orientation of the Ceylon government. We are not dealing with theoretic constructs. We are dealing with a community which through centuries of contact has been deviating toward a secular world and more recently toward an urbanity, material culture, and national consciousness of distinctively Western hue. Our problem is to make an assessment of a village's departure from the traditional way, and its movement toward the new, secular nexus of values and usages.

The Family

While it is evident that market and governmental activities encroach upon traditional family functions, there is no sign that family life is undergoing any immediate transformation or disorganization. Inrigidity and looseness in kinship groups and in marriage practices were normative in former times. There is reason for believing that marriage mores, at least, have become more firm under European influences. [2]

Were the Sinhalese followers of the joint family system, there is no doubt that the lure of the cities would be evidenced in family disorganization. So far as we know, Pelpola children have always left the household of their birth upon marriage. The fact that numbers of children, especially boys, leave their parental home to go to the city is not di-

rectly deteriorating to the old structure. This movement
has not progressed to such a point that village families are
bereft of close kin in their own and surrounding villages.
The primary significance of such change is that the city man
is no longer a stranger. [3]

Within the home the most notable deviation from traditional roles has been in the employment of men and especially
of women in wage labor. Hired labor, with money payment
has been deplored by the Sinhalese, and in remote localities
this sentiment is still expressed. In Pelpola, wage earning
by men has long been accepted, not in preference to cultivation, but as an expected part of life for those without adequate resources. For women, employment is widespread,
especially among the poor, but there is no belief that such
work is a proper expectation in life. The place for woman
is still very much in the home. Wage work is taken as an
essential supplement to the role of housewife or of mother-
assisting daughter. School teaching is perhaps the only vocation in which anything other than economic necessity makes
female employment desirable. While this career is not a
proper substitute for marriage, it is an honorable status
which redounds to the prestige of the family.

The familial institution faces its most imminent attack
from the diffusion of individualistic values which might un-
dermine the power and prerogatives of parents over children.
In its extremity, this is the battle between institutional systems which in the West has been won in the transition of marriage from institution to companionate. In Pelpola a normative marriage is one in which the spouses stand as surro-
gates of kin through arrangements made by parents which in
turn are congenial to further kin. Traditional standards are
enforced in this process. It has been indicated in Chapter
V that most marriages today meet traditional requirements,
and although romantic, undowered, and even disapproved
marriages occur, there is no reason to believe that all
these deviations are new. Romantic unions are, however,
mainly found among recent marriages. There are hints of
rebellion and the growth of attitudes inharmonious with the
old system.

Support for the "strong family" system is so strong
among adults that in the community-wide attitude survey of
household heads, no query on this point was made. Of thirty-

three wives given more intensive study, all expressed disapproval of romantic principles. We found, however, that
among younger people there was considerable idealization
of romance and self choice in mates. Explicit queries on
this matter were included in the survey of seventy-nine
male youth.

One-fourth (twenty cases) of the unmarried youths expressed unqualified preference for personal choice in a wife,
and eight others offered some qualified preference for the
romantic over the arranged system. There was little difference in attitude between different age levels although the
boys under age eighteen were slightly more prone to prefer
parental arrangement. Typical responses of the iconoclasts
indicated a definitely individualistic interpretation of marriage. "Sincerity in love comes first. " "She is for me, not
for my parents. " But the great majority of responses showed
mixture of respect for parental rights as well as recognized
advantages in the existing institution. Thus, many responded
that acceptance of an arranged spouse would win the confi-
dence of their parents or demonstrate respect. Frequently
it was said or implied that "if anything goes wrong, parents
cannot then blame the child, " and commonly, "if we abide
by their choice then they will always help us in time of need."

It is certain that not a fourth of the fathers of these youths
would agree with the rightfulness of romantic ideas as a
basis for marriage. It is also certain that not many of the
"revolutionists" would seriously consider deviating from the
traditional pattern in reference to their own marriages. No
one followed up his expressions of preference with statements of proposed action, although this was not explicitly
queried. Nor were the non-traditional views tinged with bitterness or other indications of frustration. Although girls
were not systematically queried, we feel confident that very
few indeed would express criticism of the old ways.

While the majority of youths support in both attitude and
practice the deeply embedded and moral value of parental
arrangement, attitudes toward dowry are quite different.
Two-thirds of the youths stated they were opposed to the
dowry system. Let it not be thought, however, that such opposition necessarily reflected disenchantment with the old
order of marriage relationships. The majority who professed
that they would reject a dowry, did so on grounds like the

following: "it makes a wife snobbish, " "it puts one under obligation, " "gives a wife too much power over you. " It was
the minority of the opponents who observed that "this is a
slavish practice, " or even, "it means too much strain on
the wife's people. " The type of responses which one might
expect in a society with a companionate marriage system
were notably absent. No one observed in effect that "nothing
else is important if a man really loves a woman. " Generally
the repudiation of the custom involved no rejection of the
system within which it works. It may further be noted, that
the absence of dowry in some village marriages reflects no
repudiation of the practice but rather its economic infeasi-
bility.

The most illuminating survey response indicative of
changing values among youth came in response to a question
pertaining to the treatment which should be given a daughter
who eloped to marry a man of different caste. Although this
matter involves disregard for parental authority and honor,
it is also heavily laden with status significance. As might
be expected, not one of the adult women interviewed, and
only one of the household heads, said that such a daughter
and her husband should be received by the family on a normal basis. When the identical question was posed to the male
youths, over a third believed that they should be received
and treated as other married children. While it is unlikely
that many, or any, couples will put this issue to the test in
this generation, the responses indicate a significant relax-
ation in the intense moral disfavor attached to such an action.

When questioned as to the exercise of individual choice
in one's vocation in opposition to parental desire, sympathy
does not generally fall to the son. (Vocational determination
by parents is not institutionalized but it is one of many major
choices in which a father might reasonably assert authority.)
Almost equal proportions of the adults and the youth affirm
the father's prerogative in this matter (eighty-four and
eighty-six per cent respectively). However in this society
which readily yields to the accomplished fact, it was a minority in each group who felt that a son who disobeyed his
father in such a matter should be disinherited.

Part of a strong family system is the large family ideal,
and Pelpola values a large family of children. It is improbable
that contraceptive devices are used. Abortion is a serious

sin. Expressions of ideal numbers of living children varied
widely among the household heads and the general view was
that this is a matter to be left in the hands of the gods.
Pressed for numerical responses, a fourth of the men said
simply "many. " The median number for the majority was
just under five. Less than a fifth said that they would favor
birth control if Ceylon faced a serious food shortage--assum-
ing that control were possible. Among women, superficial
responses seem to correspond to those of the men, for they
recognize the community's moral position on this subject.
However, intensive interviews with thirty-three married
women showed an undercurrent of feeling which would be
favorable to family limitation. [4] Youth react differently from
their elders. More than half (fifty-six per cent) of the young
men believed birth control would be desirable under conditions of food shortage and their ideas about optimum family
size favored somewhat fewer children than did the household
heads.

The foregoing observations speak more of a potential for
change in family values and structure than for its actuality.
The established system is in fact operative and complaints
against it are not very intense. Revolt is rare. There is undoubtedly an aura surrounding romantic marriage among a
sizable number of the youth and equally individualistic attitudes would probably not have been so frequently expressed
by any previous generation. Yet most youth, and virtually
all elders, feel that the security of the kin is vital, and this,
even apart from other restraining factors, is powerful in
preserving the old order. Under conditions wherein marriage
is not yet conceived in companionate terms and where numerous mores support large families, a spontaneous and
active acceptance of birth limitation is unlikely to appear.
The attitudinal groundwork for such a redefinition of marriage and family is being laid in a tentative fashion.

The very diffuseness of kinship reciprocities, and role
definitions and permissiveness in child-parent relationships
conspire to make the Pelpola family singularly absorbent of
new influences without necessitating major changes or creat-
ing turmoil. There is no widespread feeling that the youth
of the village are going to the dogs. And to judge by the
value judgements of most youth themselves, they are not.
Another view of the contemporary strength and deterio-

ration of traditional familial institutions can be had in the retention and neglect of various ceremonial usages. The Sinhalese are not given to the elaboration of ceremonies, nor are they meticulous in their performance. None-the-less it is possible to compose a considerable list of ritual-ized actions relative to family life which have in the past been normative expectations for both rich and poor. It may be hypothesized that deterioration in family ceremonialism indicates elemental breaks in the protective veneer of the institution. Table 3 lists six ritualized acts appropriate in

Table 3

Adherence to Traditional Practices
in Family Life

	Per Cent Practicing
Marriage ceremony held	98
Engagement ceremony held	91
Propitious fire laid on hearth on last Sinhalese New Year	65
Kinsmen visited with betel on last Sinhalese New Year	55
Auspicious day selected for first rice feeding of most recent child	47
Oil annointing ceremony held last New Year	58

all normal households and the percentage of the sample sur-vey homes practicing them. We know from observation that Pelpola has generally lost the traditional symbolic behavior of deference which wife and children still pay to the husband-father in more isolated regions.[5] Nor are honorific titles given the husband-father in the same sense as they are used in remote localities. Obedience and respect are expected, but their stylized and symbolic manifestations have weakened. We believe that actual obedience to the father is less and that an equalitarian position for wives is more nearly ap-proached in Pelpola than in isolated areas.

It is to be noted that neither an engagement ceremony
nor a marriage ceremony are essential for a legal marriage, yet these rituals of unification are almost universally
maintained. Also pertaining to the unity of the nuclear family, nearly two-thirds engaged in the annual ritual of fire
lighting at the commencement of a New Year. On the other
hand, the symbolic deference to, and renewal of bonds with
kinsmen was practiced by a little over half. The remaining
practices which might be considered as both initiatory and
protective for children were followed by about half, and
three-fifths, respectively.

Status

Pelpola, unlike many interior villages, has no recent
history of feudal gradings. They have, of course, retained
elemental caste divisions and some limited status connotations of Ge within caste. As has been observed earlier, it
is the community of caste which provides boundaries for
most interaction, and practically all equal relationships.
Caste discrimination and overt manifestations of social
distance between castes are, however, diminishing. Outside the sphere of caste, the traditional emphasis upon
ascribed status has also been affected. There has been considerable social mobility in recent years. However distaste-
ful Pelpolans may find their new-rich merchant fellows, it
is the entrepreneurs, often of humble origin, who are moving toward local power, and no doubt slowly toward esteemed
positions.

One of the pervasive myths of the caste system has been
that caste has provided historically the exclusive status system within the range of Indian influence. This is to overlook
the fact that entire castes, or segments of them, fluctuate
in their status at various times, and it is to overlook the
fact that caste position has status significance within conventionally agreed and circumscribed bounds. Caste in Pelpola is no less real today than in the past although the behavioral significance of caste membership is more circumscribed and the tabus of distance more relaxed.

In a wholly unacculturated Pelpola, inter-caste marriage
would be unthinkable. Gross symbols of social distance
would be practiced. Discriminations in opportunity and in

the administration of justice would be normative. Probably
at one time Pelpola had a system of inter-caste economic
reciprocities reminiscent of the Indian jajmani system.[6]
Pelpola has not obliterated caste, but it has come far.

Survey questions posed on ascribed and achieved status
attitudes support our less precise empirical view of the
village. The results show a wide and significant development
of democratic values in reference to status ideology. The
first three queries in Table 4 would surely have had, in each
instance, a virtually zero response under traditional conditions. The query regarding a high caste headman in a mixed
village is probably over-indicative of reactionary attitudes.
Many Pelpolans responded, much like timid Americans on
racial issues, that they personally would find no harm in a
low caste headman under such circumstances, but since others
would, the plan would be a bad thing. Only in the sphere of
marriage are most Pelpolans firm and unyielding on caste
principles. Low caste joins with high in affirming the principle of endogamy, although in our judgement the intensity of
feeling is less strong among the low castes. We must interpret the various responses as evidencing strong and continued
regard for the preservation of the caste community and general disregard for values of inequality. There is a strong tendency to limit the significance of caste difference to matters
of marriage. This is particularly true of the Badahela who
have least to lose--although had we asked if members of
other castes should be permitted to make pots, some reluctance would have been evident.

The emancipation of youth from caste ideology is even further along than with adults. A third of the young men surveyed expressed the view that a girl marrying a man of lower
caste should be received into the parental home with her husband.

The value of birth status within caste also appears to be
compromised widely. While actual behavior is not entirely
consistent with profession, the vast majority of Pelpolans
subscribe to the principle of status through personal achievement. Repugnance of wage labor as such has virtually disappeared, although it is apparent that the occupational prestige
hierarchy has somewhat different significance than in Western
society. The Pelpolan who becomes a rickshaw coolie is believed by a half to have debased his heritage--and in the crucial

Table 4

Attitudes of Male Household Heads on
Traditional Status Values*

	Per Cents Giving Affirmative Response
**Should children of the (lowest) caste (Rodi) be educated?	77
Should members of the (lowest) caste (Rodi) be permitted to vote?	70
Should qualified members of the (lowest) caste (Rodi) be permitted to hold Civil Service positions?	60
Should a village composed mainly of other castes have a headman of the (highest) caste?	22
Should a daughter who eloped to marry a man of lower caste be received with her husband by her parents?	1
- - -	
Would you permit your son to work in a factory?	86
Does a man who [rises from rags to riches] deserve greater respect than one who [inherits high class position]?	77
**If a man of your village became a rickshaw puller in the city would you treat him with as much respect as before?	49
**Would you permit your daughter to marry--	
a small shopkeeper	96
chauffeur	54
a rickshaw puller	1

*Questions asked of eighty-seven cases regardless of caste.
   Differences between Goyigama and Badahela were unim-
   portant except in regard to the "social class" questions.
   To these the Badehla gave less traditional responses.
**Derived from 1950 survey. All other questions derived from
   1951 survey.

test, that of marriage, ninety-nine per cent would not consider a rickshaw man in an alliance with their family. The principle so readily affirmed in America that the "ditch digger is as good as the banker, " is a type of hypocrisy with which Pelpolans are not familiar. Probably their conformity between value statement and action would be closer than in Middletown. It speaks much for change in a once feudal, peasant and caste based society, that nearly all Pelpola fathers would find a "small shopkeeper" a suitable son-in-law. "Suitable" is scarcely the correct word. Within the limits of probability in sons-in-law, "ideal" would be more accurate. Yet in the community esteem hierarchy, shopkeepers do not stand well. This inconsistency testifies to transitions in the status system.

Politics and Government

The rise of democratic or universalistic values in status relationships has been parallelled by the development of democratic political values. The legal system of the Low Country has been European since Dutch times, and throughout the past century of British rule there was much progress in the direction of self-government and universal suffrage. Whereas the other institutions of the Sinhalese were rarely subjected to open attack by colonial administrators, feudal monarchism was destroyed by the British.

In formal political spheres, Pelpolans assert the rights of free citizens in theory and in practice. Suffrage is exercised more fully than in many democratic Western countries. Nor are Pelpolans at all loath to write petitions to government officers and parliament members when they think grievances might be righted in those quarters. That they are perceptive of significant issues in regard to democratic processes is evidenced in Table 5. The precise issues posed are not matters that village folk normally consider or articulate. Generally spontaneous reasoning was required from the respondent's personal premises regarding government. The overwhelming civil rights viewpoint is obvious, although it should be noted that a fourth of the respondents were "undecided" on the matter of jailing the government's critic, and fourteen per cent "undecided" on the issue of freedom of the press. In spite of this indecision, nearly three-fourths

gave an unqualified affirmation to the principle of press
freedom while three-fifths gave unqualified support to the
right of open criticism by the opposition. This is a far cry
from simple trust in distant, paternalistic leadership. Pelpolans' lack of skill in the practice of democratic processes
in local organizations has been amply evidenced earlier.
But their comprehension and support of important principles
of democratic structure is clear.

Table 5

Attitudes of Male Household Heads on
Issues of Political Democracy

	Per Cents Giving Affirmative Response
Do you think it is right that a rich man be taxed for the education of a poor man's child?	99
Do you think it would be best if only people who own land had the right to vote?	3
Do you think that newspapers should be permitted to print news, even if true, which undermines people's confidence in their national leaders?	73
If your leaders assured you that it would lead Ceylon to prosperity, would you be willing to see some-one put in jail for criticising the government?	14

Naturalism and Supernaturalism

The passionless and logical search for truth embodied in
the core of Buddhist doctrine has everywhere left the wor-
shippers of Buddha to find surety in complementary religio-
magical-supernatural systems. In a society of almost static
technology the truths gained through tradition must be supplemented by the techniques of supernaturalism. Where
traditional medicines brought no relief, there were demons

to be exorcized. Where millenia old agricultural practices
could not insure crops, Hindu type gods and godlings might
be prevailed upon.

Secular thought cuts deeply into the truth of traditional
practices as well as into the supernatural accessories for
achievement and control in the sphere of nature. But the
curious structure of Sinhalese religious-supernatural institutions acts to safeguard the religious core of Buddhist
thought from disorganization through naturalism and rationalism. The Buddha's rationalism and agnosticism are probably
sufficient assurance that secularizing forces will have little
effect upon religious principles. Yet there are many legend-
ary and wondrous accoutrements to Buddhism accounted by
Pelpolans to be matters of absolute truth. At this point there
is no encroachment upon Buddhism in its central principles
nor in its lore. Attachment to their object of veneration will
long assure Pelpola's implicit belief in legends of the Buddha,
although these are in no wise central to the core of His
thought and principles.

It is as we move away from the body of Buddhism that
the forces of secular thought are most readily perceived.
Not only are scientific controls in opposition to the significance of supernatural powers, attitudes toward supernaturalism have always lacked the veneration and sacredness
held toward matters properly Buddhist. We might argue with
a Pelpolan over the existance and power of Lord Siva or
Vishnu and be neither ridiculous nor insulting, but to argue
the validity of Buddhism would be both. In actual fact, Pelpolans generally believe implicitly in the reality of the worlds
of gods and of demons. But these beliefs have not been protected by the aura of sacredness.

Almost every Pelpolan believes in the power of planet influences upon life. It is doubtful that anyone does not have
a horoscope. In regard to the existence and potency of Hindu
type deities, belief is equally general, but of less significance in daily life. The existence and disease causing powers
of demons are also accepted by a large majority. In response
to survey questioning only six out of a hundred men interviewed expressed outright disbelief in demon reality. There
has, however, been a notable reduction in the sphere of
demon activity from that which was credited them in earlier
times. No one believes that all diseases are caused in whole

or in part by demonological forces, and practically everyone asserts that all common ailments are not caused by
them. Vaguely diagnosed and especially psychosomatic and
functional symptoms are left for the demon world. However,
during 1951 approximately forty-five homes (over ten per
cent) held either bali or thovil ceremonies and it is improbable that the frequency of such events has changed much in
recent years. The incidence of these expensive ceremonies
says little regarding the prevalence of belief. On the other
hand the fact that only thirty-six per cent of the cultivators
made a harvest offering in the name of a deity undoubtedly
indicates a slackening significance of the supernatural world
in that sphere of life.

It is in matters of health that supernaturalism has held
its greatest functional importance in the past. And it is in
this sphere that modern science has made its greatest im-
pact upon village life. While the greater efficacy of bus lines
over bullock carts needs little demonstration, the efficacy
of modern medicine must prove itself over deeply rooted convictions both in supernaturalism and in the traditional practices of Ayurveda. Any discussion of supernaturalism in
respect to health is but one side of a tripartite whole.

Supernaturalism was an adjunct to the institution of Ayurveda with its great pharmacopoeia, and often learned local
practitioners. Its derivation was not from an experimental
science but from folk truths, perhaps in part deriving from
what Pareto would call "the residue of combinations." While
modern medicine has undoubtedly reduced reliance upon
exorcizing, its most direct competitor has been the indiginous
system of Ayurveda. Magic may be a suitable adjunct to either
In actual fact, Western medicine has tended to supersede both
Ayurveda and supernaturalism. The one has come to fill
something of the role of the patent medicine in the West,
while the other has become more and more confined to psychosomatic symptoms and general health protection. Pelpola has
witnessed the results of Western medicine. Regular patronage
at the government dispensary in a nearby village and at the
Kalutara medical center and the maternity hospitals testifies
to community approval. None the less, despite the impressive
record and general acceptance of the Western medical system,
two-thirds of the village men say that if they were forced to
choose, they would keep Ayurveda rather than the new system.

This is probably related to the presence of an Ayurvedic doctor in the village who stands in the role of beloved family physician, and further, it is for the most prevalent, although usually minor, ailments that the indiginous system is used. It is significant that forty-four per cent of the young unmarried males would choose the Western variety over the Eastern, if faced with the necessity of choice. Exorcizers would be the least missed of the three.

The four queries posed in Table 6 include one regarding general belief in demon possession; one regarding belief in a specific demon; another relating to astrological auspiciousness; and one related to the last but applying to a folk belief of unspecific supernatural reference. Although both questions

Table 6

Beliefs of Male Householders in
Supernatural Powers

	Believe	Per Cent who: Undecided	Disbelieve
Can (any) sickness be cured by exorcising?	84	10	6
Should first haircut of child be done at an auspicious time?	48	--	52
Do you believe in the Black Prince?	44	26	30
Does hair cutting of child delay his learning to talk?	29	21	50

pertaining to hair cutting would manifest the same basic belief that the act is dangerous, it is apparent that faith in astrological power has outlasted conviction in the traditionally attributed supernatural consequences of the act. Yet, although all Pelpolans believe in astrological influences, less than half are convinced that in this specific instance the power of the horoscope should be heeded. A similar difference

appears when we compare responses on the general question regarding demonological possession, and the specific
question of belief in a precise demon. The vast majority believe in general that demons are causal factors in disease,
yet the minority profess belief in a well known demon associated with functional ailments in women. We may draw the
tentative conclusion that the encroachment of naturalism on
supernaturalism is proceeding less upon the basis of progressive disbelief in supernatural powers per se, than in the
discarding of specific items of belief. Systems of thought
are composed both of principles and infinite numbers of particular beliefs. The evidence is that the theory or system of
supernaturalism is more immune to change than the particular beliefs and practice which form its structure.

Peasant Economy and Technology

The economy of Pelpola is mainly composed of six distinct
types of activity. By village values, paddy cultivation is the
core of the economy. This is seconded by garden cultivation,
which is general even among non-cultivators of paddy. Rubber plantings as capital operations by villagers, while not
viewed as central to the local economy, are probably in fact
the greatest source of revenue. Wage labor, especially in
the rubber estates, is a fourth type of endeavor. Potting is
a distinct craft associated with a particular caste. Finally,
there are "industrial concerns, " especially tile and brick
manufacture, and petty businesses, such as the boutiques.
Of these various modes of gaining a living, rubber is an innovation of modern times both as capital investment and as
a source of wage employment. Most retail businesses are of
recent origin. Tile and brick manufacture, while expanded
somewhat in recent years, has long been present. Potting,
paddy cultivation, and gardening are centuries old.
    It is obvious that Pelpola has had no static economy. Its
major innovation, rubber, is now more than half a century
old, and accounts for a considerable part of the growth in
petty trading. Other than expanding trade, most development
has been through the application of more capital and labor
to land, especially that turned from disuse into rubber production. Very little change has occured in the techniques of
production except as the introduction of rubber necessitated

them, and rubber production methods have changed little
since the initial period. In matters agricultural, Pelpola
has been resistent not merely to modern innovations, but
even to technics long known and practiced in some Ceylon
villages.

The occupational differentiation, and particularly the
many people not mainly dependent upon agricultural operation, makes application of the peasant concept dubious. We
may be reasonably sure however that most of this indirect
dependence upon the land is a product of the past fifty years.
Still more questionably is Pelpola a "peasantry" from the
standpoint of values and attitudes. The essentially non-
rational value which peasant people place upon their village,
their lands, their crops, their occupation in agriculture
are contradictory to the premises of a secular and urbanized
society. There is no positive assurance that Pelpola in the
past held such peasant values, but it is probable that it did.
In any event, village attitudes on such matters are of critical importance for the movement of a people toward a
rationally, rather than a traditionally, ordered economy.

Pelpola has not fully assimilated the idea of a market
economy. Rubber is the only important commercial crop,
but this, like garden produce, is usually operated with a
minimum of business acumen. As has been indicated earlier,
many well known technics to conserve trees and further
production are disregarded. In a sense rubber has come to
be regarded as another of the many fruits of nature. This is
true of the larger village producers as well as the small.
Capital investment is rarely conceived as a means of protecting and improving agricultural productive property.

The general view of savings is not fully in accord with
either the peasant or the capitalistic ethos. Savings, and
even the use of credit, are usually turned toward consumer
goods, dowry, or pilgrimages, or preserved in the form of
Post Office deposits against some time of crisis. When
householders were questioned as to how they would spend
five hundred rupees, if they were to suddenly receive it,
nearly one-third (thirty-one per cent) specified some household improvement or family expense. A fourth said that they
would use the money to start or develop some type of business
enterprise. While this response might be expected from
persons already operating a business, it is apparent that a

number of "peasants" were thinking in these terms too.
Such a response betokens secularization to be sure, but not
in reference to agricultural production. While a few (eight
per cent) said they would use the money to buy land, more
than double this number (nineteen per cent) would use it for
religious purposes. In all about two-thirds specified some
type of expenditure unrelated to capital investment. No one
mentioned the purchase of agricultural equipment.

In another question designed to test "materialism" in viewpoint, the householders were asked what they thought was
the better way of spending a gift of money to the village, to
build a new road or to improve the temple. Sixty-five per
cent chose the new road and an additional seventeen per cent
were undecided. A new road would be of more importance
as a convenience and comfort than as a feature of economic
development, but the attitude is scarcely a "sacred" one.

Unlike other crops, paddy holds a hallowed place in Sinhalese ideology. It is the traditional subsistence crop and
hence not one for which market thinking has been ingrained.
It is hence well suited for testing the extent to which economic rationality might be applied to production. Seventy-
eight of the householders (those who considered themselves
to be paddy cultivators) were asked: "If a new crop were discovered which you could sell and with the returns buy more
rice than you can produce on your paddy land, would you
(a) plant the new crop on that land? (b) continue to plant
paddy? (c) plant some of each? Presented with this problem,
the majority (fifty-two per cent) were ready to experiment
with caution, i.e. to plant part of the land to the new crop.
Forty per cent said that they would continue to plant paddy
and reject the new. Only eight per cent would turn completely
to the new crop. These responses indicate a rather high degree of economic rationality when we consider the significance of rice in Sinhalese culture.

The secularizing or rationalizing of rice production in
this century is also evident when we compare the ceremonialism surrounding it today with that current in the last century. Of around seventeen ceremonial practices described
by Bell in 1882 only one of the more simple ones appear to
have survived without reduction. [7] Seven have been lost completely. The remainder continue to be performed frequently
but with considerable loss of the details present at the period

of Bell's observations. A more precise measure of the de-
ceremonialization of paddy production may be found in the
diminished sacred vocabulary of the threshing floor. Bell
reported fifty conventional words used during threshing in
reference to objects, animals and exclamations. Today only
fourteen of the words listed by Bell are in use during the
appropriate activities.

Special forces appear to have contributed to the secularization of paddy. During World War II a complex condition
arose in the Ceylon village economy due to the related facts
of scarcity, rationing, black marketing, and the government
monopoly in rice. The peasant producer was stimulated to
"steal" part of his own paddy crop from the fields before it
could be measured and turned into government channels at
the legal price. Further stimulus to such "theft" arose from
delays in official collection machinery with the consequent
threat of theft from the fields by professional blackmarketers.
Economic circumstances were such that many honest peasants felt themselves compelled to cheat the government--
and sometimes in the same process, the landlord.

When a farmer's crop is surreptitiously divided in the
field and partially processed in secrecy, there is no room
for ceremony. As significant as physical circumstances is
the fact that paddy was now viewed in cold pecuniary colors
which held even sordid overtones. Rice became a pawn in an
unpleasant game thrust upon villagers by a war which did
not deeply concern them. The sacred object was profaned.

Rice in all forms is still respected. It commands an awe
not accorded any other product. But the cult of paddy is dying, and another generation may view it in purely rational,
instrumental terms.

It has been observed that Pelpolans take no more than
passing care of their crops and land; it is relevant also to
inquire into their love of cultivation and for the village itself.
Howsoever far from a conceptually perfect state of peasantry
these people have moved, do they idealize the village agricultural life? When householders were asked to express their
preference between continued life in the village and life in a
city or in a colonization project, other things being equal,
three-fourths chose the city! This overwhelming interest in
urban living does not reflect deep dissatisfaction with village
life. Rather it shows the positive hold of the city upon the

rural imagination. Complementary results are shown when
men express their vocational ideals for their sons. Over
nine-tenths choose government over non-governmental employments, and for precise occupation, of those who would
specify, practically all named white collar employments.
Not one of the seventy-nine youths interviewed expressed a
personal preference for agriculture and the vast majority
named professional and white collar employments, especially
teaching. Thirteen per cent mentioned "business." It is apparent that the occupational status structure has much to do
with the urban bent, despite the fact that in theory cultivation
of the soil is a highly honored work. And, although villagers
seem happy in their rural life, it is valued less than city
dwelling. Nor is the feeling for the home soil, as distinct from
the occupation of farming, much stronger. When asked if
they would move to the far-off jungle colonization schemes,
as farmers, if their economic position would thereby be improved, forty per cent of the heads gave an unequivocal "no"
but thirty per cent were as decidedly positive and the remaining forty per cent undecided. Most Pelpolans are willing to consider what looks like the "good thing" despite real
affection for their village.

Agricultural technics in paddy show a remarkable stabili-
ty in this community where agricultural ideology appears to
be very much mixed with secular conceptions. It is difficult
to find any point at which the implements of production have
changed significantly with the passage of centuries. Nor is
this because Pelpola is remote from the knowledge of improved cultivational practices both old and new. The iron
plow has been given much propaganda through government
sources, and there is one in the village itself--unused.
Various types of rakes and harrows have been recommended
by the agricultural ministry but most of these are not even
represented in the village. Other good farming practices are
known to every Pelpola cultivator: paddy transplantation,
multiple plowings, weeding, composting and fertilizing. One
farmer has transplanted, as a favor to the government production officer. Weeding of paddy is practiced by a fifth of
the cultivators. Composting is done by fewer still. Fertilizing is more or less systematically carried out by about one-
half, and three-fifths have drainage canals in their highland
gardens, a number of them having been made under the terms
of alienation in acquiring Crown land.

It is not to be supposed that Pelpolans view any of these
practices as being morally bad, harmful, or even contrary
to the ways of their forefathers. As a matter of fact some
of them have been known to the Sinhalese for centuries, e.g.
transplanting paddy. In respect to all of the mooted practices, except the iron plow, nearly all village men agree
that production would be enhanced by their use. In the matter of rubber cultivation essentially the same conditions
hold true. Why then, do Pelpolans not farm more efficiently?

There is no gainsaying the retarding effects of tenancy
and joint ownership upon careful methods of farming. Nor
is capital or credit always available. The "postage stamp"
plots operated in paddy, as well as the tenure situation, are
not conducive to the adoption of some techniques. Yet prosperous owners of large fields are also backward. Tenure
and small plots are conditioning factors, but they cannot be
viewed as determinative to the extent of being sufficient explanations. When one asks the cultivators themselves what
is responsible for their technological resistence, the most
frequent response is, "It is so troublesome to do that. "
Here we may find some clue to underlying factors.

Few if any stereotypes of Sinhalese character have failed
to portray these people as easy going, leisure loving, and
even lazy. [8] Pelpolans do in fact value verandah sitting and
"enjoying. " It is notable that most of the improved technics
call for additional labor rather than the reverse. Given such
technics in an ethos of this nature, the influences surrounding Pelpola have worked toward stasis in agriculture. Villagers have come to be concerned with making money, but
scracely out of the practice of cultivation. They see alternative uses for their labor in cash returns on the rubber estates, whether or not they actually so utilize their time. (No
research has determined whether the proceeds from improved paddy cultivation would be equal to wage returns for
the same expenditure of effort.) Further, the rise of traders
in the village has not served to help preserve an agricultural
focus during the transition from a subsistence to a market
economy. Agricultural practices are a constant, and when
this constant is inadequate, supplementation is sought outside agriculture. The farmer of Pelpola is not conservative.
He is not capitalisticly motivated toward agriculture.

For a community in which primary production is static in

technic and wholly unmechanized, popular reaction to one
mechanical innovation has been startling. The introduction
of a mechanical rice hulling machine was greeted with en-
thusiasm. This machine, introduced by a commercially
minded villager, in 1948, proved so popular that a competitor joined the field before that year was out. Within two
months after the installation of the first huller, approximately half the village housewives had tried the new device,
at a few cents per measure of rice. Nearly every home in
the village had at least a part of their rice mechanically
hulled in 1951. The movement to the new method was so
rapid, that our attempt to analyze "resistence" to this innovation proved futile. There was none. Women were directly
responsible for the shift, but men offered no objections.
When a few cents per day saves hours of back breaking toil
with the pestle, few families are so poor, and none so set
in their ways, as to cling to modes of the past. In so far as
the evidence goes, Pelpola is alert to labor saving, mechanical improvement with an avidity unsurpassed in mechanically conscious American communities.

Consumer Goods

    With an expanding money economy and adjacency to the
new standards of the coastal cities, it is to be expected that
modern, imported goods and gadgets would find their way
into village homes. Houses of any substance have unmistakable signs of Western influence--chairs, tables, a mirror,
a few large metal spoons. Likely as not, the housewife wears
a mother-hubbard while her small son, grown one stage beyond nakedness, may be clad in shorts. When mother leaves
home, however, she wears the conventional cloth and jacket,
or the Indian innovation, the saree. School girls often wear
Western style dresses. The son upon attaining full youth
will turn to a sarong, like his father, and daughter will follow the pattern set by the women. One unmistakable sign of
Western influence is the fact that all young men have their
hair cut. Sixty-three per cent of the married men wear the
old fashioned chignon.
    A prosperous adult male may wear a Western type coat
above his sarong, but generally adult male attire is simply
the sarong often topped by a knit cotton undershirt of Western

design. Among women, face powder is widely used, but ornaments are typically Sinhalese. This is not so for men. The
elderly and well-to-do villager often wears a gold watch
chain while the younger man will proudly display his jack-
knife and support his sarong with belt and buckle.

Food preferences lie solidly with traditional fare--rice
and curries. However, white potatoes in curried form have
become a luxury item, and occasionally locally grown vegetables of Western origin are used. Tinned food is used rather
widely for special items of diet. Thus in the household survey we found that a little over one-fourth (twenty-eight per
cent) of the families had used some tinned product during
the preceeding month. The most common tinned food was
milk, used in the sweetened condensed form for children and
for adults' tea. Tinned fish and biscuits were used less frequently.

The potential for mechanical implements and gadgets in
the home is limited by many factors including small money
incomes, lack of electrical power, and the general milieu
of household living. Two types of items are, however, accepted with alacrity and are limited in their spread only by
their high cost in village terms. These are the bicycle and
the sewing machine. Sixteen per cent of Pelpola households
have a bicycle, used only by the men of the family. Nearly ten
per cent of the housewives have sewing machines and these
are frequently borrowed by envious neighbors. Sixteen per
cent of the homes have clocks or watchs and a very few possess such luxury items as a phonograph or radio. It is significant for Pelpola's changing standard of living that nearly
three-fourths of the household heads chose an automobile
when asked what single piece of mechanical, powered, equipment they would want most. They did not mean "truck."

Chapter XII

SECULARIZATION: PATTERNED PROCESS

Out of a past in which Sinhalese villages conformed more
closely to the concept of the folk-Gemeinschaft, Pelpola is
meeting and absorbing the ways of a world in which traditional
verities are contravened by rationalism, technology, indivi-
duation, and market economy. Few ways of the past are deliberately repudiated, but neither are the new deliberately
rejected. Fundamentally, in our hypothesis, the new elements
stem from Western influences, but the specific adjustments
to these innovations are homespun and partially unique. Along
a path which, in broad outline, thousands of other villages
also travel, Pelpola is moving toward a way of life neither
traditionally Sinhalese nor fully Western.

It would be easy to infer that the contemporary village is
a hodge-podge of traditional and of diffused traits. Superficial observation might lend support to the hodge-podge theory
of cultural integration in Pelpola. Busses share the road
with bullock carts; castes, professedly of unequal birth,
share equally in institutional facilities; cinema-attending
men return home to participate in demon exorcizing rituals;
contractual wage workers reject employment offered by a
"bad" neighbor; peasants having their paddy machine-hulled
steadfastly reject efficient farm production techniques. But
to emphasize such a conglomeration of inconsistent traits is
fallacious. It is improbable that any society is integrated
either with perfect logic or with complete functionalism.
Certainly urban Western societies still find room for strong
primary groups, supernatural beliefs, and valuation of traditional truths.

In the present chapter we propose to make the merest attempt to explore the processes through which secular elements move into and are integrated within the village milieu.
Three closely related processes will be examined: (1) the
relationship between the peasant's contact with diffusion
channels and his acceptance of secular thought and behavior,

(2) the extent to which various facets of the secularization process are related to each other in the acceptance process, and (3) how Pelpola preserves a functional and orderly equilibrium in the midst of conflicting cultural elements.

The first of these problems may be expressed in the form of a hypothesis. Individuals in greatest contact with the sources of secularism, through participation in diffusion media, display greatest personal secularity in values and in behavior. This is to test the reality of the common assumption that worldly, especially urban, contact stimulates secularization and concomitantly de-traditionalization.

The second problem is more complex. It is a specific form of the question of functional integration. In the folk-urban continuum and related theories, it is implied that the secular trend is many faceted. It is further implied that these facets stand in functional relationship to each other-- in Durkheim's terms it might be said that all arise out of increasing social differentiation. In any case, it is hypothesized on a logical, deductive, basis that each facet of secular transition, e.g. growth of impersonal relationships, economic rationalism, and the value of status achievement, is functionally interwoven with each of the others. The hypothesis is hence suggested that secularization proceeds as a patterned system of change under whose forces, as one aspect of life is affected, all other aspects of life are similarly influenced. If movement along the folk-urban continuum is a unitary process which can be ascribed to total communities, then we may hypothesize that individuals who are secular in one sphere of life tend also to be secular in other spheres.

The third problem broaches the question of the organization and disorganization of a community moving along the path of secularization. If, as we hypothesize, an integrated set of secular values and relationships are encroaching upon a previously integrated set of folk values and relationships, it might be expected that the transition period would be one of confusion and cross purposes. The theory of the folk-urban continuum leads us to expect a period of disorganization in the life of the community, conflicts rooted in value disagreements, and moral deviation and even anomie among individuals. Yet, Pelpola shows nothing like chaos, and at least no outward signs of personal disorganization. How has Pelpola so accomodated the conflicting modes of the secular West with the sacred East?

The Channels of Secularization

The opportunities for village people to come into contact
with traits of the urban, and more Western, world are so
many and often so indirect or subtle that it is virtually impossible to measure the precise effects of differing types of
exposures. Different media of diffusion and influence undoubtedly have differing significance for the various aspects
of the transition. While Pelpolans' breadth of experience
with communication media and markets has been demonstrated, no attempt has been made to link the new traits with
actual participation in concrete situations assumed to be of
significence for change. We now propose to test, howsoever
crudely, the hypothesis that secular behavior and secular
attitudes vary with the individual's amount of participation
in the channels of diffusion. Conversely, those who participate least would be most "sacred" or "folk" in their values
and behavior.

For operational purposes, secularization is defined in
terms of (a) profession of "Westernized" values, (b) extensive knowledge of international affairs, (c) acceptance of
rational agricultural practices, (d) participation in audience
type groups, (e) possession of Western type material objects,
and (f) disregard for folk beliefs and practices. Each of
these aspects of secularization is further defined operationally
so that a series of indexes results permitting classification
of respondents into levels of "secularism" (or traditionalism) in respect to each facet of the concept. (For the actual
tests used as a basis for classification, see Appendix B.)
Dealing as we are with the responses of eighty-seven heads
of families, no attempt at refined analysis can be made. It
is to be noted that one of the secularization facets is negative
in that it does not test for secularization but for lack of traditionalism. This, in a sense, is a validity check upon positive items, although the folk beliefs and practices tested are
in no instances merely the antitheses of those included under
the various secular facets. They are largely ritualized practices having supernatural or familistic significance. It is
conceivable that persons standing high in secular values and
Westernization in other measures might be highly traditional
in the magical and folk beliefs and practices composing our
index of folk adherence. If this were so it would at least

suggest some personality inconsistencies and would also imply closely conventionalized acceptance of new values.

Table 7 demonstrates that in reference to every communication process we are able to measure, there is some positive relationship between participation and secularization. Not only does each communication activity show positive relationship to secularization generally, this relationship is maintained in almost every aspect of the secularization process treated separately. Only in regard to the negative criterion, that of breakdown in traditional beliefs and practices, is there a much qualified relationship between the two sets of variables. Even here the most secular are clearly more in contact than are others in regard to most measures. Trips to the city, newspaper reading, and education is each associated with highly secular value profession, acceptance of rational agricultural practices, audience participation, and use of Western material culture traits.

For a number of reasons it is hazardous to make internal comparisons regarding the relative importance of different diffusion media for various facets of the secularization process. Our discrimination of degrees of secularization varies between categories and no attempt has been made to equate intensities of contact, and we may be sure that the variables are much inter-related. In general, we are justified in viewing newspaper reading and schooling as the most persistently related factors. While it is not to be suggested that education per se has yielded the modes of conduct and thinking noted, it has undoubtedly stimulated interests and provided the skills essential to widening contact. When we use what is in effect an overall test of perceptive contact with the outer world, knowledge of affairs in other countries, there is also marked difference between the traditionalists and the secular in every facet of life measured, including breakdown of folk practices and beliefs. There is no evidence, however, that direct contact with the city is more crucial for changing points of view than indirect, impersonal contacts. Personal participation in some media is the decisive factor.

While no extensive attempt has been made to determine the background characteristics of persons most susceptible to secularization, these persons were found to be among

Table 7

Relationship between Various Aspects of Secularization
and Contacts with the Outer World*

Type of Secular Behavior	No. of Cases	Mean Trips to City	Per cent Reading Newspapers Reg.	Per cent Reading Newspapers Never	Mean Years in School	Mean Score or Internation Knowledg
Value Statements						
Traditional	23	24	8	39	3. 6	2. 2
Moderate	40	33	25	30	4. 6	3. 4
Secular	24	42	54	4	5. 3	6. 2
Technical Innovations**						
Traditional	27	28	22	33	4. 3	3. 3
Moderate	27	32	22	18	4. 9	4. 0
Secular	21	35	38	19	5. 4	4. 3
Audience Participation						
Traditional	63	28	21	32	4. 2	3. 4
Secular	24	45	50	8	5. 4	5. 2
Retention of Folk Beliefs and Practices						
Traditional	34	31	29	26	3. 5	3. 2
Moderate	22	29	9	36	4. 0	3. 5
Secular	31	39	39	16	5. 4	4. 9
Western Material Culture						
Traditional	58	28	22	31	4. 0	3. 1
Moderate	14	33	28	22	4. 6	4. 2
Secular	15	50	53	7	6. 8	6. 7

*For bases of classification in reference to traditionalism and secu
larization see Appendix B. Note that audience participation is operationally defined as cinema attendance. This might be considered a typ
of contact as well as a form of secular behavior. Conversely extensiv
knowledge is both an indication of contact and a manifestation of secul
interest. Divisions of responses into categories was made to achieve
three groups of nearest possible equal size.
    **Cultivators only.

the economically well-off and also the youthful. (It has already been noted that unmarried youth are especially non-
traditional.) There is no persistent tendency, however,
throughout every facet of secularization. A fifteen year difference in average age exists between the most "traditional"
third and the most "secularized" third in reference to value
statements, and about ten years difference between audience
participators and non-participators. There is a similar difference between those retaining and rejecting traditional beliefs and practices. On the other hand, age appears to be no
factor in reference to agricultural practices, and use of
Western material culture items. The "good" farmers and
the gadget conscious came disproportionately from the upper financial levels. [1]

It is interesting to note that when analysis of piety ratings
was made for the traditional and the secular, the latter were
not judged as more impious than others except in reference
to the retention of folk beliefs and practices. Thirty-eight
per cent of the traditionalists in folk practices were from
the ranks of the two highest piety classes, compared with
ten per cent of the most secularized. [2] It may be inferred
that little moral censure is placed upon those who depart
from the traditional culture and values so long as ancient
ritualism and associated beliefs are also maintained. Since
the measure of adherence to traditional practices is weighted
by ritualistic observances, it may be suggested, that censure
is not applied to the more secular persons provided they do
not flout the ancient forms and ceremonies. Since such a
possibility was not foreseen in study planning, this suggestion cannot be precisely tested.

Secularization as a Multidimensional Continuum

The great transition occurring among economically underdeveloped folk peoples meeting the secularizing forces of
Western ideology and market and technical influences is
multidimensional. We have essayed to study the encroachment of these new modes of thinking and of living upon social
participation, values, technology, and other phases of culture and the deteriorating effects upon traditional beliefs and
rituals. In the assumptions of many anthropologists and
sociologists, such differing phases of life and culture stand

in functionally integrative relationships to each other phase.
It is widely inferred that in the broad sweeps of history,
various institutions and technologies move almost as a single
unity or as the multiple effect of change in some particular
segment of the culture. Implicit in much of the writing upon
the continua from folk to urban, or sacred to secular or
Gemeinschaft to Gesellschaft is the assumption of functional
unity in values, social organization, and culture. Does the
movement toward the qualities of the urban society which is
now underway in Asian countries imply consistency in change
between the various component parts of the socio-cultural
system? Are individuals who are converted to secular value
positions also prone to accept Western technology, urban
social participation patterns, and "materialistic" comforts
of modern life? Can communities and individuals be "placed"
upon a meaningful continuum of change, or must we deal
with change as it occurs in discrete spheres of activity? .

There is unmistakable evidence that the secularization
process, as conceived here, moves forward as at least a
partially integrated pattern. In Pelpola, individuals who are
secular in certain facets of life tend also to be secular in
others. (See Table 8.) Singularly enough, despite a popular
tendency to view the introduction of Western technology as
the core of the Asian transition, the use of improved technical practices in agriculture is the only facet of the secularization process which is unrelated to most others, and apparently least advanced. It should be recognized, however,
that the agricultural technics used here as a measure are
not mechanical ones, nor do they give account of the effects
of rubber production. None-the-less there is no support for
any theory of direct technological determinism. The lack of
mechanical devices in our measure of technological innova-
tiveness was dictated by the paucity of such devices in the
production systems of the community.

With research instruments so crudely designed, it is not
surprising that the evidence of configuration in the secularization process is not definitive. Yet in Table 8, out of thirty
comparisons twenty-five differ in the expected direction and
only two are negative. Obviously most of the individual differences, particularly those relative to technological innovations, would be statistically non-significant. The only
strong evidence for configuration arises in reference to the

Table 8

Inter-relationships among Different Facets of Secularization

Per cent in Most Secular Third in respect to:

	Values	Audience Participation	Technology	Traditional Practices	Western Material Culture	Knowledge
Values						
Most Conservative 23 cases*	--	9	36	9	31	13
Most Secular 24 cases	--	33	29	63	69	68
Audience Participation						
Most Conservative 63 cases	25	--	28	32	33	25
Most Secular 24 cases	33	--	28	46	33	46
Technology						
Most Conservative 27 cases	22	15	--	33	33	22
Most Secular 21 cases	29	24	--	24	38	29
Traditional Practices						
Most Conservative 34 cases	9	29	29	--	38	24
Most Secular 31 cases	35	36	25	--	40	42
Western Material Culture						
Most Conservative 58 cases	10	28	27	31	--	31
Most Secular 29 cases	44	28	29	41	--	52
Knowledge						
Most conservative 30 cases	10	13	15	20	13	--
Most secular 27 cases	63	41	27	48	46	--

*The 23 lowest cases in respect to value secularization score. Wherever possible the groups chosen for comparison in this column constitute the bottom and top thirds of all scores in the designated secularization facet.

correlates of secular values and extensive knowledge. When persons who are most secular in social values are compared with the least secular the former are also strikingly more secular in regard to audience participation, western material culture, knowledge, and belief in, or performance of traditional practices. While extensive knowledge shows general relation with further secularity, knowledge is as much a measure of outside contact as it is an element in secularity and hence such relationships are not entirely comparable with others. Although the evidence will not carry us far into the question of configuration in facets of Westernization or secularization processes, it seems clear that persons meeting the standards of high secularity in knowledge and values tend also to be secular in most other respects. The data further suggest the possibility that the basic forces within the broader secularization movement in this community lie in extensive knowledge of the world and in conversion to the secular-democratic value nexus of Western society.

The tendency for traditionalists to be consistently traditional and for the secular to be consistently secular lends support to the idea of social types in reference to cultural change. Leo Silberman has developed the concept of the "social entrepreneur" in reference to persons in another traditional culture who are accepting Western, rational family orientations.[3] With qualifications notably in regard to agricultural technology, the evidence of Pelpola supports in tentative fashion the existence of such an innovative social type in regard to a wider range of non-traditional values and behavior patterns.[4] Conversely, our findings hint at the existence of traditionalists who may be consistent in a wide range of cultural and social responses. If we would go beyond the realm of suggestive findings, Pelpola must be studied with more refined techniques than those justified in the present exploration.

Socio-Cultural Integration

If Pelpola is pursuing an unsteady but persistent course in the implanting of secular traits in its traditional milieu, the introduction of these new and logically conflicting modes has yielded nothing remotely resembling community chaos. Value conflicts have given rise to petty disagreements over

the relationships between high and low castes; businessmen
do not have an esteem commensurate with their economic
power. Peasants appear to idealize urban living. But these,
and other conditions of their ilk, are minor ruffles on the
surface of a placid village life. Caste relationships are no
source of serious conflict, businessmen have not brought
cleavages in leadership and peasants do not beat their
breasts in hopelessness at village life. That Pelpola has its
erring sons, its thieves, factional disputes, and some poverty, there is no doubt. But such problem groups which
might testify to disorganization are insignificant in the overwhelming evidence of responsible children, honest and economically solvent citizens, neighborliness and village pride.
Nor is it unreasonable that minor bits of disorganization
would not have appeared under conditions of stasis as well
as change. Yet, at scores of points, logically we might
look for serious disorganization arising from new values
and new organizational forms. Wage labor by women might
have, but has not in fact, disordered patriarchal authority:
Hollywood movies might have yielded romance-demanding
sons, but in fact the marriage arrangement system is strong.
The firm introduction of Western medicine might have
broken faith in supernaturalism and Ayurveda, but demon
dancers, astrologers and the "native doctor" still prosper.
The content of institutions has been modified drastically,
but with minor effect upon their smooth functioning. And in
these transitions, not even the conservative elders of the
village cry out that youth are going to the dogs or that the
best of life is being lost. Much as Sinhalese revere their
historic past, most recognize that life today is preferable.
Pelpolans do not see that they have lost much in their transitions. A few reactionary high caste men deplore the equali-
zation movement in caste, but the things that matter most
stand unharmed though changed. Family life is secure and
satisfying; serenity in the worship of Lord Buddha is as before; few people live less well than their fathers, and most
live better; the neighborliness of the lanes, fields and tea
shops is a constant joy. Yet, by our evidence, Pelpola is in
the process of a revolutionary transition. How can the good
things of the old life be preserved in such a time? How can
conflicting norms, conflicting values, and conflicting systems of truth fail to yield internal tensions, dissatisfactions,

and even normlessness and anti-social deviance? The answer, we believe, lies in a long record of historic accident
conjoined with the "loose structuring" of Sinhalese culture
and social organization.

Although this study has viewed Pelpola at a single point
in time, i. e. the period 1948-1957, the transition which we
visualize has been underway for a great many years--and
will no doubt be projected many years into the future. The
immediacy of certain dramatic developments in Asia has an
effect of over-emphasizing the recency of modernization.
In fact, Pelpola has long been affected by Western contacts.
To say that this village has been subjected to persistent
European influences for four hundred years is no exaggeration. Family names, as well as several hundred Portuguese
words incorporated into common Sinhalese usage attest pervasive Western contacts, even before Western civilization
itself had acquired fully a distinctively secular flavor. Feudal
structure had disappeared from this region by the early
British period at least, and likely was in disuse in the immediate locality well before that. From early British times
onward, caste was given no legal status and, although sometimes utilized for purposes of rule, has been fairly consistently discouraged for more than a century. In economic
matters, Pelpola's small ceramic industry was prospering
probably in Dutch times and certainly more than a century
ago. Even rubber, the most important stimulus to a market
economy, appeared in this village at the beginning of the
present century. Limited political suffrage in regard to
colonial legislative bodies was instituted in 1910, and was
related to a government which had long been of Western
constitutional design. [6] Experience with the products of science in medicine was widespread by the time of World War I.
An extensive hookworm eradication campaign by the Rockefeller Foundation had been initiated in 1916, and in 1926 a
model health and medical center was established in nearby
Kalutara. [7] The fact that contemporary stimuli and communication processes are more intense and more pervasive
than in the past should not obscure the historical perspective
from which we must view Pelpola's transition.

At no time in the history of colonial rule in Low Country
Ceylon has there been traumatic disruption of local institutions by action of a conqueror or even by unplanned economic

or social forces. Whereas in India the introduction of a
centralized governmental mechanism overshadowing the village panchayat had disorganizing consequences, nothing
comparable occurred in Ceylon. The Portuguese, and for
the most part the Dutch, accepted the society they found,
using it for their own purposes usually with regard for traditional usage. Although the Portuguese brought rabid
Christianity and the Dutch, capitalistic bureaucracy and
schools, nominal conversion could satisfy the former, and
the potentially disrupting influences of the Dutch were closely
limited in their application and the limits probably did not
include Pelpola.

Significant for the ease of subsequent changes was the
application of Roman-Dutch law, especially under the
British. This legal system applied particularly to Low Country Sinhalese and served to widen the small cultural differences between the Low Country and the Kandyan Provinces.
Rather than disrupting the traditional order of civil processes,
the new code appears to have operated more toward regu-
larizing certain of the traditional norms, narrowing the
range of normative behavior rather than supplanting traditional customs by arbitrary European standards. Hayley
has observed that the introduction of Roman-Dutch law in
the Low Country was easily effected.[8] In fact, there is
reason to believe that the new code was introduced gradually
and was deliberately developed in those spheres not explicitly covered by custom and where customary usage could
be brought into disuse most readily. And in regard to criminal law, Hayley has observed the striking similarity between native Sinhalese conceptions and those of the English
which were instituted as statute law.

Western economic interests in Ceylon were at no period
served by policies directly disruptive to local traditional
economy.[9] Portuguese and Dutch were well served by the
feudal-caste order. The British were exploiters of land
more than of Ceylonese. While the plantation system introduced by them was a revolutionary economic structure, the
plantation world was relatively self-contained and non-competitive with village agricultural life. Whereas in India,
British economic policy had forced drastic changes in many
aspects of local economy, Ceylon was valued for its plantation crops rather than for village agricultural production and

tax revenue. [10] A money economy was stimulated, but the impersonal contacts which it brought were largely super- imposed upon the age-old design of traditional crops and traditional crafts. Unlike India, Ceylon had little to offer England by way of village agricultural producers or textile consumers. Ceylon's appeal lay in the plantation crops chiefly worked by a culturally isolated, immigrant labor force. Villages like Pelpola have taken on limited participa- tion in plantation work but as an adjunct to, rather than as a substitute for, village life.

The outer world has been penetrating the village with al- most imperceptible graduality; legal code upon custom modi- fication, rubber upon ceramics, equal suffrage upon equal rights before the law, socialized medicine upon sporadic health programs.

Beyond the great period of time which the Sinhalese have had for the absorption of new ways, their ethos is peculiarly flexible and adjustive. New values do not seem to overturn old ones. Instead, old values, when not fully retained, are eaten away bit by bit. On the side of material culture, the only potentially traumatic innovation has been that of rubber, and this was happily integrated with paddy cultivation during a period of increasing population. While the money economy it presaged no doubt disrupted the traditional harvest work group, and decreased peasant independence, the individual- ized nature of village farm economy generally was not up- set. Nor do many of the more recent changes show replace- ment power. Thus the cinema seems to be additive rather than a substitute for primary forms of recreation. Modern medicine has served to limit but neither to push out nor dis- credit the Ayurvedic practitioner. People are getting more medical attention, by the Western type added to the Eastern. Rational "materialism" has limited the power of demons but very slightly affected the principle of demon possession. Nowhere have Pelpolans found disillusionment with the past. And in very few areas have the central, core, moral values been subjected to violent wrenching. Even in caste, a sphere wherein traditional and modern status values are irreconcil- ible, the new values are entirely consistent with the deep tolerance in Buddhist thought--and it is mainly in the sense of a discrimination system that caste reality has faded in Pelpola today. The older economic reciprocities of caste, reminiscent of the Indian jajmani system have been so long withered in this region that no memory of them persists.

The unstudied ease with which the Sinhalese village preserves the old, while adopting the new was described by Emerson Tennent in the mid-nineteenth century. [11] He observed that the Sinhalese were like a "yielding fluid which adapts its shape to that of the vessel into which it may happen to be poured, without any change in its quality or any modification of its character. " This analogy symbolizes the struggle of an outstanding scholar and observer to articulate the penetrable yet resilient character of Sinhalese society and culture.

It has been suggested elsewhere that this apparent paradox is explicable through the concept of "loose structuring." [12] Permissiveness of individual behavior in the sense of many alternative norms, imprecisely defined role patterning, and tolerance even to non-normative deviation combine with weak norms of group solidarity to yield the condition of "loose structure. " As Embree has pointed out for Thailand, "The permissiveness of individual behavior variation in the culture does not mean that the society is poorly integrated. On the contrary, the loose integration is a functional one, allowing not only variation in individual behavior but also in national behavior. It has survival value...that is, a loosely integrated structure such as the Thai may adjust to external cultural influences with less drastic over-all changes than a more rigid structure such as the Japanese or Vietnamese. "[13] Thus, for the Sinhalese, it has been argued that colonial rule had immediate organizing effects upon Sinhalese institutions rather than degenerative or disorganizing effects. [14] While this observation requires qualification in reference to the caste system, for the familial institution, European influence was never disorganizing in spite of deliberate statutory restriction upon customary marriage practices. There is every indication that European influence had a formalizing and rigidifying effect through the partial limitation of old alternatives rather than the demolition of old norms in favor of new. The fact that the norms of Sinhalese life, as evidenced throughout Pelpola's institutions, are matters of principle rather than specifications of conduct offers wide latitude for change so long as it is consistent with the nonspecific normative principles.

It is significant that basic principles of Theravada Buddhism are consistent with both loose structuring and smooth social transitions. Buddhism has no deep alignment with any particular secular order of society. Its force is toward the preservation of ultimate values more than specific norms of behavior or specific forms of social organization. Whatever overtones are introduced by syncretism, the nature of truth in the Buddha's teaching lies in reason rather than faith. Rather than absolutism and a straight and narrow way, there is here a relativism of tolerance and the middle way.

Pelpola has suffered no emotional or abrupt conversions to a new way of life nor repudiations of an old one. The new creeps in upon the old, growing much as Charles Horton Cooley described in "the tentative social process."[15] There is indeed a strain toward consistency as evidenced in the partially integrated advance of various facets of secularism, but the advances are slow wherever the hard moral core of values is encountered (as in strong family ideology) and rapid where new norms are consistent with core values (as in the use of Western medicine).[16] How far will Pelpola move? How individualized will matters of marriage become? How inconsequential will be the marital mixing of castes? How far will commercialized recreations and special interest groups weaken the functions of primary associations?

These are questions now unanswerable but the evidence is that the selection of marriage partners will long remain a conventionalized exclusion from increasing individualization generally. Individualization in occupational choices, or in places of residence may be sloughed off as group concerns. Doctrines of equality are acceptable and integratable with Buddhist tolerance and kindliness and conceptions of spiritual attainment. They may pervade economic and civic relationships, and even inter-household affairs. But inter-caste marriage will be divorced from questions of equality and preserved on grounds of family integrity in something of the same way that ethnic group endogamy need imply no status inequality.

Nor is the integrity of the going family system in any immediate threat from individuating forces. Evidence in other areas supports the view that encroaching urbanism has minimal effects upon family values.[17] The very looseness of kin structuring and family organization patterns has permitted the reduction of production functions in the home without ap-

parent disorganization. There is no reason to believe that
the firm but flexible unit of the nuclear family is not adapt-
able to the secular order. Here the contrast with the Hindu
joint family is pronounced.

So in other institutions. Barring catastrophic change
such as might occur with industrialized paddy production
or collectivization of land or concerted external attack upon
paternal authority and honor, Pelpola will go on, modifying
readily the subordinate norms, and very slowly some of the
deeper ones, and continue to accept new blessings of an in-
ventive world in matters of consumption and health. But
though the shape of the container changes, there is no evidence that Pelpola loses or even seriously compromises
the things that matter most to Pelpolans: the serenity arising from worship of Lord Buddha, the tolerant individualism honoring the dignity of others, security in the strong-
hold of family, and the ultimate appeal to the supernatural,
the joys of pilgrimages, and perhaps most precious of all,
the daily fellowship of neighbors and kinsmen.

NOTES

Chapter I

1. Land use and type of ownership for the village of Pelpola, as a political unit, have been estimated from the village vel vidane's figures and the Ceylon Surveyor General's records. The following tabular presentation is the basis for textual statements.

Type of Ownership and Extent in Acres

	Local Villagers	Estates	Other Absentee	Total
Rubber	158	550	98	806
Paddy	302	223*	--	525
Garden Land	679**	---	--	679

*Including a small but undetermined amount owned by "Other Absentee."

**Including a small amount of land owned by the Crown for ultimate distribution.

2. For the basis of statistical statements see Appendix A. Most statistical statements, unless otherwise indicated, refer to conditions as of 1950 and 1951. Where observation since that time suggests that conditions have changed by 1957, this has been noted in the text. A few migrant families living as resident labor on a rubber estate within the political boundaries of Pelpola have not been considered. These persons are not part of the Pelpola community and have little significance to it.

3. See Chapter VIII for definitions of economic categories.

Chapter II

1. For the bases upon which statistical data are cited throughout this work, see Appendix A.

2. Regular employment has been defined as wage work or engagement in family productive enterprise for 120 days or more during 1950.

3. H. C. P. Bell: "Sinhalese Customs and Ceremonies Connected with Paddy Cultivation in the Low Country. " Paper read February 15, 1882, Royal Asiatic Society (Ceylon Branch), Colombo. Available in the Colombo Museum, printed and bound with other papers on this subject. See also below, Chapter XI.

4. See Chapter VII.

5. Robert Knox: An Historical Relation of Ceylon (1681). Glasgow: James MacLehose and Sons, 1911, p. 140.

Chapter III.

1. This count is based upon a special survey designed only to determine the extent of crowding in these poorest and smallest homes which include all of simple thatch construction and some of the most inadequate "wattle and daub." The average (mean) household size for the entire village, based on the sample of 100 households, is 5. 2 persons.

2. It should be recalled that the Sinhalese caste system was highly organized on vocational and craft lines. The long tradition is toward craft specialization and interdependence rather than toward family economic self-sufficiency. Cf. Bryce Ryan: Caste in Modern Ceylon: The Sinhalese System in Transition. New Brunswick: Rutgers University Press, 1953.

3. Cf. Bryce Ryan: "Institutional Factors in Sinhalese Fertility, " Milbank Memorial Fund Quarterly, Vol. XXX, 1952, pp. 359-381.

4. See M. A. Straus: "Childhood Experience and Emotional Security in the Context of Sinhalese Social Organization, " Social Forces, Vol. 33, 1954, pp. 152-160. Straus has noted symptoms of emotional insecurity in children which, he hypothesizes, arise from feelings of rejection when the parents withdraw overt signs of affection. Within a milieu of loose structuring, this generally yields a high incidence of insecurity feeling. The existence of such insecurity is demonstrated in Rorschach evidence. See Murray A. Straus and Jacqueline H. Straus: "Personal Insecurity and Sinhalese Social Structure: Rorschach Evidence for Primary School Children, " Eastern Anthropologist, Vol. X, No. 2, December, 1956-February, 1957, pp. 97-111. Accepting Straus' evidence, we are inclined to conclude that Pelpola children appear to enjoy their insecurity.

Chapter IV

1. E. B. Denham: Ceylon at the Census of 1911. Colombo: "Govt. Printer, " 1912, pp. 178-189. Other aspects of naming not relevant to Pelpola but to other Sinhalese localities are also described by Denham.

2. For a description of Sinhalese kinship terminology, see F. A. Hayley: Laws and Customs of the Sinhalese or... Kandyan Law. Colombo: Cave and Co. , 1923.

3. Cf. Bryce Ryan: "Primary and Secondary Contacts in a Ceylonese Peasant Community, " Rural Sociology, Vol. 17, 1952, pp. 311-321.

4. Murray A. Straus: unpublished datum derived from a study of child training practices among mothers having children in the third form (grade).

Chapter V

1. See Bryce Ryan: Caste in Modern Ceylon, op. cit.

2. Statistical data on marriages are derived from analysis of all marital units within the households drawn in the household survey sample of 100 homes.

Chapter VI

1. For further discussion of Buddhist sectarianism and its relationship to caste, see Bryce Ryan: Caste in Modern Ceylon, op. cit., Chapter 2.

2. The dagoba, a solid, dome-shaped structure, containing Buddhist relics, is considered an integral part of a complete temple. Relics for the Pelpola dagoba were brought from Anuradhapura. The word dagoba is derived from dhatu (relic) and garbha (a receptacle).

3. See also Bryce Ryan: "Primary and Secondary Contacts in a Ceylonese Peasant Community, " op. cit.

4. Hell is conceived as a place of flames and intense heat with threatening tortures at every turn. Male adulterers, for example, would in this place continuously climb a tree with great thorns, at the top of which is a woman. Village people are vague in fitting the concept of "hell" into the kammatic cycle.

5. Devas are discussed subsequently. In general, supernatural beings cannot acquire merit by their own action. Hence merit is bestowed upon them through offerings by human beings.

6. Adam's Peak and the "footprint" are revered by Hindus, Buddhists, and Muslims, and historically by Christians. Each group has its own version of the mark's origin. See J. E. Tennent: Ceylon; an Account of the Island; Physical, Historical, and Topographical. Second edition. London: Longman, Green, Longman, and Roberts, 1859, Volume II, pp. 132-141.

Chapter VII
  1. C. J. Seligman and B. Z. Seligman: The Veddas. Cambridge: Cambridge University Press, 1911. S. C. Dube: Indian Village. Ithaca: Cornell University Press, 1955.
  2. It may be wondered how one's life can be determined both by kamma and by astrological position. While this poses something of a paradox, the answer is simple for the villager: astrological position is determined by kamma. A good kamma yields a good horoscope. Further, it is apparent that one's stars cannot affect ascribed statuses, e. g. sex, or caste, while kamma is determinative of such matters.
  3. There is a Hindu legend that the footprint on this holy mountain is that of Siva, and another version in which it is the footprint of Vishnu. For some evidence of religious syncretism in Ceylon, see E. B. Denham: Ceylon at the Census of 1911, op. cit., Chapter IX.
  4. Probably the only exception among the Sinhalese generally is in reference to Gara Yaka, a benevolent demon. See E. R. Sarathchandra: The Sinhalese Folk Play. Colombo: University of Ceylon Press, 1953. Although chiefly concerned with art forms, Sarathchandra gives a superb account of relations between Buddhism and "folk religion." His descriptions of exorcizing ceremonies are also excellent.
  5. The demonology implied here is imperfect from a general, informed Sinhalese viewpoint. Cf. E. R. Sarathchandra, ibid., especially Chapter II.
  6. For varieties of peretayas, see Arthur A. Perera: Sinhalese Folklore Notes, Ceylon. Bombay: British India Press, 1917, p. 14.
  7. See Perera, ibid. Literally a mantram or mantra is a sacred text or passage used as an incantation. See also The Oxford Universal Dictionary. Third Edition. Oxford: Oxford University Press, 1955, p. 1202.

8. Supernatural techniques for dealing with a disease do not imply that the disorder is not also subject to "natural" medical treatment. Under somé circumstances, as in chronic illness, it often appears that some evil power must be removed before medication can prove effective.

9. Additional diagnostic practices are used in other regions. Thus, especially in Kandyan areas, certain spiritually pure individuals are subject to trances in which a god or goddess, e.g. Kataragama or Pattini, takes possession of them and reveals the source of trouble and the procedure for alleviating it. Persons subject to possession are unknown in the vicinity of Pelpola and while the technique has been heard of, it is rarely if ever utilized.

10. Cf. Sarathchandra, op. cit.

11. This datum would have been considered "privileged information" had not this magician died during the preparation of this monograph.

Chapter VIII

1. The Vahumpera family has been disregarded in this account since it has no particular significance in village life. In status theory the Vahumpera are about equal to the Badahela and Hena. Members of this family live in friendly relations with Goyigama neighbors, give alms to the "Goyigama temple, " and send their children to the village school. The husband-father is an agricultural laborer. Their most intimate contacts are outside the village.

2. The following anecdote appeared in different form in Bryce Ryan: Caste in Modern Ceylon, op. cit., in reference to a village given the pseudonym of Kalugama. "Kalugama" is Pelpola.

3. Economic class determination is described subsequently in this chapter.

4. Villagers are reluctant to provide wealth and income data and no systematic effort was made to collect such data. It is probable that persons classified in the upper three per cent would have annual incomes of over 10, 000 rupees, but only in one or two cases so much as say 50, 000 rupees. By way of comparison, 8, 000-10, 000 rupees would be approximately the salary of the equivalent of an Assistant Professor at the University of Ceylon.

5. Names of friends were derived from the sample survey of 100 households, but include only cases for whom complete data were secured, i.e. 91 cases. The two highest status groups have been combined here since only 3 cases in the sample fell into the highest category. The number of sample cases in each economic class were, from top to bottom, respectively, 3, 15, 35, 38. The economic class of friends was derived from the panel ratings of all village households.

Chapter IX
1. Portuguese naming has no implication of miscegenation although much undoubtedly occurred in the Low Country. Such names are widely found among Low Country Sinhalese.

2. The original knowledge survey was reported in Bryce Ryan: "The Ceylonese Village and the New Value System, " Rural Sociology, Vol. 17, 1952, pp. 9-28. A more carefully chosen sample was utilized in the 1951 study which was conducted as part of the general household survey. See Appendices. All results reported here are from the latter study except in reference to knowledge of Ceylon affairs and scientific-mechanical knowledge, topics not broached in the resurvey. Eighty male youths, age 15-24, were studied separately. One of these cases has frequently been omitted because of lack of full information. Women were studied as part of the fertility attitude inquiry reported upon in Bryce F. Ryan: "Institutional Factors in Sinhalese Fertility, " op. cit.

Chapter XI
1. See bibliography at end of this volume.

2. Cf. Bryce Ryan: "West and East in Ceylon, " Journal of Educational Sociology, Vol. 26, 1953, pp. 342-355; and Bryce F. Ryan and M. A. Straus: "The Integration of Sinhalese Society, " Research Studies of the State College of Washington, Vol. XXII, 1954, pp. 179-227.

3. Unlike India there is little migration of males to the city, leaving wife and children in the village home. While there is some intermittent migration of this sort, the pattern is not typical. Most migrants settle in the city but maintain close affective contacts with the home village.

4. Reported upon in Bryce Ryan: "Institutional Factors in Sinhalese Fertility, " op. cit.

5. Cf. S. J. Tambiah and Bryce Ryan: "Secularization of Family Values in Ceylon, " American Sociological Review, Vol. 22, 1957, pp. 292-299.

6. Cf. Bryce Ryan: Caste in Modern Ceylon, op. cit., Chapter 8.

7. H. C. P. Bell: "Sinhalese Customs and Ceremonies Connected with Paddy Cultivation in the Low Country, " op. cit. (See above, Chapter II.)

8. Cf. Bryce Ryan and M. A. Straus: "The Integration of Sinhalese Society, " op. cit.

Chapter XII

1. For a statistical analysis of similar data for this village, see Bryce Ryan: "The Ceylonese Village and the New Value System, " op. cit.

2. See supra, pp. 128-129.

3. "Social Entrepreneurship--The Mauritian Case, " (mimeographed) Chicago: University of Chicago, 1955. Silberman's stimulating paper develops this concept in relationship to changes in family life in Mauritius.

4. The qualification upon consistency in secularism in reference to agricultural techniques might prove to be more apparent than real. The production techniques used as a measure of secularism did not involve labor saving devices. Most of them required further labor in the production of crops other than rubber, especially paddy. It is possible that the peasant's refusal to put further labor inputs into peasant agriculture is economically rational. This would be true in so far as alternative uses of labor are more rewarding. Cf. Chapter XI above.

5. Cf. Bryce Ryan and M. A. Straus: "The Integration of Sinhalese Society, " op. cit.

6. S. Namasivayam: The Legislatures of Ceylon. London: Faber and Faber Ltd., 1951.

7. Jane Philips: "The Hookworm Campaign in Ceylon, " in Howard M. Teaf, Jr. and Peter G. Franck (editors), Hands Across Frontiers: Case Studies in Technical Cooperation, Ithaca: Cornell University Press, 1955, pp. 265-306.

8. F. A. Hayley: Laws and Customs of the Sinhalese or... Kandyan Law, op. cit., p. 25.

9. Cf. Bryce Ryan: Caste in Modern Ceylon, op. cit., Chapter 3.

10. Thus see Daniel Thorner: "India and Pakistan" in Ralph Linton (ed.), Most of the World. New York: Columbia University Press, 1949, pp. 548-653.

11. J. E. Tennent: Ceylon; an Account of the Island; Physical, Historical, and Topographical. Fifth edition, London: Longman, Green, Longmann, and Roberts, 1860, Vol. I, p. 544.

12. Bryce F. Ryan and M. A. Straus: "The Integration of Sinhalese Society, " op. cit.

13. J. F. Embree: "Thailand--A Loosely Structured Social System, " American Anthropologist, Vol. 52, 1950, pp. 181-193.

14. Bryce Ryan: "West and East in Ceylon, " op. cit.

15. C. H. Cooley: Social Process. New York: Scribners, 1918, Chapter I.

16. Cf. S. J. Tambiah and Bryce Ryan: "Secularization of Family Values in Ceylon, " op. cit.; and S. J. Tambiah: "Patterns of Secularization in Three Sinhalese Communities, " unpublished Ph. D. dissertation, Cornell University. Ithaca, 1953.

17. S. J. Tambiah and Bryce Ryan: "Secularization of Family Values in Ceylon, " op. cit.

APPENDIX A

General Research Procedure

Field study basic to this work combined unstructured research techniques with survey and other structured approaches. Most statistical references in the text are based upon a sample of one hundred cases, chosen by taking every fourth entry on the Village Headman's list of all households in the community. Substitution was made in only one instance. This case was that of a non-Sinhalese household, the only one in the area, the head of which was the superintendent on one of the large rubber estates. For most purposes only households having male heads have been utilized. These numbered eighty-seven. All but five of these homes were "normal families" in the sense of having a living husband-wife nucleus. For certain purposes it has been most reasonable to make calculations only for "normal families." At other points, notably in reference to household composition, the entire sample forms the base for analysis. In statistical matters pertaining to marriages, the sample becomes all living marital units found in the households covered by the survey. Unless otherwise indicated, percentage statements throughout the text relate to a base of eighty-seven cases, i.e. the total number of residential families (households) headed by a male in a one-fourth sample of all village households.

The main household survey was conducted in 1951. Included were basic data on household composition, marriage, economic activities, social participation, practice of ceremonies, and attitudes and beliefs of the head on matters relevant to secularization (see Appendix B). A previous survey of similar type but less exhaustive and based upon less experience in the village and less careful sampling has been utilized at a few points as noted in the text.

In addition to the one hundred case sample survey, several other more or less structured inquiries were undertaken. A separate study was made of attitudes, values and practices of significance to family planning and birth control. In this connection thirty-three mothers were interviewed

intensively by three carefully chosen female assistants,
each of whom was a graduate of the University of Ceylon.
The main results of this inquiry have been reported in "Institutional Factors in Sinhalese Fertility, " Milbank Memorial Fund Quarterly, October 1952.

In 1951 and 1952 a statistical survey was conducted of
eighty unmarried male village youth, age 15-24 inclusive.
This pertained principally to matters relevant to social
change and especially to secular values and attitudes. Sampling was done on an approximate neighborhood quota plan.
Value questions posed to the youth were selected from the
battery used in the survey of household heads. Based on the
household sample a statistical inquiry into local leadership
also was made in 1951. The results of that study have been
used here in impressionistic rather than in formal statistical presentation.

As a separate inquiry an unsystematically selected sample
of one hundred household heads were surveyed as to their
belief in supernatural powers and especially the causative
importance of demons in cases of illness. This study pre-
ceeded the general household survey and several questions
from it were utilized in the latter, especially in regard to
the retention of traditional beliefs and practices.

The exploration in structured analysis of social status
described in Chapter VIII was carried out in 1952 in an attempt to gain insight into the complexities of status determination which had remained obscure despite intensive qualitative research.

Structured research utilized as part of this program has
at several points been supplemented by the separate inquiries
conducted in Pelpola by Dr. Murray A. Straus.

For all surveys, schedules were mimeographed in English and responses recorded in English. Interviewers were
perfectly bilingual and the significance of each query had
been discussed at length and Sinhalese equivalents agreed
upon. In all questions it was understood that literal meanings
were to be subordinated to proper comprehension by the
respondents. Survey interviewing was done largely by Messrs.
Jayasena and Wickremesinghe; the fertility study required
much female assistance and some further student help was
also needed in completing the general household survey. All
interviewing was done by senior or graduate "majors" in
Sociology.

Although the study in general, as well as its constituent parts, was designed and planned by the senior author, all operational procedures were developed in full collaboration. Practically all unstructured, as well as most structured, interviewing was conducted by Messrs. Jayasena and Wickremesinghe. Survey research was not attempted until the conclusion of more than a year of unstructured observation and questioning, and participant observing. The fact that one of the authors was born and reared in Pelpola and looks upon that village as his familial home was of immense value. During 1949 and 1950 field work was conducted intermittently. During these years, Messrs. Jayasena and Wickremesinghe spent at various periods approximately ten months in the village, with frequent periodic visits by the senior author. In 1951, thanks to a grant from the Rockefeller Foundation, Mr. Wickremesinghe was able to live most of the year in the village and through the cooperation of the Ceylon Department of Social Service, Mr. Jayasena again had several uninterrupted months in Pelpola. During most of 1951, and into 1952, the senior author averaged perhaps two days or more each week in the village, some visits being simply overnight, others for as long as a week. Subsequent to March 1952 systematic work in the village ceased, although both Mr. Jayasena and Mr. Wickremesinghe remained in close touch with the community and paid it periodic visits. In 1957, armed with the present manuscript in preliminary form, Mr. Jayasena returned to Pelpola for the purpose of assessing it in reference to changes which might have occurred since 1952. At a number of points the manuscript was modified to include events and changes since that time. Survey data of course still relate to conditions as of 1951-1952.

APPENDIX B

Indices of Knowledge, Attitudes, and Traditionalism

Knowledge and attitude (value) questions were included as one schedule in the basic household survey and applied to male household heads. The index of knowledge used in Chapter XII was taken as the sum of correct answers to the following queries:

1. What Asian country fought on the same side as Germany in the last war?
2. Name as many Asian countries as you can which became independent during the last five years (excluding Ceylon). (Maximum 4 points).
3. Which of the following pairs of countries have the most unfriendly relations?
     a. America and England
     b. England and France
     c. America and Soviet Russia
4. What is the religion of the majority of people in India?
5. What is the religion of the majority of people in Pakistan?
6. What is the religion of the majority of the people in Burma?
7. In the Korean conflict are American and Chinese troops fighting on
     a. the same side
     b. different sides
     c. doesn't know

* * * * * * *

The index of secularization in values was derived by giving a score of one point for each starred answer to the following questions:

1. Other things being equal (economic), where would you prefer to live?
     City*
     Village
     Colonization scheme
     Undecided

2. If you could be sure of bettering your economic po-
   sition would you move to:
   Colonization scheme*
   Remain in the village
   Undecided
   Inapplicable (not a farmer)
3. If you were forced to choose, which of the following
   would you be least willing to give up?
   Western medicine*
   Ayurvedic medicine
   Undecided
4. If the village were given a large sum of money, which
   do you think would be the better way of spend-
   ing it?
   Improving the temple
   Building a new road*
   Undecided
5. If a new crop were discovered which you could plant on
   your paddy land and from its returns buy more
   rice than you are able to grow on that land what
   would you do?
   Plant new crop entirely*
   Plant some of the new crop
   Stick to paddy entirely
6. If a father wants his son to become a doctor but the
   son wishes to become an airline pilot, is the
   son right or wrong in following his own desire?
   Right*
   Wrong
   Undecided
7. Do you think a qualified Rodiya ("untouchable") should
   be given a position in the civil service?
   Yes*
   No
   Undecided
8. If you had a daughter who eloped with a man of lower
   caste, would you
   Accept him and her too*
   Accept her but shun him
   Shun both but finally accept
   Shun both but not disown
   Disown (disinherit)

9. Which of the following men do you think deserves
        greater respect?
        Man A*   Son of a poor man who rose to be
                   managing director of a company
        Man B   Son of a wealthy man who manages
                   his own inherited estates.
        Undecided
10. If conditions became such that Ceylon did not have
        enough food to go around, would you approve
        of people practicing birth control (assuming
        that it would be possible)
        Yes*
        No
        Undecided

* * * * * * *

The index of technological receptiveness in agricultural
practice was derived by giving one point for each of the
following:
        1. Transplants all or part of paddy
        2. Ploughs three times or more
        3. Weeds all paddy land
        4. Uses compost in garden
        5. Uses bone meal or other fertilizer
        6. Has drains in highland gardens

* * * * * * *

The index of receptiveness to Western material culture
traits in the household was derived by giving one point for
each of the following:
        1. Sewing machine
        2. Bicycle
        3. Phonograph
        4. Radio
        5. Clock or watch in family
        6. Use of tinned food in past month

* * * * * * *

The index of retention of traditional practices was derived by giving one point for each starred answer below:

1. At your last harvest did you make an offering of the first harvested grain to a god?
   Yes*   No   Inapplicable
2. Do you believe that cutting the hair of a young child prevents or delays his talking?
   Yes*   No   Undecided
3. Do you believe in the Black Prince?
   Yes*   No   Undecided
4. Do you believe that a first hair cut should be given at an auspicious time?
   Yes*   No   Undecided
5. Do you believe that women should be permitted on the threshing floor?
   Yes*   No   Undecided
6. Do you believe that sickness (some or any) can be cured by exorcizing?
   Yes*   No   Undecided
7. Did you visit (important) relatives with betel last Sinhalese New Year?
   Yes*   No   Inapplicable
8. Did you light a fire propitiously on last Sinhalese New Year?
   Yes*   No
9. Does the head of the household (male) get his hair cut?
   Yes   No*   Inapplicable
10. Did you select an auspicious day for the first rice feeding for your last child?
    Yes*   No   Inapplicable
11. Did you have an oil annointing ceremony last Sinhalese New Year?
    Yes*   No   Inapplicable

Do you think worship (obeisance) is called for:

12. When a man of low caste comes to the home of a high caste
    Yes*   No   Undecided
13. When a son takes leave of his father for a long journey
    Yes*   No   Undecided

14. When a wife takes leave of her husband for a long journey
       Yes*   No   Undecided
15. By children to schoolmaster at beginning or end of school year
       Yes*   No   Undecided
16. By villager to village Headman
       Yes*   No   Undecided

GLOSSARY

Adam's Peak--See "Sri Pada. "

Ahimsa--Buddhist doctrine of non-harming, especially non-killing.

Amarapura Sect--A sect or ordination of Buddhist monks, the name of which (Amarapura) is derived from the capital of the Burmese Empire. This ordination was introduced into Ceylon about 1800.

Appuhamy--A moderate honorific: formerly a term applied to the sons of a chief.

Ata Sil--Eight precepts of Buddhism, see "Sil. "

Ayurveda--An indiginous system of medicine based upon traditional, especially herbal compounds.

B.

Badahela--The Sinhalese caste having pottery-making as their traditional occupation.

Bahirava Devathava--God in charge of "treasures of the earth, " e.g. soil productivity.

Bali--A ceremony propitiating the planet gods.

Bana--Sermon derived from Buddhist Scriptures.

Bazaar--A permanent market or street of shops.

Betel--A substance commonly chewed: usually composed of areca nut, "betel" leaf, and chunam (lime).

Berava--The caste of "tom-tom beaters, " which in the Pelpola area also provides bali dancers.

Bhikkhu--A Buddhist monk (priest).

Black Prince--A demon affecting adolescent girls and yielding symptoms of "madness. "

Boutique--A small shop or booth.

C.

Cadjan--The plaited leaf of the palm, used for thatching houses, etc.

Chena--High jungle land cultivated periodically by slashing and burning.

D.

Dayakaya--A regular contributor of alms to the temple, especially food for the priests.
Deva--Any of a wide category of supernatural beings, including gods and nature spirits.
Devale--A temple of a deity.
Dhamma--(Skt: Dharma) The teachings of the Buddha.
Dhobi--(Dhoby) A washerman; persons of castes having washing as their traditional occupation.

G.

Gama--A village.
Gamsabha--Historically the village council, i.e. panchayat.
Ge--Unilinear name group.
Goyigama--The largest and highest caste among the Sinhalese.
Gurunnanse--Leader of pilgrimages to holy sites.

H.

Hela--A white cloth, especially that given the bride in a marriage ceremony.
Hinayana Buddhism--Theravada, one of the great branches of Buddhist thought found today in Ceylon, Burma, Thailand, and Cambodia.
Hooniyam--Black magic; also the demon responsible for the power of sorcery.
House--See "Ge."

J.

Jatakas--The stories of the different existances of Gautama (Buddha) of which several hundred are recorded.

K.

Kabook--Clayish earth which when exposed to the air hardens to a rocklike consistency and is used as blocks in house construction.
Kaiya--A traditional cooperative work group, i.e. voluntary group of unpaid workers.

Kaluganga--A major river immediately south of Pelpola.
Kalukumaraya--See "Black Prince."
Kamma--(Skt: Karma) The Buddhist law of causation, es-
    pecially the doctrine of rebirth.
Kandyan--Pertaining to the interior Sinhalese Provinces.
Kapu Ela--The canal built in Dutch times which skirts the
    village of Pelpola.
Kataragama--One of the important deities of Ceylon, said
    to be related to Skanda, the Hindu God.
Kodivina--See "Hooniyam."

L.

Low Country--The Western and Southern coastal Provinces.

M.

Maha--Season of the Southwest Monsoon: the major paddy
    season in Pelpola.
Mamoty--A heavy hoe, any one of several types, used in
    tilling and other agricultural operations.
Merit--Good kamma stored up by the individual through the
    practice of "Right Action."

N.

Nibbana--(Skt: Nirvana) Personal goal of Buddhism: final
    spiritual attainment and cessation of rebirth.

P.

Pansil--Five precepts of Buddhism, see "Sil."
Pattini--One of the important "Hindu" deities in Ceylon: a
    goddess.
Perahera--A procession or parade, especially one with re-
    ligious significance.
Pereteya--See "Pratha."
Piligeneema--Sinhalese word equivalent to the concept of
    "general social status."
Pin--See "Merit."
Pingo--A pliant length of wood carried on the shoulders, from
    the two ends of which burdens are carried.

Pinkama--Meritorious act or a religious festival (unspecific).

Pirith--Collection of Pali hymns and sermons publicly read
with a view to warding off evil influences.

Poruva--Covered platform upon which marriage ceremonies
are performed.

Poya Day--The holy day of the Buddhists.

Pratha--A maleficent ghost.

R.

Rupee--Monetary unit worth about twenty U.S. cents.

S.

Sadhu--A holy exclamation of Buddhism.

Saman--An important deity of the Sinhalese associated with
Adam's Peak (Sri Pada).

Sambol--A flavorful relish used with rice.

Sangha--The Buddhist "priesthood."

Sansara--(Samsara) Worldly existence, contrasting with
Nibbana.

Siamese Sect--The largest sect or ordination of Buddhist
monks in Ceylon. Membership is limited to persons of
Goyigama caste.

Sil--Precepts of Buddhism, especially as recited in worship.

Sri Pada--Adam's Peak, the holy mountain upon which the
Buddha's footprint is said to be.

T.

Thattamaru--A system of non-partitioned inheritance of
productive property in which heirs rotate in the right
of operation and returns.

Theravada--See "Hinayana."

Thovil--A ceremony of demon exorcism.

Toddy--The fermented sap of the palm, drawn from the
blossom.

Tomba--Register, especially of land or population.

U.

Upasaka--A layman of great piety.
Upasika--Feminine of <u>Upasaka</u>.
Upasikavi--Feminine of <u>Upasaka</u>.

V.

Vel Vidane--(Vel Vidana) Irrigation headman.
Vihare--A temple of Buddha.

Y.

Yaka--Generic term for demons, a number of which are
    associated with diseases.
Yala--Season of the Northeast Monsoon.

BIBLIOGRAPHY

Works Arising from the Ceylon Village Study
Program and Related Researchs in the
Department of Sociology
University of Ceylon
Initiated 1948-1952

1950

Ryan, Bryce--"Sociocultural Regions of Ceylon, " Rural
Sociology, Vol. 15, pp. 3-19.
_____--"People, People, More People, " New Lanka
(Ceylon), Vol. 2, pp. 53-59.

1951

Ryan, Bryce and Sylvia Fernando--"The Female Factory
Worker in Colombo, " International Labour Review, Vol.
64. Reprinted as separate by the International Labour
Organization, Geneva, 1952, pp. 1-24.
Straus, Murray A.--"Mental Ability and Cultural Needs: A
Psychocultural Interpretation of the Intelligence Test
Performance of Ceylon University Entrants, " American
Sociological Review, Vol. 16, pp. 371-375.
_____--Family Characteristics and Occupational Choice
of University Entrants as Clues to the Social Structure of
Ceylon, " University of Ceylon Review, Vol. 9, pp. 125-
136.

1952

Ryan, Bryce--"The Ceylonese Village and the New Value
System, " Rural Sociology, Vol. 17, pp. 9-28.
_____--"Primary and Secondary Contacts in a Ceylonese
Peasant Community, " Rural Sociology, Vol. 17, pp. 311-
321.
_____--"Institutional Factors in Sinhalese Fertility, " Mil-
bank Memorial Fund Quarterly, Vol. 30, pp. 359-381.

Reprinted in revised form in Broom, Leonard and Phillip
Selznick, Sociology; a Text with Adapted Readings, Row,
Peterson, and Co., Evanston, Ill., 1956.

1953

Ryan, Bryce--Caste in Modern Ceylon, the Sinhalese System
in Transition, Rutgers University Press, New Brunswick.
_____ --"West and East in Ceylon, " Journal of Educational
Sociology, Vol. 26, pp. 342-355.
_____ --"The Sinhalese Family System, " Eastern Anthro-
pologist, Vol. 6, pp. 143-163.
Straus, Murray A.--"Cultural Factors in the Functioning of
Agricultural Extension in Ceylon, " Rural Sociology, Vol.
18, pp. 249-256.
_____ and Jacqueline H. Straus--"Suicide, Homicide,
and Ceylonese Social Structure, " American Journal of
Sociology, Vol. 58, pp. 461-469.

1954

Ryan, Bryce--"Hinayana Buddhism and Family Planning in
Ceylon. " In: The Interrelations of Demographic, Eco-
nomic, and Social Problems in Selected Underdeveloped
Areas, Milbank Memorial Fund, New York, pp. 90-102.
_____ and Murray A. Straus--"The Integration of Sinhalese
Society, " Research Studies of the State College of Wash-
ington, Vol. 22, pp. 179-227.
Straus, Murray A.--"Subcultural Variation in Ceylonese
Mental Ability: a Study in National Character, " Journal
of Social Psychology, Vol. 39, pp. 129-141.
_____ --"Childhood Experience and Emotional Security in
the Context of Sinhalese Social Organization, " Social
Forces, Vol. 33, pp. 152-160.
Tambiah, S. J.--"The Process of Secularization in Three
Ceylonese Peasant Communities, " unpublished Ph.D.
thesis, Cornell University, Ithaca.

1955

Ryan, Bryce--"The Agricultural Systems of Ceylon, " Rural
Sociology, Vol. 20, pp. 16-24.

_____, Chandra Arulpragasam, and Cuda Bibile--"The Agricultural System of a Ceylon Jungle Village, " Eastern Anthropologist, Vol. 8, pp. 151-160. Reprinted in Rural Profiles (edited by D. N. Majumdar) The Ethnographic and Folk Culture Society, U. P., Lucknow, 1955, pp. 23-32.

1956

Straus, Murray A. --"Child Training and Child Personality in a Rural and Urban Area of Ceylon, " unpublished Ph. D. thesis, University of Wisconsin, Madison.

1957

Straus, Murray A. --"Thematic Apperception Test Protocols of Ceylon University Entrants, " Microcard Publications of Primary Records in Culture and Personality (in press).

_____ --"Thematic Apperception Test Protocols of Third Standard Children in a Low Country Sinhalese Village, " Microcard Publications of Primary Records in Culture and Personality (in press).

_____ --"Anal and Oral Frustration in Relation to Sinhalese Personality, " Sociometry, Vol. 20, pp. 21-31.

_____ and Jacqueline H. Straus--"Personal Insecurity and Sinhalese Social Structure: Rorschach Evidence for Primary School Children, " Eastern Anthropologist, Vol. 10, pp. 97-111.

Tambiah, S. J. and Bryce Ryan--"Secularization of Family Values in Ceylon, " American Sociological Review, Vol. 22, pp. 292-299.

INDEX